Nesrin Ozatac • Nigar Taspinar
Bezhan Rustamov
Editors

Sustainable Development in Banking and Finance

7th International Conference on Banking and Finance Perspectives, Famagusta, Northern Cyprus

Springer

Editors
Nesrin Ozatac
Department of Banking and Finance
Eastern Mediterranean University
Famagusta, Cyprus

Nigar Taspinar
Department of Banking & Finance
Eastern Mediterranean University
Famagusta, Cyprus

Bezhan Rustamov
Banking and Finance
Rauf Denktas University
Nicosia, Türkiye

ISSN 2198-7246 ISSN 2198-7254 (electronic)
Springer Proceedings in Business and Economics
ISBN 978-3-031-65532-6 ISBN 978-3-031-65533-3 (eBook)
https://doi.org/10.1007/978-3-031-65533-3

This Springer imprint is published by the registered company Springer Nature Switzerland AG
The registered company address is: Gewerbestrasse 11, 6330 Cham, Switzerland

Contents

The Effect of COVID-19 on the Relationship Between Environmental Performance and Financial Performance: Insight from the US Tourism Sector

Mohamad Kaakeh and Korhan K. Gokmenoglu

1 Introduction

The tourism industry is currently responsible for 8% of global greenhouse gas emissions (Lenzen et al., 2018). Therefore, environmental sustainability in the tourism sector has received growing attention from researchers and practitioners (Galeazzo et al., 2021). However, tourism firms are reluctant to enhance their environmental performance (EP) as the effect on financial performance (FP) is still uncertain (Galeazzo et al., 2021).

Investigation of the empirical literature reveals two stylized facts: First, the empirical findings regarding the nature of the relationship between EP and FP are mixed; that is, researchers provide evidence for a positive (Tan et al., 2017), negative (Duque-Grisales & Aguilera-Caracuel, 2021) or neutral (Lahouel et al., 2019) relationship between these variables. Second, the majority of the empirical literature uses linear models and neglects non-linear possible explanations for the association between EP and FP (Trumpp & Guenther, 2017). Moreover, most literature examined the link between EP and FP under normal economic conditions. However, the dramatic economic consequences of the COVID-19 pandemic on the tourism and leisure sector (Duro et al., 2021) have made necessary the re-evaluation of the relationship between EP and FP in this sector during financial distress.

This research aims to fill the existing gap in the literature by investigating the effect of EP on the FP of the US tourism and leisure sector in a non-linear framework

M. Kaakeh
Utrecht University, School of Economics and Finance, Utrecht, The Netherlands

K. K. Gokmenoglu (✉)
Ankara HBV University, Faculty of Financial Sciences,
Department of Capital Markets, Ankara, Turkey
e-mail: korhan.gokmenoglu@hbv.edu.tr

N. Ozatac et al. (eds.), *Sustainable Development in Banking and Finance*, Springer Proceedings in Business and Economics,
https://doi.org/10.1007/978-3-031-65533-3_1

under unfavorable economic conditions resulting from the COVID-19 pandemic. Several control variables and methods are used to ensure the robustness of the results.

2 Data and Methodology

The suggested non-linear framework can be represented by a quadratic form of the regression model, where EP is represented by both linear and quadratic terms (Trumpp & Guenther, 2017). The two equations formulated using different proxies to represent FP are presented below:

$$\mathrm{ROA}_{it} = \alpha + \beta_1 \mathrm{EP}_{it} + \beta_2 \mathrm{EP}^2{}_{it} + \beta_3 \mathrm{COV}_{it} + \beta_4 \mathrm{COVEP}_{it} + \sum_{n=1}^{m} \beta_n X_{n,it} + \varepsilon_{it} \quad (1)$$

$$\mathrm{ROC}_{it} = \alpha + \beta_1 \mathrm{EP}_{it} + \beta_2 \mathrm{EP}^2{}_{it} + \beta_3 \mathrm{COV}_{it} + \beta_4 \mathrm{COVEP}_{it} + \sum_{n=1}^{m} \beta_n X_{n,it} + \varepsilon_{it} \quad (2)$$

Where return on assets (ROA) and return on capital (ROC) represent FP, the environmental pillar score of environmental, social, and governance (ESG) Refinitiv Eikon database was selected to measure EP, COV is a COVID-19 dummy variable taking the value of 1 in 2020 and 0 otherwise, COVEP is an interaction variable representing EP during COVID-19, X represents control variables including size (a logarithmic form of market value), liquidity (current ratio), and leverage (a logarithmic form of long-term debt), and ε_{it} is the error term. After filtration and exclusion of firms that did not have environmental performance scores, a panel of 115 US travel and leisure firms was utilized from 2017 to 2020. All data was gathered from the Refinitiv Eikon database.

To investigate models (1) and (2), we employed a fixed-effects regression model preventing any correlation between regressors and information related to fixed-effects. The model is considered suitable due to the similar characteristics of tourism firms included in the analysis. Moreover, we used robust least squares (Robust LS) and panel corrected standard errors (PCSE) to validate our findings. Robust LS reduces the sensitivity of conventional regression methods to outliers and reflects the correct statistical relationship between the variables (Yohai, 1987), while PCSE corrects for any autocorrelation, heteroscedasticity, and multicollinearity in the residuals (Wooldridge, 2003).

Table 1 Determinants of financial performance in US tourism firms (ROA)

ROA	Fixed-effects	Robust LS	PCSE
Constant	0.258337*	−0.297271*	−0.15055**
EP	−0.00188**	−0.001608*	−0.001544*
EP^2	0.000031*	0.000013*	0.000018*
Leverage	−0.019885*	−0.002528*	−0.0014620
Size	0.006047*	0.027842*	0.017588*
Liquidity	−0.0037***	−0.000014*	−0.0013949
Cov	−0.071766*	−0.082354*	−0.096818*
Covep	−0.000865*	−0.000414*	−0.000556*
R^2/Rw^2	0.812626	0.522845	0.6250
F-statistic/Rn^2/Wald	12.1147*	2770000*	1017.68*

*, **, ****represent significance at 1%, 5%, and 10% respectively. R^2 is the R-squared statistic for both Random effects and PCSE, Rw^2 is a better measure of fit in the case of Robust-LS (Renaud & Victoria-Feser,* 2010*). F-statistic, Rn^2, and Wald tests measure if the model is best fitted for fixed-effects, Robust-LS, and PCSE, respectively*

3 Empirical Findings

Table 1 presents the empirical findings of the fixed-effects regression, Robust LS, and PCSE for model (1). According to the obtained results, the linear form of EP has a significant negative effect on FP. However, EP2 is found to have a significant positive impact on FP. Thus, the relationship between FP and EP is best represented by a U-shaped pattern. This finding indicates that an increase in EP investments affects FP negatively until EP reaches a certain threshold value. Still, after this threshold is exceeded, the relationship becomes positive and higher investment in EP enhances FP. The COV dummy variable has a significant negative relationship with FP, as expected. In addition, the significant negative link between FP and the interaction variable COVEP points out that increased spending on EP during financial distress reduces FP of tourism firms. The models are all best fitted and have adequate R-squared values.

Empirical findings for model (2) are presented in Table 2. Results for model 2 confirm the U-shaped association between EP and FP. This finding also aligns with Tan et al. (2017). Besides, Robust LS estimations signify that an increase in EP during the COVID-19 pandemic can decrease the FP of the firms. All control variables have expected signs aligning with the theoretical literature.

4 Discussion

Our research confirms that investment in EP inhibits AP until EP reaches a certain level. This might be due to two reasons. The first one is related to the stakeholder theory, which asserts that stakeholders' attention and reward depend on the level of

Table 2 Determinants of financial performance in US tourism firms (ROC)

ROC	Fixed-effects	Robust LS	PCSE
Constant	1.587011**	−0.434074*	−0.30342**
EP	−0.00341**	−0.001834*	−0.00299**
EP^2	0.000079*	0.000015*	0.000038*
Leverage	−0.142483*	−0.006172*	−0.0103***
Size	0.027132*	0.042774*	0.037948*
Liquidity	0.0016200	−0.000409*	0.0027420
Cov	−0.156906*	−0.137027*	−0.232647*
Covep	−0.0006280	−0.000384*	−0.0001520
R^2/Rw^2	0.761178	0.446157	0.4067
F-statistic/Rn^2/Wald	8.90314*	1240000*	6568.35*

*, **, ****represent significance at 1%, 5%, and 10% respectively. R^2 is the R-squared statistic for both Random effects and PCSE, Rw^2 is a better measure of fit in the case of Robust-LS (Renaud & Victoria-Feser,* 2010*). F-statistic, $Rn^{2,}$ and Wald tests measure if the model is best fitted for fixed-effects, Robust-LS, and PCSE, respectively*

firms' EP. When a firm reaches the level of EP compatible with stakeholders' expectations, it will reap financial gains through competitive advantage and goodwill. The second explanation is related to tourism companies' environmental strategies. If firms only react to new regulations and compliance requirements and try to minimize costs (reactive environmental strategies), this strategy may accrue more costs than benefits. However, the firms that use the development of dynamic capabilities and market leadership (proactive environmental strategies) improve competitive advantage and, in turn, can have higher benefits than costs (Alonso-Almeida et al., 2015; Tan et al., 2017).

Our research also provides evidence of a negative association between EP and FP during the COVID-19 economic downturn. Investment in corporate social responsibility, particularly in the tourism and leisure sector, should be postponed in situations of economic distress that deteriorate firms' balance sheets. Under crisis conditions, an investment reduction in environmental and sustainable practices can reduce costs and maintain or even improve FP (Karaibrahimolu, 2010). Results are in line with Petitjean (2019), who argued that investors are more focused on short-term survival than higher EP in crisis conditions.

5 Conclusion

This study utilizes fixed-effects, robust LS, and PCSE estimation methods to examine the non-linear relation between EP and FP in the tourism and leisure sector of the United States from 2017 to 2020. The fact that the sample used covers the period of COVID-19 allows us to present more comprehensive findings regarding our research question. We propose a U-shaped relationship between EP and FP; that is, the relationship is negative until EP reaches a certain threshold, and the effect becomes positive thereafter. In addition, the finding that the impact of EP on FP during the COVID-19 period was negative implies that a decrease in EP investments under adverse economic conditions would support FP.

The findings that were obtained lead us to several policy recommendations. The U-shaped relationship between EP and FP suggests that during adverse financial conditions, it is advisable to reduce investment in environmental performance and focus on the survival of the firm. However, making progress in environmentally sound and sustainable business practices should remain the long-term strategic goal of companies. Managers need to pay closer attention to the stakeholders' sustainability expectations and design a proactive environmental strategy to increase benefits. Moreover, governments should motivate tourist firms to invest in environmental protection by designing a subsidy policy to enhance environmental performance.

References

Alonso-Almeida, M. D. M., Bremser, K., & Llach, J. (2015). Proactive and reactive strategies deployed by restaurants in times of crisis: Effects on capabilities, organization and competitive advantage. *International Journal of Contemporary Hospitality Management, 27*(7), 1641–1661.

Duque-Grisales, E., & Aguilera-Caracuel, J. (2021). Environmental, social and governance (ESG) scores and financial performance of multilatinas: Moderating effects of geographic international diversification and financial slack. *Journal of Business Ethics, 168*(2), 315–334.

Duro, J. A., Perez-Laborda, A., Turrion-Prats, J., & Fernández-Fernández, M. (2021). Covid-19 and tourism vulnerability. *Tourism Management Perspectives, 38*, 100819.

Galeazzo, A., Ortiz-de-Mandojana, N., & Delgado-Ceballos, J. (2021). Green procurement and financial performance in the tourism industry: The moderating role of tourists' green purchasing behaviour. *Current Issues in Tourism, 24*(5), 700–716.

Karaibrahimolu, Y. Z. (2010). Corporate social responsibility in times of financial crisis. *African Journal of Business Management, 4*(4), 382–389.

Lahouel, B. B., Gaies, B., Zaied, Y. B., & Jahmane, A. (2019). Accounting for endogeneity and the dynamics of corporate social–corporate financial performance relationship. *Journal of Cleaner Production, 230*, 352–364.

Lenzen, M., Sun, Y. Y., Faturay, F., Ting, Y. P., Geschke, A., & Malik, A. (2018). The carbon footprint of global tourism. *Nature climate change, 8*(6), 522–528.

Petitjean, M. (2019). Eco-friendly policies and financial performance: Was the financial crisis a game-changer for large US companies? *Energy Economics, 80*, 502–511.

Renaud, O., & Victoria-Feser, M. P. (2010). A robust coefficient of determination for regression. Journal of *Statistical Planning and Inference, 140*(7), 1852–1862.

Tan, S. H., Habibullah, M. S., Tan, S. K., & Choon, S. W. (2017). The impact of the dimensions of environmental performance on firm performance in travel and tourism industry. *Journal of Environmental Management, 203*, 603–611.

Trumpp, C., & Guenther, T. (2017). Too little or too much? Exploring U-shaped relationships between corporate environmental performance and corporate financial performance. *Business Strategy and the Environment, 26*(1), 49–68.

Wooldridge, J. M. (2003). Cluster-sample methods in applied econometrics. *American Economic Review, 93*(2), 133–138.

Yohai, V. J. (1987). High breakdown-point and high-efficiency robust estimates for regression. *The Annals of Statistics, 15*, 642–656.

Understanding Drivers of Boom and Bust in Cryptocurrency Markets

Ibrahim Yagli and Ozkan Haykir

1 Introduction

Cryptocurrency is a new unit of digital assets that employs online ledgers with robust cryptographic algorithms to secure transactions. Even though this distinguished digital currency overcomes several issues that fiat money cannot solve, such as time constraints and requirements for a bank or a government, it also brings certain problems. First, its decentralized structure makes the cryptocurrency market vulnerable to manipulation (Gandal et al., 2018; Hamrick et al., 2018). The excessive use of digital platforms by crypto traders also makes the cryptocurrency market prone to manipulation (Cumming et al., 2019). Second, the lack of intrinsic value (Cheah & Fry, 2015) sparks a debate about whether cryptocurrencies are a medium of exchange or speculative assets (Baur et al., 2018), and they seem speculative assets rather a real currency (Baek & Elbeck, 2015; Yermack, 2015). These facts, combined with scarce cryptocurrency knowledge among investors (Cardify, 2021), make the cryptocurrency market susceptible to financial bubbles (Corbet et al., 2018; Bouri et al., 2019a; Geuder et al., 2019; Kyriazis et al., 2020). In addition, the absence of fundamental models for their price assessments leaves the cryptocurrency market open to the formation of pump-and-dump schemes (Shahzad et al., 2022). Last but not least, crypto traders have lottery-type preferences (Ozdamar et al., 2021). The distinctive nature of cryptocurrencies causes the cryptocurrency market to be more volatile than other financial markets (Dwyer, 2015). In fact, the volatility

I. Yagli (✉)
Nevsehir Haci Bektas Veli University, Faculty of Economics and Administrative Science, Business Administration Department, Nevsehir, Turkey

O. Haykir
Nigde Omer Halisdemir University, Faculty of Economics and Administrative Science, Finance and Banking Department, Niğde, Turkey

N. Ozatac et al. (eds.), *Sustainable Development in Banking and Finance*, Springer Proceedings in Business and Economics,
https://doi.org/10.1007/978-3-031-65533-3_2

of cryptocurrency prices is ten times higher than equity prices and five times higher than commodity prices (Caporale & Plastun, 2019).

Despite the aforementioned risks that cryptocurrencies pose, the cryptocurrency market has been growing at a blazing pace following the invention of Bitcoin. The total cryptocurrency market capitalization reached $2.9 trillion in November 2021, with more than fifteen thousand cryptocurrencies[1] (coinmarketcap, 2021). The market capitalization in the last year has just increased more than five times. Furthermore, it is expected that cryptocurrency market growth will continue and the total market capitalization of the cryptocurrency market is estimated to be 250 trillion US dollars by 2030 (Nahar, 2022).

The increasing cryptocurrency prices attract new investors to invest in these brand-new digital assets. However, the risk-return tradeoff states that a higher return brings higher risk. Therefore, identifying the underlying factors behind the price formation of cryptocurrencies can help investors to minimize their risks. Given that price changes in the cryptocurrency market are in large magnitude and recurring phenomena, the current study attempts to discover relevant factors behind large price changes of cryptocurrencies by adopting recurrent event analysis. Analyzing factors behind large-price swings in this volatile market provides important implications for both individual and institutional cryptocurrency traders.

The current study contributes to the literature in several distinct ways. First, although recent papers address either cryptocurrency pricing (Shahzad, 2021; Wang & Chong, 2021; Derbentsev et al., 2020; Shen et al., 2020) or explosiveness in cryptocurrency prices (Cheah & Fry, 2015; Corbet et al., 2018; Bouri et al., 2019a; Cagli, 2019; Gronwald, 2021), no prior study directly investigates the determinants of large price changes, as far as we know. Second, we consider the recurrence of large price changes since cryptocurrency prices have experienced multiple ups and downs. Third, we analyze the asymmetric effects of size on large price changes since the heterogeneous cryptocurrency market and full sample results do not reflect the overall picture. Fourth, a bulk of studies reveal that the uncertainty has an impact on the cryptocurrency market (Demir et al., 2018; Aysan et al., 2019; Akyildirim et al., 2021; Gozgor et al., 2019); hence, we investigate whether uncertainty moderates the impact of covariates on large price movements. Lastly, unlike prior studies analyzing cryptocurrency pricing using a limited sample (Gregoriou, 2019; Wang & Chong, 2021; Liu & Tsyvinski, 2021), we use approximately 1000 cryptocurrencies with a trading volume of over $5 million (Ozdamar et al., 2021) which allow us to obtain more robust results.

Our results reveal several distinct points: (i) the probability of experiencing large price increases (decreases) is higher (lower) if the return of cryptocurrency is positive on the previous day. On the other hand, the likelihood of facing large price increases (decreases) is lower (higher) if the market return of cryptocurrency is positive on the previous day. (ii) the probability of experiencing large price increases (decreases) is not affected by the sign of the previous day's large price

[1]The overall market capitalization expect Bitcoin has surpassed $1.3 trillion in December, 2021.

movements for 10 highest market capitalization cryptocurrencies. (iii) sub-size groups show that the probability of facing large price increases is mixed for both previous day return and market return. Conversely, the results do not alter for large price decreases. (iv) Uncertainty periods also do not affect the probability of experiencing large price increases and decreases. (v) Lastly, our models have superior predictive power compared to random models.

We organize the paper into five sections. The following section discusses the studies addressing cryptocurrency asset pricing or returns. Section 3 presents the data and methodology, and Sect. 4 reports empirical findings. Section 5 gives concluding remarks.

2 Literature Review

The pricing of cryptocurrencies is a puzzle because they do not have intrinsic value or offer fixed payments. Therefore, no conventional fundamental pricing models exist for cryptocurrencies. Nevertheless, recent finance literature attempts to solve this puzzle. A strand of studies directly addresses cryptocurrency pricing employing conventional pricing models basically generated for stocks (Gregoriou, 2019; Shen et al., 2020; Shahzad et al., 2021; Wang & Chong, 2021), while the bulk of studies attempts to estimate cryptocurrency prices using deep learning techniques (Valencia et al., 2019; Patel et al., 2020; Wang, 2021; Zhang et al., 2021; among others). In addition, several studies investigate other pricing issues, such as financial bubbles, co-explosivity, and herding in the cryptocurrency market (Bouri et al., 2019b; Vidal-Tomás et al., 2019; Kurt Gumus et al., 2019; Haykir & Yagli, 2022; Yousaf & Yarovaya, 2022).

The Efficient Market Hypothesis (EMH) states that asset prices properly reflect all available information, and therefore, investors are unable to obtain excess return by analyzing for undervalued assets. However, cryptocurrency is a new investment tool, and there are still concerns regarding the efficiency of the cryptocurrency market. Urquhart (2016), for instance, analyzed the informational efficiency of Bitcoin and revealed that the Bitcoin market is inefficient in general. Zhang et al. (2018a, b) investigated inefficiency for a wider group of cryptocurrencies (Bitcoin, Ripple, Ethereum, Nem, Stellar, Litecoin, Dash, Monero and Verge) by adopting a battery of efficiency tests and showed that all these cryptocurrencies are inefficient. Al-Yahyaee et al. (2020) also confirmed the inefficiency in six major cryptocurrencies (Bitcoin, Ethereum, Monero, Dash, Litecoin, and Ripple). Furthermore, several studies have analyzed the impact of COVID-19 on the efficiency of the cryptocurrency market. By adopting multifractal detrended fluctuation analysis, Naeem et al. (2021) showed that the pandemic impaired the efficiency of Bitcoin, Ethereum, Litecoin, and Ripple. Kakinaka and Umeno (2022) also analyzed the efficiency of Bitcoin and Ethereum markets in different short- and long-term horizons. Their results reveal that the COVID-19 pandemic deteriorates efficiency in the short-term but not in the long-term.

Inspired by the Capital Asset Pricing Model (CAPM), many studies employed a factor pricing model for cryptocurrencies. For instance, Shen et al. (2020) proposed a three-factor model for cryptocurrency pricing by addressing market, size and reversal factors. Their results showed that size and reversal factors are useful indicators for cryptocurrency pricing. More clearly, cryptocurrencies with smaller market capitalization tend to generate higher returns, and losers perform better than winners. Along the same line, Shahzad et al. (2021) propounded the four-factor pricing model by adding contagion risk into the three factor model and suggesting that the new model performs better than cryptocurrency-CAPM and three-factor models. Gregoriou (2019) constructed the pricing model by using size, value to growth, momentum, profitability, and investment risk factors to estimate cryptocurrency prices and showed that investors could generate an excessive return with the proposed model. Wang and Chong (2021) also addressed five groups of variables for cryptocurrency pricing; market-based factors (market return), equity-based factors (size, momentum and value to growth), volatility-based factors (realized volatility, jump, and skewness), liquidity-based factors (bid-ask price, volume growth, and Roll's liquidity measure), macro-based factors (LIBOR, Hash rate, fundamental build-up), and attention factor (Twitter number), respectively. They revealed that market, equity, volatility, and liquidity factors have explanatory power for excess return in the cryptocurrency market, whereas macro factors do not. Besides, their results show that the explanatory power of attention factors on excess return is time-varying.

Not only liquidity and volatility have explanatory power, but size can also be considered one of the most important factors in estimating excess return. Following this notion, Zhang and Li (2021) state that the return predictability is primarily due to cryptocurrencies with small market capitalizations. In furtherance, Zaremba et al. (2021) state that market capitalization of crypto assets affects the direction of return predictability. More specifically, they elicit that the daily reversal pattern is present in the overwhelming majority of cryptocurrencies, whereas a small fraction of the largest cryptocurrencies does not show any discernible reversal effect. A series of studies also report that cryptocurrency returns vary by size, implying that size is one of the main factors affecting price dynamics in crypto assets. For instance, Li et al. (2020) show that small cryptocurrencies are more likely to generate higher returns than large ones. Shen et al. (2020) also provide evidence that reversal returns rise when the size of the cryptocurrency decreases.

Furthermore, several studies have examined the impact of uncertainty on the cryptocurrency market. According to Demir et al. (2018), the Economic Policy Uncertainty (EPU) index has the power to forecast Bitcoin returns. Akyildirim et al. (2021) have used the VIX index as a proxy for investors' fear and have shown that when investors' fear is high, the cryptocurrency markets become more volatile. In addition to the EPU or VIX index, Aysan et al. (2019) find that Bitcoin returns and volatility can be predicted using the Geopolitical Uncertainty Index. Gozgor et al. (2020) also show that the Trade Policy Uncertainty Index is positively correlated with Bitcoin returns.

Machine learning and deep learning mechanisms such as Neural Networks (NN), Convolutional Neural Network (CNN), Gated Recurrent Unit (GRU), Long Short-Term Memory (LSTM), Support Vector Machines (SVM) have also been utilized to estimate the cryptocurrency prices. Valencia et al. (2019), for example, applied sentiment analysis and machine learning to predict the prices of Bitcoin, Ethereum, Ripple, and Litecoin and found that these tools can assist investors in cryptocurrency price predictions. Patel et al. (2020) proposed a hybrid pricing model combining machine learning and deep learning mechanisms to estimate the price of Litecoin and Monero. They revealed that the proposed algorithm can accurately forecast cryptocurrency prices. Wang (2021) also employed machine learning to estimate the pricing of 58 coins and 1 token by addressing market, equity, volatility, liquidity, cross-category, and crypto-related factors. The results show that machine learning models can explain much of the cryptocurrency's extreme returns.

Overall, even though the finance literature deals with the return predictability of cryptocurrencies from different perspectives, there is still room to explore the factors behind recurring large price changes, especially given the highly volatile nature of cryptocurrency prices. In doing so, the current study utilizes recurrent event analysis to understand the determinants of large-magnitude rising and falling cryptocurrency prices.

3 Data and Methodology

Cryptocurrencies are decentralized digital assets that are not subject to government or financial institution control. Thus, they are often subject to high fluctuation, which can lead to large daily price movements. Several factors, including cryptocurrency-specific or market factors, influence the large price movements of cryptocurrencies. These factors can cause sudden and significant shifts in demand for cryptocurrencies, leading to sharp price increases or decreases.

The primary aim of the study is to determine whether past or market return has the power to predict subsequent daily large price movements ("jumps" or "dumps") in cryptocurrency. To achieve this, we have initially downloaded the daily price, market capitalization, and volume of the largest 1200 cryptocurrencies (excluding stable coins) based on their market capitalization from CoinMarketCap (https://coinmarketcap.com/coins/). Ozdamar et al. (2021) state that empirically, the cryptocurrencies should have reasonable size to include in the regression analysis since low market capitalization cryptocurrencies mostly have low liquidity, which may complicate the interpretations of the results. Additionally, a coin's initial price behavior may be highly unusual until consumers, miners, and traders accept it. It takes time for it to become widely accepted and liquid. Hence, they exclude cryptocurrencies with a lower market capitalization than $5 million and an initial 6 months of cryptocurrencies after they are launched to invest. Following Ozdamar et al. (2021), we impose the same two restrictions on our sample. The sample period spans between 1 January 2015 and 30 November 2022. The study's sample size begins with 25 cryptocurrencies and ends with 1007.

3.1 Variables Construction

In this study, the primary variables of interest are the past and the market returns. Following Shieh et al. (2012) and Yildiz and Karan (2019), we proxy the past return of a cryptocurrency as a one-day lag of stock return ($Return_{t-1}$), and the value-weighted average return of all cryptocurrencies is used as a one-day lag market return ($Market_{t-1}$).

To boost the validity of the estimation results, we include several control variables. The first set of control variables are the most common factors that affect the return of cryptocurrencies. The second set of control variables captures the systematic and the tail risk of cryptocurrencies. First, we measure the daily liquidity of cryptocurrency as a one-day lag of trading volume divided by the shares outstanding ($Liquidity_{t-1}$). Second, we use a one-day lag of the logarithm of market capitalization ($Size_{t-1}$), which is calculated as the logarithm of price multiple by shares outstanding. Third, to estimate daily volatility, we follow Garman and Klass's (1980) calculation as follows:

$$\text{Volatility}_{i,t} = \sqrt{\frac{1}{2}(h_{i,t} - \text{l}_{i,t})^2 - (2\log 2 - 1)c_{i,t}^2} \tag{1}$$

where $c_{i,t} = \log(\text{close}_{i,t}) - \log(\text{open}_{i,t})$, $l_{i,t} = \log(\text{low}_{i,t}) - \log(\text{open}_{i,t})$ and $h_t = \log(\text{high}_{i,t}) - \log(\text{open}_{i,t})$.

To estimate beta, we mainly follow Scholes and Williams (1977), Dimson (1979), and Ozdamar et al. (2021) and estimate one-day lag beta ($Beta_{t-1}$) using lag, current, and lead returns of the market index within a month as follows:

$$\begin{aligned} R_{i,d} - rf_d = \alpha_i + \beta_{1,i}(R_{m,d-1} - rf_{d-1}) + \beta_{2,i}(R_{m,d} - rf_d) \\ + \beta_{3,i}\left(R_{m,d+1} - rf_{d+1}\right) \end{aligned} \tag{2}$$

where $R_{m,\ d}$ is the cryptocurrency market return on day d, and rf_d refers to the risk free-rate, which is the 1-month T-bill return.[2]

Following Bali et al. (2011), we use one-day lag maximum return (Max_{t-1}) as the maximum daily return within the past week. Lastly, we use one-day lag total skewness ($Skewness_{t-1}$), which is constructed as follows:

[2]One-month T-bill return is obtained from Kenneth French's website.

Table 1 Descriptive statistics

Variables	Observations	Mean	Std.dev.	Minimum	Maximum
$Return_{t-1}$	838,979	−0.002	0.064	−0.778	0.594
$Market\ Return_{t-1}$	838,979	0.0004	0.040	−0.475	0.176
$Liquidity_{t-1}$	838,979	0.108	0.171	0.000	2.096
$Volatility_{t-1}$	838,979	0.065	0.049	0.002	0.855
$Size_{t-1}$	838,979	17.542	1.916	10.209	23.692
$Beta_{t-1}$	838,979	0.917	0.705	−8.205	16.036
Max_{t-1}	838,979	0.092	0.076	−0.018	0.972
$Skewness_{t-1}$	838,979	0.069	0.888	−3.984	3.543

$$\text{Skewness}_{i,d} = \frac{1}{D_m} \sum_{d=1}^{D} \left(\frac{R_{i,d} - \mu_i}{\sigma_i} \right)^3 \tag{3}$$

where D_m is the number of days in a month, $R_{i,\ d}$ is the daily return of cryptocurrency, μ_i is the average return of cryptocurrency in a month, σ_i is the standard deviation of returns of cryptocurrency in a month.

Table 1 presents the descriptive statistics of our variables of interest. The average return of cryptocurrencies in our sample period is −0.002, and the value-weighted average market return is 0.004. The average daily beta is close to 1 and the maximum daily return is 0.092. The average skewness is 0.069.

3.2 Methodology

The primary objective of this research is to determine whether one-day lag return or one-day lag market return is a significant factor in explaining large price movements. We use recurrent event analysis to answer the problem since cryptocurrencies may suffer significant price fluctuations more than once. We handle the time aspect of the data and overcome the event dependence problem by using recurrent event analysis. Recurrent event analysis is based on the Cox proportional hazards model. Thus, we first introduce the Cox Proportional hazard model and then describe recurrent event analysis.

One of the most commonly used models in survival analysis to investigate time-to-event findings between variables and survival time is the Cox proportional hazards model. Cox (1972) develops a model for predicting event timings that include one event per subject and allows for the inclusion of censored observations that would otherwise be ignored in typical regression models. At the same time, the model seeks to analyze the impact of covariates on survival. In other words, hazard rate allows one to analyze how various factors affect the rate at which a specific occurrence occurs at a given point in time.

Although the Cox proportional hazards model is the most commonly used approach for time to event, it has drawbacks when the stocks face several incidents. Due to a violation of the independence assumption, the Cox proportional hazards model may not produce reliable results if a stock has numerous big price movements throughout the sample period (Cox, 1972). As a result, the Cox model is inapplicable when there are several events per subject. Because of this restriction, numerous adaptations to the Cox model have been proposed to counteract recurring events more effectively.

There are several approaches in the literature that address the event dependency issue caused by the existence of numerous events per subject, such as the Andersen-Gill model (Andersen & Gill, 1982), marginal models (Wei et al., 1989), and conditional risk models (Prentice et al., 1981). Andersen and Gill (1982) developed the Andersen-Gill model, also known as the proportional intensity model, as a generalization of the Cox proportional hazards model to allow for the study of recurrent data. The traditional Cox model studies only the first event when each stock has the potential for big price movements until the event occurs. In a recurrent event model, a stock has the potential to see big price movements during the follow-up period, regardless of whether the event has already occurred. However, the baseline proportional intensity function is assumed to be the same for all events in the Andersen and Gill model, regardless of their order. Prentice et al. (1981) provide an approach that separately investigates each sequential event (first, second, etc.). Because the time scale employed in this model is the period from event entry, it is also known as the conditional risk model. Because the model is stratified by event series, the baseline hazard function will differ across consecutive occurrences.

Following Shieh et al. (2012) and Yildiz and Karan (2019), we determine the large price movements as 10%, 15%, and 20% jumps and dumps in a day and adopt a conditional risk model which assumes that events per subject have a natural order and the hazard rates of the ordered events may differ. We adopt the estimation model with shared frailty effects to handle unobservable effects and use robust standard errors to control the heterogeneity problem. To understand the driving factors of large price movements, we estimate the hazard model using $Return_{t-1}$, $Market\ Return_{t-1}$, $Liquidity_{t-1}$, $Volatility_{t-1}$, $Size_{t-1}$, $Beta_{t-1}$, Max_{t-1}, and $Skewness_{t-1}$. The estimated Hazard model can be formulated as follows:

$$h(t) = \begin{aligned} & h_{0i}(t) * \exp\big(b_1 \text{Return}_{i,t-1} + b_2 \text{Market Return}_{i,t-1} + b_3 \text{Liquidity}_{i,t-1} \\ & + b_4 \text{Volatility}_{i,t-1} + b_5 \text{Size}_{i,t-1} + b_6 \text{Beta}_{i,t-1} + b_7 \text{Max}_{i,t-1} \\ & + b_8 \text{Skewness}_{i,t-1} + \mu_i\big) \end{aligned} \tag{4}$$

We standardize the covariates to capture the relative importance of variables in estimating large price movements.

4 Empirical Analysis

The empirical section is divided into five parts: (i) adopt recurrent event analysis to determine whether past return or market return drives the large price movements, (ii) examine whether the co-explosivity has significant impact on large price movements, (iii) investigate the role of the size of cryptocurrencies in terms of the impact of main covariates on large price movements, (iv) examine whether the dominant covariate alters during high and low uncertainty periods, and (v) investigate predictive power of recurrent event analysis as a robustness analysis.

4.1 Estimation Results for Main Analysis

Table 2 presents the results of the recurrent event analysis for large price movements of more than 10%, 15%, and 20%. We first begin with the simple analysis and use only the covariates of interest, one-day lag return, and one-day lag market return. Columns 1–3 show the large price increases and columns 4–6 present the large price decreases. The positive and statistically significant results of past returns *($Return_{t-1}$)* indicate that the likelihood of experiencing large price increases is higher if cryptocurrency returns are positive on the previous day. Conversely, the probability of facing large price decreases is lower when a one-day previous cryptocurrency return is positive. The results align with the previous findings (Shieh et al., 2012; Yıldız & Karan, 2019). When we turn our attention to the second main covariate, market return *($Market\ Return_{t-1}$)*, we have unanticipated outcomes that suggest that the likelihood of facing large price increases (decreases) is lower (higher) when the market return is positive on the previous day. Since the covariates are standardized, the coefficients of magnitudes infer that the dominant factor of large price increases and decreases is a one-day lag return of cryptocurrencies.

Table 2 Recurrent event COX model

Variables	Poz10	Poz15	Poz20	Neg10	Neg15	Neg20
$Return_{t-1}$	0.218[a] (0.000)	0.140[a] (0.000)	0.094[a] (0.000)	−0.156[a] (0.000)	−0.056[a] (0.000)	0.015[c] (0.096)
$Market\ Return_{t-1}$	−0.083[a] (0.000)	−0.071[a] (0.000)	−0.093[a] (0.000)	0.032[a] (0.000)	0.070[a] (0.000)	0.018[c] (0.071)
Likelihood	−341264.7	−166540.7	−93058.8	−353148.6	−150941.9	−74801.8
Wald	2052.9[a] (0.000)	452.49[a] (0.000)	143.7[a] (0.000)	1160.2[a] (0.000)	104.4[a] (0.000)	12.6[a] (0.002)
# of Obs.	56,674	28,382	16,480	58,574	25,864	13,555

Notes: The dependent variable is large price movements of 10%, 15%, and 20% of cryptocurrencies. Independent variables are $Return_{t-1}$, *which* is the one-day lag of stock return, and $Market\ Return_{t-1}$ is the one-day lag of market return. a, b, and c represent the significance level of 1%, 5%, and 10%, respectively

Table 3 Recurrent event COX model with fundamental control variables

Variables	Poz10	Poz15	Poz20	Neg10	Neg15	Neg20
$Return_{t-1}$	0.261[a] (0.000)	0.185[a] (0.000)	0.125[a] (0.000)	−0.269[a] (0.000)	−0.166[a] (0.000)	−0.091[a] (0.000)
Market $Return_{t-1}$	−0.005 (0.241)	0.013[b] (0.036)	0.002 (0.803)	0.103[a] (0.000)	0.142[a] (0.000)	0.112[a] (0.000)
$Liquidity_{t-1}$	0.042[a] (0.000)	0.027[a] (0.000)	0.019[a] (0.005)	−0.069[a] (0.000)	−0.081[a] (0.000)	−0.088[a] (0.000)
$Volatility_{t-1}$	0.289[a] (0.000)	0.309[a] (0.000)	0.298[a] (0.000)	0.307[a] (0.000)	0.292[a] (0.000)	0.283[a] (0.000)
$Size_{t-1}$	0.165[a] (0.000)	0.215[a] (0.000)	0.228[a] (0.000)	0.042[a] (0.000)	0.023[a] (0.000)	0.032[a] (0.000)
Likelihood	– 336335.62	– 163535.3	– 91378.812	– 349778.48	– 149,603	– 74146.35
Wald	14355.68[a] (0.000)	7459.97[a] (0.000)	3905.63[a] (0.000)	9537.03[a] (0.000)	3062.84[a] (0.000)	1421.60[a] (0.000)
# of Obs.	56,674	28,382	16,480	58,574	25,864	13,555

Notes: The dependent variable is large price movements of 10%, 15%, and 20% of cryptocurrencies. Independent variables are $Return_{t-1}$, *which* is the one-day lag of stock return. *Market* $Return_{t-1}$ is the one-day lag of market return, one-day lag size ($Size_{t-1}$), as the natural logarithm of price multiplied by shares outstanding of cryptocurrency, one-day lag liquidity ($Liquidity_{t-1}$), as trading volume divided by the shares outstanding and one-day lag volatility ($Volatility_{t-1}$), as Garman and Klass (1980) volatility measure, of cryptocurrencies. a, b, and c represent the significance level of 1%, 5%, and 10% level, respectively

In addition to univariate specifications, we also adopt multivariate analysis. We include two sets of control variables: (i) we use fundamental control variables such as *size* ($Size_{t-1}$), as measured by the log market value of cryptocurrency, *liquidity* ($Liquidity_{t-1}$), as trading volume divided by the shares outstanding, and *volatility* ($Volatility_{t-1}$), as Garman and Klass (1980) volatility measure, of cryptocurrencies (ii) we control the higher moments, as *skewness* ($Skewness_{t-1}$), extreme returns, as *maximum return* (Max_{t-1}), and systematic risk, *beta* ($Beta_{t-1}$), of cryptocurrencies.

Table 3 shows the estimation results of the recurrent event analysis with control variables for large price movements of more than 10%, 15%, and 20%. Controlling cryptocurrency-specific fundamental variables neither signs nor significantly alters the level of one-day lag return in large price increases (decreases). The positive (negative) coefficient indicates that if the one-day lag return is positive, the probability of experiencing a large price increase (decrease) is higher (lower). Unlike the one-day lag return, the coefficients of the one-day lag market return are insignificant for large price increases of more than 10% and 20%, and the coefficient is positive and statistically significant at a 5% level for 15% increases. The coefficients of large price increases of one-day market return remain positive and statistically significant for large price decreases. Regarding the other covariates, the positive (negative) coefficients of one-day lag liquidity suggest that the likelihood of experiencing a large price increase (decreases) is higher (lower). The findings indicate that before the large price increases (decreases) the investors buy (sell) and increase (decrease)

Table 4 Recurrent event COX model with additional control variables

Variables	Poz10	Poz15	Poz20	Neg10	Neg15	Neg20
Return$_{t-1}$	0.144[a] (0.000)	0.044[a] (0.000)	−0.027[a] (0.000)	−0.258[a] (0.000)	−0.173[a] (0.000)	−0.120[a] (0.000)
Market Return$_{t-1}$	−0.033[a] (0.000)	−0.017[a] (0.004)	−0.019[b] (0.018)	0.068[a] (0.000)	0.116[a] (0.000)	0.098[a] (0.000)
Liquidity$_{t-1}$	−0.003 (0.413)	−0.010[b] (0.045)	−0.021[a] (0.003)	−0.066[a] (0.000)	−0.078[a] (0.000)	−0.089[a] (0.000)
Volatility$_{t-1}$	0.144[a] (0.000)	0.157[a] (0.000)	0.153[a] (0.000)	0.235[a] (0.000)	0.214[a] (0.000)	0.182[a] (0.000)
Size$_{t-1}$	0.059[a] (0.000)	0.070[a] (0.000)	0.062[a] (0.000)	0.060[a] (0.000)	0.054[a] (0.000)	0.045[a] (0.000)
Beta$_{t-1}$	0.038[a] (0.000)	0.042[a] (0.000)	0.050[a] (0.000)	0.118[a] (0.000)	0.123[a] (0.000)	0.088[a] (0.000)
Max$_{t-1}$	0.501[a] (0.000)	0.595[a] (0.000)	0.663[a] (0.000)	0.208[a] (0.000)	0.275[a] (0.000)	0.320[a] (0.000)
Skewness$_{t-1}$	0.153[a] (0.000)	0.252[a] (0.000)	0.324[a] (0.000)	−0.292[a] (0.000)	−0.385[a] (0.000)	−0.325[a] (0.000)
Likelihood	− 325066.95	− 155693.42	− 86328.88	− 346429.55	− 147580.57	− 73349.44
Wald	48092.36[a] (0.000)	30128.16[a] (0.000)	17371.62[a] (0.000)	17286.66[a] (0.000)	7507.68[a] (0.000)	3104.18[a] (0.000)
# of Obs.	56,674	28,382	16,480	58,574	25,864	13,555

Notes: The dependent variable is large price movements of 10%, 15%, and 20% of cryptocurrencies. Independent variables are *Return$_{t-1}$, which* is the one-day lag of stock return. *Market Return$_{t-1}$* is the one-day lag of market return, one-day lag size (*Size$_{t-1}$*), as the natural logarithm of price multiplied by shares outstanding of cryptocurrency, one-day lag liquidity (*Liquidity$_{t-1}$*), as trading volume divided by the shares outstanding, one-day lag volatility (*Volatility$_{t-1}$*), as Garman and Klass (1980) volatility measure, one-day lag beta (*Beta$_{t-1}$*), as systematic risk estimated by lag, current and lead returns of the market index within a month, one-day lag maximum daily return (*Max$_{t-1}$*), as the maximum daily return within the past week, and one-day lag skewness (*Skewness$_{t-1}$*), as total skewness of cryptocurrencies. a, b, and c represent the significance level of 1%, 5%, and 10% level, respectively

the trading volume of cryptocurrencies. One-day lag volatility and size exhibit similar patterns. The coefficients of volatility and size are positive and statistically significant regardless of large price increases or decreases. This indicates that an increase in volatility or size has a positive impact on the probability of experiencing large price movements.

Ozdamar et al. (2021) show that extreme and higher moments returns have a significant impact on cryptocurrency returns. Following these studies, we decide to include additional control variables. Table 4 reports the effect of our covariates on the large price movements, including the second set of control variables, namely, skewness, maximum daily return, and beta, in addition to the fundamental control variables. The sign and significant level of one-day lag return remain positive (negative) and significant for large price increases (decreases) expect higher than positive 20% increases. Adding lottery-like control variables affects the significant level of coefficients one-day lag market return for large price increases. Unlike Table 3, the coefficients of one-day lag market return are negative and statistically significant, suggesting that the likelihood of observing large price increases (decreases) is lower (higher) when the market return is positive on the previous day. When we turn our attention to control variables, volatility and size have a similar impact as in Table 3. However, the coefficient of one-day lag liquidity becomes negative in large price increases and insignificant for 10% large price increases. The coefficients of one-day lag beta, max, and skewness are positive for large price increases, indicating that the probability of facing large price increases is higher when the one-day lag beta, skewness, and max are positive. The coefficients of beta and max remain positive and significant for large price decreases, whereas the coefficients are negative and statistically significant for skewness. The magnitude of coefficients suggests that one-day lag return is still the dominant factor compared to one-day lag market return.

To show that the estimation results are not driven by the choice of variables, we use alternative measures for market return, liquidity, and volatility. In the main analysis, we proxy market return as the value-weighted average return of all cryptocurrencies in the sample. Alternatively, we measure market return using the Crypto Currencies Index (which can be downloaded at https://cci30.com/), which is the average return of the 30 largest cryptocurrencies in the market. The index has been used as a cryptocurrency market return in finance literature (Kurt Gümüş et al., 2019; Haykir & Yagli, 2022).

Brauneis et al. (2021) present evidence that Amihud (2002) illiquidity measure is one of the best proxies among low-frequency liquidity measures to capture the price impact in the cryptocurrency market. Thus, we use Amihud (2002) as a proxy for liquidity instead of volume. To construct daily Amihud measure, we use 30-day rolling windows calculation as follows:

$$\text{Amihud}_{i,m} = \frac{1}{D_{im}} \sum_{d=1}^{D_{im}} \frac{|\text{Return}_{id}|}{\text{Dvol}_{id} * 10^6} \tag{5}$$

Return_{id} is the daily return, and Dvol_{id} is the dollar value of the trading volume on day d for cryptocurrency i. The Amihud measure captures the illiquidity; hence, increases in the Amihud measure indicate low liquidity.

Since the cryptocurrency market is open 24/7, it is difficult to determine a fair opening and closing price for each cryptocurrency. To address this concern, we construct an alternative volatility proxy: realized (historical) volatility. Following Figlewski (1994), we use a 30-day rolling window standard deviation of historical return to construct a daily realized volatility measure.

Table 5 presents the estimation results of the recurrent event model with alternative proxies for market return, liquidity, and volatility. At first glance, the estimation coefficients of one-day lag return remain similar to previous findings. The coefficients are positive (negative) and statistically significant for large price increases (decreases). On the contrary, the proxy for market return, one-day lag CCI Return, is

Table 5 Recurrent event COX model with alternative proxies for fundamental control variables

Variables	Poz10	Poz15	Poz20	Neg10	Neg15	Neg20
$Return_{t-1}$	0.175[a] (0.000)	0.095[a] (0.000)	0.040[a] (0.000)	−0.209[a] (0.000)	−0.124[a] (0.000)	−0.079[a] (0.000)
$CCI\ Return_{t-1}$	−0.080[a] (0.000)	−0.068[a] (0.000)	−0.060[a] (0.000)	−0.005 (0.286)	0.013[c] (0.087)	0.0001 (0.999)
$Amihud_{t-1}$	0.038[a] (0.000)	0.021[a] (0.000)	0.008 (0.352)	−0.024[a] (0.000)	−0.022[a] (0.002)	−0.016[c] (0.083)
$Realized\ Volatility_{t-1}$	0.274[a] (0.000)	0.393[a] (0.000)	0.500[a] (0.000)	0.457[a] (0.000)	0.627[a] (0.000)	0.726[a] (0.000)
$Size_{t-1}$	0.073[a] (0.000)	0.075[a] (0.000)	0.057[a] (0.000)	0.020[a] (0.000)	0.010 (0.150)	0.008 (0.406)
$Beta_{t-1}$	−0.002 (0.507)	−0.015[a] (0.006)	−0.017[b] (0.019)	0.038[a] (0.000)	0.037[a] (0.000)	0.013 (0.123)
Max_{t-1}	0.426[a] (0.000)	0.469[a] (0.000)	0.480[a] (0.000)	0.071[a] (0.000)	0.042[a] (0.000)	0.042[a] (0.000)
$Skewness_{t-1}$	0.124[a] (0.000)	0.226[a] (0.000)	0.309[a] (0.000)	−0.218[a] (0.000)	−0.342[a] (0.000)	−0.367[a] (0.000)
Likelihood	– 324065.4	– 154431.9	– 85110.7	– 343078.5	– 144560.8	– 71457.7
Wald	48338.5[a] (0.000)	32059.4[a] (0.000)	19982.1[a] (0.000)	24673.2[a] (0.000)	14936.2[a] (0.000)	7563.5[a] (0.000)
# of Obs.	56,674	28,382	16,480	58,574	25,864	13,555

Notes: The dependent variable is large price movements of 10%, 15%, and 20% of cryptocurrencies. Independent variables are $Return_{t-1}$, *which* is the one-day lag of stock return. $Market\ Return_{t-1}$ is the one-day lag of CCI index return, one-day lag size ($Size_{t-1}$), as the natural logarithm of price multiplied by shares outstanding of cryptocurrency, one-day lag Amihud ($Amihud_{t-1}$), as 30 days average of the price changes per dollar of the volume unit of trade one-day lag realized volatility ($Realized\ Volatility_{t-1}$), as 30-day rolling window standard deviation of the daily return, one-day lag beta ($Beta_{t-1}$), as systematic risk estimated by lag, current and lead returns of the market index within a month, one-day lag maximum daily return (Max_{t-1}), as the maximum daily return within the past week, and one-day lag skewness ($Skewness_{t-1}$), as total skewness of cryptocurrencies. a, b, and c represent the significance level of 1%, 5%, and 10% level, respectively

insignificant for large price decreases, whereas negative and significant for large price increases. Compared to volume-based liquidity measures, the coefficients of Amihud are positive (negative) and significant for 10% and 15% large price increases (decreases). The sign and significant level of realized volatility are similar to the Garman and Klass (1980) volatility measure. Including alternative proxies for market return, volatility, and liquidity does not alter the estimation results for size, max, and skewness variables, whereas beta has become negative for large price increases.

4.2 Co-explosivity Analysis

Prior literature demonstrates that explosive behavior in one cryptocurrency influences others since the lack of fundamental methodologies to determine the fair value of cryptocurrencies and the lack of financial literacy among cryptocurrency investors (Bouri et al., 2019a, b; Haykir & Yagli, 2022). Thus, to capture the effect of large price movements in the ten highest market capitalization cryptocurrencies on altcoins large price movements, we investigate co-explosivity analysis. We construct a dummy variable that gets one if large price increases (decreases) occur in the ten highest market capitalization cryptocurrencies and zero otherwise. Specifically, we first identify the highest market capitalization cryptocurrencies each day, and then we determine the large price movements for these 10 highest market capitalization cryptocurrencies and name them co-explosivity. Table 6 shows the results of the co-explosivity analysis. The estimation results indicate that the probability of experiencing large price increases in the ten highest market capitalization coins does not have a significant impact on large price increases.

4.3 Size Quintile Analysis

Banz (1981) claims that smaller stocks tend to yield higher returns than larger stocks. This phenomenon has gained attention afterward; other studies have also found similar results in international and US stock markets (Roll, 1981; Lakonishok & Shapiro, 1986; Fama & French, 1992, 2012). Li et al. (2020) investigate the size effect in the cryptocurrency market and reveal that the size effect exists in the cryptocurrency market. Thus, to eliminate the size effect, we construct quintiles for each day based on the market capitalization of cryptocurrencies and our baseline estimation as in Eq. (4) for each sub-group. We only present small-cap, mid-cap, and large-cap sub-group results for brevity. Table 7 shows the results of size sub-groups. The estimation results of one-day lag return differ in sub-groups for large price increases of more than 15% and 20%. On the other hand, the coefficients are negative and statistically significant for large price decreases. The results of one-day lag market return are mostly insignificant in size sub-groups for large price increases, whereas mostly positive and significant (except for small-cap group) for large price decreases.

4.4 Uncertainty Analysis

To understand the dynamics of large price movements under uncertainty, we divide the sample into two sub-periods based on the median value of Cryptocurrency Policy Uncertainty Index (UCRY Policy). The index value is weekly and constructed using

Table 6 Recurrent event COX model: co-explosivity analysis

Variables	Poz10	Poz15	Poz20	Neg10	Neg15	Neg20
Co-explosivity$_{t-1}$	−0.005 (0.897)	0.102 (0.134)	0.144 (0.152)	−0.143[a] (0.001)	−0.062 (0.414)	−0.194[c] (0.088)
Return$_{t-1}$	0.144[a] (0.000)	0.044[a] (0.000)	−0.027[a] (0.000)	−0.258[a] (0.000)	−0.173[a] (0.000)	−0.120[a] (0.000)
Market Return$_{t-1}$	−0.032[a] (0.000)	−0.017[a] (0.004)	−0.019[b] (0.018)	0.068[a] (0.000)	0.116[a] (0.000)	0.098[a] (0.000)
Liquidity$_{t-1}$	−0.003 (0.412)	−0.010[b] (0.047)	−0.021[a] (0.003)	−0.066[a] (0.000)	−0.078[a] (0.000)	−0.090[a] (0.000)
Volatility$_{t-1}$	0.145[a] (0.000)	0.157[a] (0.000)	0.153[a] (0.000)	0.235[a] (0.000)	0.214[a] (0.000)	0.182[a] (0.000)
Size$_{t-1}$	0.059[a] (0.000)	0.069[a] (0.000)	0.062[a] (0.000)	0.060[a] (0.000)	0.054[a] (0.000)	0.045[a] (0.000)
Beta$_{t-1}$	0.038[a] (0.000)	0.042[a] (0.000)	0.051[a] (0.000)	0.118[a] (0.000)	0.123[a] (0.000)	0.089[a] (0.000)
Max$_{t-1}$	0.501[a] (0.000)	0.595[a] (0.000)	0.662[a] (0.000)	0.209[a] (0.000)	0.275[a] (0.000)	0.321[a] (0.000)
Skewness$_{t-1}$	0.152[a] (0.000)	0.251[a] (0.000)	0.324[a] (0.000)	−0.291[a] (0.000)	−0.385[a] (0.000)	−0.324[a] (0.000)
Likelihood	− 325066.9	− 155692.3	− 86327.8	− 346424.4	− 147580.2	− 73347.9
Wald	48091.7[a] (0.000)	30132.8[a] (0.000)	17374.3[a] (0.000)	17287.1[a] (0.000)	7505.5[a] (0.000)	3103.9[a] (0.000)
# of Obs.	56,674	28,382	16,480	58,574	25,864	13,555

Notes: The dependent variable is large price movements of 10%, 15%, and 20% of cryptocurrencies. Independent variables are *Co-explosivity$_{t-1}$* is a one-day lag of a dummy variable that gets one if large price increases (decreases) occur in the ten highest market capitalization cryptocurrencies and zero otherwise. *Return$_{t-1}$* is the one-day lag of stock return, *Market Return$_{t-1}$* is the one-day lag of market return, one-day lag size (*Size$_{t-1}$*), as the natural logarithm of price multiplied by shares outstanding of cryptocurrency, one-day lag liquidity (*Liquidity$_{t-1}$*), as trading volume divided by the shares outstanding, one-day lag volatility (*Volatility$_{t-1}$*), as Garman and Klass (1980) volatility measure, one-day lag beta (*Beta$_{t-1}$*), as systematic risk estimated by lag, current and lead returns of the market index within a month, one-day lag maximum daily return (*Max$_{t-1}$*), as the maximum daily return within the past week, and one-day lag skewness (*Skewness$_{t-1}$*), as total skewness of cryptocurrencies. a, b, and c represent the significance level of 1%, 5%, and 10%, respectively

news from the LexisNexis database. If the UCRY Policy index in a week is higher than the median of the index, we define that week as a high UCRY period. On the other hand, if the UCRY Policy index in a week is lower than the median of the index, we define that week as a low UCRY period and estimate Eq. (4).

Table 8 presents the results of the uncertainty sub-periods analysis. The coefficients of one-day lag return are positive and significant for large price increases of more than 10% and 15%, whereas the coefficient is insignificant for more than 20% increases during a high uncertainty period. One-day market return is negative (positive) for large price increases (decreases) during the high uncertainty period. During the low uncertainty sub-period, one-day lag return is positive and significant

Table 7 Recurrent event COX model: size sorting analysis

Variables	POZ10 Small cap	POZ10 Mid-cap	POZ10 Large cap	POZ15 Small cap	POZ15 Mid-cap	POZ15 Large cap	POZ20 Small cap	POZ20 Mid-cap	POZ20 Large cap	NEG10 Small cap	NEG10 Mid-cap	NEG10 Large cap	NEG15 Small cap	NEG15 Mid-cap	NEG15 Large cap	NEG20 Small cap	NEG20 Mid-cap	NEG20 Large cap
$Return_{t-1}$	0.135^{a}	0.050^{a}	0.102^{a}	0.044^{a}	−0.046^{a}	0.020	0.009	−0.080^{a}	−0.031	−0.183^{a}	−0.233^{a}	−0.215^{a}	−0.130^{a}	−0.138^{a}	−0.223^{a}	−0.089^{a}	−0.105^{a}	−0.299^{a}
	(0.000)	(0.000)	(0.000)	(0.000)	(0.000)	(0.238)	(0.532)	(0.000)	(0.191)	(0.000)	(0.000)	(0.000)	(0.000)	(0.000)	(0.000)	(0.000)	(0.000)	(0.000)
$Market\ Return_{t-1}$	−0.028^{a}	−0.001	−0.021^{c}	−0.023^{c}	0.017	−0.021	−0.016	−0.003	−0.057^{b}	0.007	0.048^{a}	0.076^{a}	0.044^{a}	0.074^{a}	0.190^{a}	0.029^{c}	0.057^{b}	0.250^{a}
	(0.002)	(0.968)	(0.096)	(0.058)	(0.221)	(0.249)	(0.274)	(0.873)	(0.041)	(0.431)	(0.000)	(0.000)	(0.000)	(0.000)	(0.000)	(0.078)	(0.036)	(0.000)
$Liquidity_{t-1}$	−0.024^{a}	−0.027^{a}	0.071^{a}	−0.022^{b}	−0.040^{a}	0.005	−0.019	−0.024	0.026	−0.059^{a}	−0.061^{a}	−0.036^{a}	−0.069^{a}	−0.057^{a}	−0.009	−0.072^{a}	−0.028	−0.002
	(0.004)	(0.003)	(0.000)	(0.048)	(0.002)	(0.721)	(0.195)	(0.130)	(0.209)	(0.000)	(0.000)	(0.000)	(0.000)	(0.000)	(0.518)	(0.000)	(0.123)	(0.941)
$Volatility_{t-1}$	0.140^{a}	0.112^{a}	0.106^{a}	0.142^{a}	0.105^{a}	0.128^{a}	0.127^{a}	0.138^{a}	0.117^{a}	0.165^{a}	0.230^{a}	0.265^{a}	0.146^{a}	0.223^{a}	0.257^{a}	0.159^{a}	0.194^{a}	0.282^{a}
	(0.000)	(0.000)	(0.000)	(0.000)	(0.000)	(0.000)	(0.000)	(0.000)	(0.000)	(0.000)	(0.000)	(0.000)	(0.000)	(0.000)	(0.000)	(0.000)	(0.000)	(0.000)
$Size_{t-1}$	0.016	0.012^{a}	0.205^{a}	0.006	0.142^{a}	0.297^{a}	−0.018	0.121^{a}	0.326^{a}	0.025^{a}	0.164^{a}	0.166^{a}	0.033^{b}	0.228^{a}	0.314^{a}	0.070^{a}	0.299^{a}	0.520^{a}
	(0.135)	(0.000)	(0.000)	(0.687)	(0.000)	(0.000)	(0.379)	(0.000)	(0.000)	(0.007)	(0.000)	(0.000)	(0.013)	(0.000)	(0.000)	(0.000)	(0.000)	(0.000)
$Beta_{t-1}$	0.025^{a}	0.042^{a}	0.037^{a}	0.046^{a}	0.048^{a}	0.016	0.033^{b}	0.039^{b}	−0.014	0.070^{a}	0.110^{a}	0.141^{a}	0.073^{a}	0.144^{a}	0.132^{a}	0.058^{a}	0.166^{a}	0.065^{b}
	(0.002)	(0.000)	(0.000)	(0.000)	(0.000)	(0.327)	(0.026)	(0.043)	(0.548)	(0.000)	(0.000)	(0.000)	(0.000)	(0.000)	(0.000)	(0.000)	(0.000)	(0.038)
Max_{t-1}	0.503^{a}	0.453^{a}	0.438^{a}	0.601^{a}	0.504^{a}	0.505^{a}	0.677^{a}	0.482^{a}	0.483^{a}	0.233^{a}	0.165^{a}	0.135^{a}	0.321^{a}	0.163^{a}	0.127^{a}	0.366^{a}	0.159^{a}	0.061^{c}
	(0.000)	(0.000)	(0.000)	(0.000)	(0.000)	(0.000)	(0.000)	(0.000)	(0.000)	(0.000)	(0.000)	(0.000)	(0.000)	(0.000)	(0.000)	(0.000)	(0.000)	(0.057)
$Skewness_{t-1}$	0.078^{a}	0.118^{a}	0.177^{a}	0.141^{a}	0.199^{a}	0.238^{a}	0.199^{a}	0.265^{a}	0.359^{a}	−0.218^{a}	−0.249^{a}	−0.376^{a}	−0.327^{a}	−0.279^{a}	−0.413^{a}	−0.366^{a}	−0.202^{a}	−0.131^{a}
	(0.000)	(0.000)	(0.000)	(0.000)	(0.000)	(0.000)	(0.000)	(0.000)	(0.000)	(0.000)	(0.000)	(0.000)	(0.000)	(0.000)	(0.000)	(0.000)	(0.000)	(0.000)
Likelihood	−64907.9	−58294.4	−39586.3	−33369.8	−28232.3	−17028.6	−19785.9	−15677.3	−8542.6	−80198.5	−60086.9	−36847.1	−40226.6	−24191.2	−13023.4	−22339.4	−11397.9	−5673.1
Wald	7209.9^{a}	5514.7^{a}	6462.9^{a}	4813.4^{a}	3015.5^{a}	3133.1^{a}	3138.1^{a}	1707.1^{a}	1643.3^{a}	2848.4^{a}	2704.9^{a}	2977.5^{a}	1897.2^{a}	1033.1^{a}	958.4^{a}	1259.4^{a}	451.6^{a}	400.36^{a}
	(0.000)	(0.000)	(0.000)	(0.000)	(0.000)	(0.000)	(0.000)	(0.000)	(0.000)	(0.000)	(0.000)	(0.000)	(0.000)	(0.000)	(0.000)	(0.000)	(0.000)	(0.000)
# of Obs.	14,175	11,406	8989	7785	5901	4075	4940	3584	2227	16,678	11,648	8373	8804	5103	3190	5262	2771	1600

Notes: We construct quintiles for each day based on the market capitalization of cryptocurrencies. The dependent variable is large price movements of 10%, 15%, and 20% of cryptocurrencies. Independent variables are $Return_{t-1}$, which is the one-day lag of stock return, $Market\ Return_{t-1}$ is the one-day lag of market return, one-day lag size ($Size_{t-1}$), as the natural logarithm of price multiplied by shares outstanding of cryptocurrency, one-day lag liquidity ($Liquidity_{t-1}$), as trading volume divided by the shares outstanding, one-day lag volatility ($Volatility_{t-1}$), as Garman and Klass (1980) volatility measure, one-day lag beta ($Beta_{t-1}$), as systematic risk estimated by lag, current and lead returns of the market index within a month, one-day lag maximum daily return (Max_{t-1}), as the maximum daily return within the past week, and one-day lag skewness ($Skewness_{t-1}$), as total skewness of cryptocurrencies. a, b, and c represent the significance level of 1%, 5%, and 10%, respectively

Table 8 Recurrent event COX model: uncertainty analysis

	High uncertainty						Low uncertainty					
Variables	Poz10	Poz15	Poz20	Neg10	Neg15	Neg20	Poz10	Poz15	Poz20	Neg10	Neg15	Neg20
$Return_{t-1}$	0.161[a] (0.000)	0.071[a] (0.000)	0.007 (0.364)	−0.270[a] (0.000)	−0.188[a] (0.000)	−0.131[a] (0.000)	0.124[a] (0.000)	0.031[b] (0.019)	−0.044[b] (0.013)	−0.181[a] (0.000)	−0.108[a] (0.000)	−0.063[a] (0.004)
Market $Return_{t-1}$	−0.038[a] (0.000)	−0.025[a] (0.000)	−0.027[a] (0.003)	0.081[a] (0.000)	0.148[a] (0.000)	0.121[a] (0.000)	−0.035[a] (0.006)	0.004 (0.827)	−0.020 (0.467)	0.042[a] (0.001)	0.086[a] (0.000)	0.067[b] (0.034)
$Liquidity_{t-1}$	0.003 (0.446)	−0.002 (0.701)	0.002 (0.793)	−0.069[a] (0.000)	−0.074[a] (0.000)	−0.092[a] (0.000)	−0.004 (0.610)	0.016 (0.231)	−0.003 (0.835)	−0.064[a] (0.000)	−0.094[a] (0.000)	−0.117[a] (0.000)
$Volatility_{t-1}$	0.139[a] (0.000)	0.159[a] (0.000)	0.161[a] (0.000)	0.248[a] (0.000)	0.229[a] (0.000)	0.202[a] (0.000)	0.187[a] (0.000)	0.187[a] (0.000)	0.225[a] (0.000)	0.167[a] (0.000)	0.150[a] (0.000)	0.136[a] (0.000)
$Size_{t-1}$	0.065[a] (0.000)	0.079[a] (0.000)	0.090[a] (0.000)	0.057[a] (0.000)	0.062[a] (0.000)	0.063[a] (0.000)	0.104[a] (0.000)	0.114[a] (0.000)	0.049[c] (0.075)	0.073[a] (0.000)	0.031 (0.121)	−0.072[b] (0.019)
$Beta_{t-1}$	0.056[a] (0.000)	0.052[a] (0.000)	0.044[a] (0.000)	0.127[a] (0.000)	0.134[a] (0.000)	0.105[a] (0.000)	0.005 (0.510)	0.022[b] (0.046)	0.031[c] (0.051)	0.044[a] (0.000)	0.033[a] (0.008)	0.013 (0.470)
Max_{t-1}	0.489[a] (0.000)	0.573[a] (0.000)	0.629[a] (0.000)	0.186[a] (0.000)	0.254[a] (0.000)	0.291[a] (0.000)	0.429[a] (0.000)	0.525[a] (0.000)	0.603[a] (0.000)	0.218[a] (0.000)	0.279[a] (0.000)	0.388[a] (0.000)
$Skewness_{t-1}$	0.129[a] (0.000)	0.228[a] (0.000)	0.294[a] (0.000)	−0.269[a] (0.000)	−0.364[a] (0.000)	−0.292[a] (0.000)	0.114[a] (0.000)	0.136[a] (0.000)	0.179[a] (0.000)	−0.224[a] (0.000)	−0.300[a] (0.000)	−0.357[a] (0.000)
Likelihood	−266066.2	−129162.4	−71774.7	−289482.1	−124533.7	−62881.7	−62288.4	−28726.8	−15674.7	−59724.8	−24409.1	−11267.2
Wald	33570.6[a]	20962.8[a]	12735.2[a]	13891.1[a]	5938.7[a]	2265.3[a]	6274.1[a]	3442.4[a]	2095.4[a]	1430.8[a]	698.2[a]	519.6[a]
# of Obs.	44,469	22,594	13,236	47,154	21,095	11,259	12,586	6187	3648	11,815	5172	2701

Notes: If the UCRY Policy index is used to distinguish high and low uncertainty periods. If the UCRY Policy Index in a week is higher (lower) than the median of the index, we define that week as a high (low) UCRY period. The dependent variable is large price movements of 10%, 15%, and 20% of cryptocurrencies. Independent variables are $Return_{t-1}$, which is the one-day lag of stock return, *Market* $Return_{t-1}$ is the one-day lag of market return, one-day lag size ($Size_{t-1}$), as the natural logarithm of price multiplied by shares outstanding of cryptocurrency, one-day lag liquidity ($Liquidity_{t-1}$), as trading volume divided by the shares outstanding, one-day lag volatility ($Volatility_{t-1}$), as Garman and Klass (1980) volatility measure, one-day lag beta ($Beta_{t-1}$), as systematic risk estimated by lag, current and lead returns of the market index within a month, one-day lag maximum daily return (Max_{t-1}), as the maximum daily return within the past week, and one-day lag skewness ($Skewness_{t-1}$), as total skewness of cryptocurrencies. a, b, and c represent the significance level of 1%, 5%, and 10%, respectively

for more than 10% and 15% large price increases; however, it is negative and significant for more than 20% large price increases. One-day lag market return is insignificant for more than 15% and 20% large price increases but negative and significant for more than 10% increases. The coefficients of large price decreases are positive and significant for a one-day lag market return.

4.5 *Predictive Power of Recurrent Event Analysis*

To enhance the accuracy and predictive capability of our models, we utilize both in-sample and out-of-sample prediction techniques. In assessing the efficacy of our risk models within the realm of survival analysis, we employ one of the most widely recognized metrics—Harrell's C, introduced by Harrell et al. in 1982. Also known as the concordance index, this metric serves as a robust measure of goodness of fit for models that calculate risk scores. A value exceeding 0.5 signifies the model's strong predictive capacity. To implement an out-of-sample model evaluation, we employ a random categorization process, segregating companies into treatment and control groups within each country. Subsequently, we assess the predictive performance of our model using the treatment groups. Table 9 displays the outcomes of the predictive power analysis results for the entire sample, market capitalization sub-groups, and high-low uncertainty periods. The results reveal that Harrell's C score consistently surpasses the 0.5 threshold for almost all the analyses, indicating that our models possess superior predictive capability compared to random selection. Both in-sample and out-of-sample assessments affirm that our estimation models exhibit comparable predictive power. Notably, estimation results show superior predictive accuracy in identifying large price increases except small-cap model.

5 Conclusion

Cryptocurrencies are high-yield investment assets that attract new investors to be part of the cryptocurrency market. However, the risk-return tradeoff states that investors desire higher returns for higher risk. Therefore, determining factors affecting cryptocurrency prices assists investors in balancing between risk and return. The implications of cryptocurrency pricing extend beyond the financial markets. They impact investment strategies, influence regulatory decisions, and stimulate innovation in blockchain technology. As cryptocurrencies continue to evolve, understanding their pricing dynamics becomes increasingly crucial for investors, policymakers, and businesses seeking to navigate the digital economy.

The study investigates determinants of large-price changes considering the high volatility structure of the cryptocurrency market. To do so, we employ recurrent event analysis based on the Cox proportional hazards model in accordance with frequent high-price changes in the cryptocurrency market. Among the covariates,

Table 9 Predictive power analysis

Harrell's C	Entire sample		Small cap		Mid-cap		Large cap		High uncertainty		Low uncertainty	
	In-sample	Out-of-sample	In-sample	Out-of-sample	In-sample	Out-of-sample	In-sample	Out-of-sample	In-sample	Out-of-sample	In-sample	Out-of-sample
Poz10	0.515	0.516	0.511	0.510	0.565	0.568	0.548	0.549	0.538	0.540	0.497	0.500
Poz15	0.516	0.516	0.520	0.518	0.577	0.580	0.559	0.558	0.542	0.543	0.505	0.513
Poz20	0.522	0.524	0.531	0.538	0.593	0.588	0.579	0.573	0.553	0.544	0.531	0.526
Neg10	0.506	0.507	0.518	0.520	0.524	0.524	0.496	0.498	0.522	0.522	0.507	0.506
Neg15	0.504	0.508	0.514	0.513	0.540	0.537	0.503	0.506	0.521	0.517	0.521	0.522
Neg20	0.516	0.518	0.522	0.523	0.580	0.577	0.577	0.585	0.536	0.531	0.555	0.549

Notes: The table presents the results of in-sample and out-of-sample predictive power analysis using a 10%, 15%, and 20% large price increase and decrease for the full sample period, market capitalization sub-groups, and high-low uncertainty periods past return, market return, liquidity, volatility, size, beta, maximum return, and skewness are used to estimate the hazard model. We also consider the effect of size and market conditions and co-explosivity analysis. Our analysis encompasses a dataset comprising 1200 cryptocurrencies, with the sample period spanning from January 1, 2015, to November 30, 2022.

Our results show that (i) the likelihood of encountering significant price increases (decreases) is greater (lower) when the cryptocurrency's return is positive the day before. Conversely, the chance of experiencing notable price increases (decreases) is lower (higher) when the overall market return for the cryptocurrency is positive on the previous day, (ii) the direction of the previous day's large price movements of the top 10 cryptocurrencies does not affect the probability of facing substantial price changes, (iii) analysis of sub-size groups reveals a mixed impact on the probability of encountering significant price increases for both previous day return and market return, while the results remain consistent for large price decreases, (iv) the effect of covariates on large price changes do not sensitive to the market conditions, (v) lastly, our models exhibit superior predictive capabilities compared to random models.

The empirical findings of this study offer valuable insights with significant policy implications for cryptocurrency investors. Firstly, investors may consider adjusting their investment strategies based on the observed lag effect, where the likelihood of encountering significant price increases (decreases) is greater (lower) when the cryptocurrency's return is positive the day before. This suggests that investors could potentially capitalize on positive momentum by strategically timing their trades to align with positive historical returns. Secondly, the inverse relationship between overall market return and the likelihood of notable price increases (decreases) indicates that investors should be attuned to broader market conditions. When the overall market return is positive, exercising caution or employing risk mitigation strategies may be prudent to navigate the higher likelihood of subsequent notable price decreases. Moreover, the results suggest that the direction of the previous day's large price movements in the price of the 10 largest cryptocurrencies may have limited predictive power regarding substantial price changes in altcoins. As such, investors in these top cryptocurrencies might benefit from diversifying their analytical approach beyond short-term historical price movements. In addition, the nuanced impact observed within sub-size groups underscores the importance of tailored strategies. Investors should carefully analyze the specific characteristics of cryptocurrencies within different sub-size groups, considering both previous day return and market return, to optimize decision-making. This approach acknowledges the heterogeneous nature of the cryptocurrency market and provides a more nuanced understanding for investors seeking to navigate various segments within it. Given that uncertainty periods do not significantly influence the probability of experiencing significant price increases or decreases, investors may find it beneficial to maintain a steady investment approach during such periods rather than altering their strategies based on perceived uncertainties. This stability-oriented approach aligns with the observed resilience of price dynamics during uncertainty periods.

In conclusion, our study's policy implications suggest that investors stand to benefit from adopting a nuanced and adaptive approach that considers lag effects, market conditions, cryptocurrency characteristics, and predictive modeling enhancements. These insights contribute to the evolving discourse on effective investment strategies in the dynamic and complex landscape of cryptocurrency markets. As a future study, the sample period can be extended, and the effect of covariates is investigated for different magnitudes of price changes.

References

Akyildirim, E., Aysan, A. F., Cepni, O., & Darendeli, S. P. C. (2021). Do investor sentiments drive cryptocurrency prices? *Economics Letters, 206*, 109980. https://doi.org/10.1016/j.econlet.2021.109980

Al-Yahyaee, K. H., Mensi, W., Ko, H. U., Yoon, S. M., & Kang, S. H. (2020). Why cryptocurrency markets are inefficient: The impact of liquidity and volatility. *The North American Journal of Economics and Finance, 52*, 101168. https://doi.org/10.1016/j.najef.2020.101168

Andersen, P. K., & Gill, R. D. (1982). Cox's regression model for counting processes: A large sample study. *The Annals of Statistics*, 1100–1120.

Amihud, Y. (2002). Illiquidity and stock returns: Cross-section and time-series effects. *Journal of Financial Markets, 5*(1), 31–56. https://doi.org/10.1111/j.2517-6161.1972.tb00899.x

Aysan, A. F., Demir, E., Gozgor, G., & Lau, C. K. M. (2019). Effects of the geopolitical risks on Bitcoin returns and volatility. *Research in International Business and Finance, 47*, 511–518. https://doi.org/10.1016/j.ribaf.2018.09.011

Baek, C., & Elbeck, M. (2015). Bitcoins as an investment or speculative vehicle? A first look. *Applied Economics Letters, 22*(1), 30–34. https://doi.org/10.1080/13504851.2014.916379

Bali, T. G., Cakici, N., & Whitelaw, R. F. (2011). Maxing out: Stocks as lotteries and the cross-section of expected returns. *Journal of Financial Economics, 99*(2), 427–446. https://doi.org/10.1016/j.jfineco.2010.08.014

Banz, R. W. (1981). The relationship between return and market value of common stocks. *Journal of Financial Economics, 9*(1), 3–18. https://doi.org/10.1016/0304-405X(81)90018-0

Baur, D. G., Hong, K., & Lee, A. D. (2018). Bitcoin: Medium of exchange or speculative assets? *Journal of International Financial Markets, Institutions and Money, 54*, 177–189. https://doi.org/10.1016/j.intfin.2017.12.004

Bouri, E., Gupta, R., & Roubaud, D. (2019b). Herding behaviour in cryptocurrencies. *Finance Research Letters, 29*, 216–221. https://doi.org/10.1016/j.frl.2018.07.008

Bouri, E., Shahzad, S. J. H., & Roubaud, D. (2019a). Co-explosivity in the cryptocurrency market. *Finance Research Letters, 29*, 178–183. https://doi.org/10.1016/j.frl.2018.07.005

Brauneis, A., Mestel, R., Riordan, R., & Theissen, E. (2021). How to measure the liquidity of cryptocurrency markets? *Journal of Banking & Finance, 124*, 106041. https://doi.org/10.1016/j.jbankfin.2020.106041

Cagli, E. C. (2019). Explosive behavior in the prices of Bitcoin and altcoins. *Finance Research Letters, 29*, 398–403. https://doi.org/10.1016/j.frl.2018.09.007

Cardify. (2021). All aboard the crypto train: Who are the latest crypto investors?. https://www.cardify.ai/reports/crypto

Caporale, G. M., & Plastun, A. (2019). Price overreactions in the cryptocurrency market. *Journal of Economic Studies, 46*(5), 1137–1155. https://doi.org/10.1108/JES-09-2018-0310

Cheah, E. T., & Fry, J. (2015). Speculative bubbles in Bitcoin markets? An empirical investigation into the fundamental value of Bitcoin. *Economics Letters, 130*, 32–36. https://doi.org/10.1016/j.econlet.2015.02.029

Cox, D. R. (1972). Regression models and life-tables. *Journal of the Royal Statistical Society: Series B (Methodological), 34*(2), 187–202.

Corbet, S., Lucey, B., & Yarovaya, L. (2018). Datestamping the Bitcoin and Ethereum bubbles. *Finance Research Letters, 26*, 81–88. https://doi.org/10.1016/j.frl.2017.12.006
Cumming, D. J., Johan, S., & Pant, A. (2019). Regulation of the crypto-economy: Managing risks, challenges, and regulatory uncertainty. *Journal of Risk and Financial Management, 12*(3), 126. https://doi.org/10.3390/jrfm12030126
Demir, E., Gozgor, G., Lau, C. K. M., & Vigne, S. A. (2018). Does economic policy uncertainty predict the Bitcoin returns? An empirical investigation. *Finance Research Letters, 26*, 145–149. https://doi.org/10.1016/j.frl.2018.01.005
Derbentsev, V., Matviychuk, A., & Soloviev, V. N. (2020). Forecasting of cryptocurrency prices using machine learning. In *Advanced studies of financial technologies and cryptocurrency markets* (pp. 211–231). Springer. https://doi.org/10.1007/978-981-15-4498-9_12
Dimson, E. (1979). Risk measurement when shares are subject to infrequent trading. *Journal of Financial Economics, 7*(2), 197–226. https://doi.org/10.1016/0304-405X(79)90013-8
Dwyer, G. P. (2015). The economics of Bitcoin and similar private digital currencies. *Journal of Financial Stability, 17*, 81–91. https://doi.org/10.1016/j.jfs.2014.11.006
Fama, E. F., & French, K. R. (1992). The cross-section of expected stock returns. *Journal of Finance, 47*(2), 427–465.
Fama, E. F., & French, K. R. (2012). Size, value, and momentum in international stock returns. *Journal of Financial Economics, 105*(3), 457–472. https://doi.org/10.1016/j.jfineco.2012.05.011
Figlewski, S. (1994). Forecasting volatility using historical data. NYU Working Paper No. FIN-94-032.
Gandal, N., Hamrick, J. T., Moore, T., & Oberman, T. (2018). Price manipulation in the Bitcoin ecosystem. *Journal of Monetary Economics, 95*, 86–96. https://doi.org/10.1016/j.jmoneco.2017.12.004
Garman, M. B., & Klass, M. J. (1980). On the estimation of security price volatilities from historical data. *Journal of Business*, 67–78.
Geuder, J., Kinateder, H., & Wagner, N. F. (2019). Cryptocurrencies as financial bubbles: The case of Bitcoin. *Finance Research Letters, 31*. https://doi.org/10.1016/j.frl.2018.11.011
Gozgor, G., Tiwari, A. K., Demir, E., & Akron, S. (2019). The relationship between Bitcoin returns and trade policy uncertainty. *Finance Research Letters, 29*, 75–82. https://doi.org/10.1016/j.frl.2019.03.016
Gregoriou, A. (2019). Cryptocurrencies and asset pricing. *Applied Economics Letters, 26*(12), 995–998. https://doi.org/10.1080/13504851.2018.1527439
Gronwald, M. (2021). How explosive are cryptocurrency prices? *Finance Research Letters, 38*, 101603. https://doi.org/10.1016/j.frl.2020.101603
Hamrick, J. T., Rouhi, F., Mukherjee, A., Feder, A., Gandal, N., Moore, T., & Vasek, M. (2018). *The economics of cryptocurrency pump and dump schemes*. CEPR Discussion Paper No. DP13404, Available at SSRN: https://ssrn.com/abstract=3310307
Haykir, O., & Yagli, I. (2022). Speculative bubbles and herding in cryptocurrencies. *Financial Innovation, 8*(1), 78. https://doi.org/10.1186/s40854-022-00383-0
Kakinaka, S., & Umeno, K. (2022). Cryptocurrency market efficiency in short-and long-term horizons during COVID-19: An asymmetric multifractal analysis approach. *Finance Research Letters, 46*, 102319. https://doi.org/10.1016/j.frl.2021.102319
Kurt Gümüş, G., Gümüş, Y., & Çimen, A. (2019). Herding behaviour in cryptocurrency market: CSSD and CSAD analysis. *Blockchain Economics and Financial Market Innovation: Financial Innovations in the Digital Age*, 103–114. https://doi.org/10.1007/978-3-030-25275-5_6
Kyriazis, N., Papadamou, S., & Corbet, S. (2020). A systematic review of the bubble dynamics of cryptocurrency prices. *Research in International Business and Finance, 54*, 101254. https://doi.org/10.1016/j.ribaf.2020.101254
Lakonishok, J., & Shapiro, A. C. (1986). Systematic risk, total risk and size as determinants of stock market returns. *Journal of Banking & Finance, 10*(1), 115–132. https://doi.org/10.1016/0378-4266(86)90023-3

Li, Y., Zhang, W., Xiong, X., & Wang, P. (2020). Does size matter in the cryptocurrency market? *Applied Economics Letters, 27*(14), 1141–1149. https://doi.org/10.1080/13504851.2019.1673298

Liu, Y., & Tsyvinski, A. (2021). Risks and returns of cryptocurrency. *The Review of Financial Studies, 34*(6), 2689–2727. https://doi.org/10.1093/rfs/hhaa113

Naeem, M. A., Bouri, E., Peng, Z., Shahzad, S. J. H., & Vo, X. V. (2021). Asymmetric efficiency of cryptocurrencies during COVID19. *Physica A: Statistical Mechanics and its Applications, 565*, 125562. https://doi.org/10.1016/j.physa.2020.125562

Nahar, P. (2022). *Can crypto mart's m-cap zoom 100 times by 2030? Here's what experts say.* https://economictimes.indiatimes.com/markets/cryptocurrency/can-crypto-marts-m-cap-zoom-100-times-by-2030-heres-what-experts-say/articleshow/88755153.cms.

Ozdamar, M., Akdeniz, L., & Sensoy, A. (2021). Lottery-like preferences and the MAX effect in the cryptocurrency market. *Financial Innovation, 7*(1), 1–27. https://doi.org/10.1186/s40854-021-00291-9

Patel, M. M., Tanwar, S., Gupta, R., & Kumar, N. (2020). A deep learning-based cryptocurrency price prediction scheme for financial institutions. *Journal of Information Security and Applications, 55*, 102583. https://doi.org/10.1016/j.jisa.2020.102583

Prentice, R. L., Williams, B. J., & Peterson, A. V. (1981). On the regression analysis of multivariate failure time data. *Biometrika, 68*(2), 373–379. https://doi.org/10.1093/biomet/68.2.373

Roll, R. (1981). A possible explanation of the small firm effect. *The Journal of Finance, 36*(4), 879–888. https://doi.org/10.1111/j.1540-6261.1981.tb04890.x

Scholes, M., & Williams, J. (1977). Estimating betas from nonsynchronous data. *Journal of Financial Economics, 5*(3), 309–327. https://doi.org/10.1016/0304-405X(77)90041-1

Shahzad, S. J. H., Anas, M., & Bouri, E. (2022). Price explosiveness in cryptocurrencies and Elon Musk's Tweets. *Finance Research Letters, 47*, 102695. https://doi.org/10.1016/j.frl.2022.102695

Shahzad, S. J. H., Bouri, E., Ahmad, T., Naeem, M. A., & Vo, X. V. (2021). The pricing of bad contagion in cryptocurrencies: A four-factor pricing model. *Finance Research Letters, 41*, 101797. https://doi.org/10.1016/j.frl.2020.101797

Shen, D., Urquhart, A., & Wang, P. (2020). A three-factor pricing model for cryptocurrencies. *Finance Research Letters, 34*, 101248. https://doi.org/10.1016/j.frl.2019.07.021

Shieh, S. J., Lin, C. Y., & Ho, P. H. (2012). Large changes in stock prices: Market, liquidity, and momentum effect. *The Quarterly Review of Economics and Finance, 52*(2), 183–197. https://doi.org/10.1016/j.qref.2012.02.003

Urquhart, A. (2016). The inefficiency of Bitcoin. *Economics Letters, 148*, 80–82. https://doi.org/10.1016/j.econlet.2016.09.019

Valencia, F., Gómez-Espinosa, A., & Valdés-Aguirre, B. (2019). Price movement prediction of cryptocurrencies using sentiment analysis and machine learning. *Entropy, 21*(6), 589. https://doi.org/10.3390/e21060589

Vidal-Tomás, D., Ibáñez, A. M., & Farinós, J. E. (2019). Herding in the cryptocurrency market: CSSD and CSAD approaches. *Finance Research Letters, 30*, 181–186. https://doi.org/10.1016/j.frl.2018.09.008

Wang, Q. (2021). Cryptocurrencies asset pricing via machine learning. *International Journal of Data Science and Analytics, 12*, 175–183. https://doi.org/10.1007/s41060-021-00252-6

Wang, Q., & Chong, T. T. L. (2021). Factor pricing of cryptocurrencies. *The North American Journal of Economics and Finance, 57*, 101348. https://doi.org/10.1016/j.najef.2020.101348

Wei, L. J., Lin, D. Y., & Weissfeld, L. (1989). Regression analysis of multivariate incomplete failure time data by modeling marginal distributions. *Journal of the American Statistical Association, 84*(408), 1065–1073.

Yermack, D. (2015). Is Bitcoin a real currency? An economic appraisal. *Handbook of digital currency. Elsevier, 31–43*. https://doi.org/10.1016/B978-0-12-802117-0.00002-3

Yildiz, Y., & Karan, M. B. (2019). Momentum or market? Determinants of large stock price changes in an emerging market. *Applied Economics, 51*(7), 731–742. https://doi.org/10.1080/00036846.2018.1524128

Yousaf, I., & Yarovaya, L. (2022). Herding behavior in conventional cryptocurrency market, non-fungible tokens, and DeFi assets. *Finance Research Letters, 50*, 103299. https://doi.org/10.1016/j.frl.2022.103299

Zaremba, A., Bilgin, M. H., Long, H., Mercik, A., & Szczygielski, J. J. (2021). Up or down? Short-term reversal, momentum, and liquidity effects in cryptocurrency markets. *International Review of Financial Analysis, 78*, 101908. https://doi.org/10.1016/j.irfa.2021.101908

Zhang, W., & Li, Y. (2021). Liquidity risk and expected cryptocurrency returns. *International Journal of Finance & Economics*. https://doi.org/10.1002/ijfe.2431

Zhang, W., Wang, P., Li, X., & Shen, D. (2018a). Some stylized facts of the cryptocurrency market. *Applied Economics, 50*(55), 5950–5965. https://doi.org/10.1080/00036846.2018.1488076

Zhang, W., Wang, P., Li, X., & Shen, D. (2018b). The inefficiency of cryptocurrency and its cross-correlation with Dow Jones Industrial Average. *Physica A: Statistical Mechanics and its Applications, 510*, 658–670. https://doi.org/10.1016/j.physa.2018.07.032

Zhang, Z., Dai, H. N., Zhou, J., Mondal, S. K., García, M. M., & Wang, H. (2021). Forecasting cryptocurrency price using convolutional neural networks with weighted and attentive memory channels. *Expert Systems with Applications, 183*, 115378. https://doi.org/10.1016/j.eswa.2021.115378

Unraveling Profitability Determinants of Insurance Companies in Kazakhstan: Exploring Firm-Specific and Macroeconomic Factors

Almas Kalaubay, Alimshan Faizulayev, and Nejat Capar

1 Introduction

In the service-based economy, the insurance sector is crucial and is gradually included in the larger financial sector. Insurance companies in Kazakhstan offer a variety of insurance services and products, including property insurance, annuity insurance, life insurance, third-party liability for motor vehicles, and many others. The financial sector in Kazakhstan has proven to be very resilient in the face of difficult macroeconomic conditions and international developments. Banks, the insurance industry, the stock market, non-bank financial institutions (NBFIs), and other financial institutions comprise the nation's financial sector.

Additionally, the insurance industry performs important intermediary functions in terms of risk transmission, boosting private investment, job creation, and securing numerous initiatives related to development. To be viable in the competitive, international environment, profit-making is a must for firms operating in the insurance market. Insurance companies cannot raise outside funds to accomplish their goals without profit. Numerous variables, such as inflation rate, size, leverage ratio, tangibility ratio, market share and many others, can impact an insurance company's profitability. While some of these variables may affect the insurers' profitability favorably, others may affect negatively. Furthermore, some of these factors are internal, which can be taken under the control of management, while others are external, and insurers have no control over them. Regulators, insurance managers, and supervisors find it crucial to comprehend the internal and external elements affecting insurers' profitability.

A. Kalaubay · A. Faizulayev (✉) · N. Capar
Bang College of Business, KIMEP University, Almaty, Republic of Kazakhstan
e-mail: a.faizulayev@kimep.kz

N. Ozatac et al. (eds.), *Sustainable Development in Banking and Finance*, Springer Proceedings in Business and Economics,
https://doi.org/10.1007/978-3-031-65533-3_3

Consequently, this research aims to pinpoint the crucial factors affecting insurance businesses' financial performance in Kazakhstan. Moreover, to determine the profitability, this study considered both firm-specific variables such as gross written premiums, firm size, capital adequacy, and liquidity ratio, as well as macroeconomic variables such as GDP growth rate and population growth. The choice of companies and time period is largely motivated by data availability. Thirty-two listed companies were selected for this research for the past 10 years, from 2011 to 2021.

This study is structured as follows: The first section discusses a review of the literature on the factors that affect the profitability of the insurance sector, then the data and methodology, as well as the hypotheses is provided in the next section, followed by results and their interpretation, and the study's conclusion with some recommendations and limitations of the study is presented in the final section.

2 Literature Review

Numerous studies have empirically determined the elements that affect the profitability of traditional banks, Islamic banks, manufacturing firms, mining companies, and other businesses. In fact, the number of publications is gradually increasing due to analysts' and scientists' rising interest in the variables affecting the insurance industry's profitability. However, there still seems to be a tiny number of published papers regarding the insurance sector in Kazakhstan. In the past, the following literature reviews were performed in other countries in terms of variables that influenced the financial performance of insurance companies. The studies are (Berhe & Kaur, 2017; Murungi, 2014; Guendouz & Ouassaf, 2018; Kramaric et al., 2017; Kozak, 2011; Malik, 2011; Nebolsina, 2020) and other similar studies but on other industries were conducted.

There was a research article in which the researcher investigated the profitability determinants of Pakistan's insurance industry. Moreover, a list of variables, such as age, size of the company, leverage and loss ratios, has been examined to observe the impact of these firm-specific variables on the profitability of companies. The 35 listed companies of Pakistan were used in the paper from 2005 to 2009. One of the study's conclusions demonstrated no correlation between profitability and firm age but a strong correlation between profitability and company size. Also, the researcher proposed that, as independent variables, the link between leverage and loss ratios should be reversed and significant to increase profitability (Malik, 2011).

Another researcher investigated variables that mostly impact Ethiopian insurance companies' profitability. In particular, it looks at the firm-specific variables of insurance company size, capital adequacy, leverage ratio and inflation rate. Following the results of the Hausman test, the fixed effect model was employed. Panel data for 17 insurance companies were analyzed over a 10-year period from 2005 to 2014 (Berhe & Kaur, 2017).

According to one of the researchers that have examined how macroeconomic factors, insurance-specific factors, and insurance industry-specific factors affect the performance of the insurance markets in a few Central and Eastern European nations. The study specifically examined the insurance industries in Croatia, Slovenia, Hungary, and Poland from 2010 to 2014. In the model, return on equity (ROE) and return on assets (ROA) were used as dependent performance variables. As a result, the age variable had a significant and positive effect on ROA and ROE. Moreover, real GDP per capita growth is another factor that has a major and favorable impact on performance in terms of ROE, not ROA. This indicates that the profitability of an insurance firm is influenced by both company-specific and macroeconomic factors (Kramaric et al., 2017).

Another researcher used panel data from 25 non-life insurance businesses from 2002 to 2009 to examine the factors that affected the non-life insurance companies' profitability in Poland. The findings of an estimated regression model showed that the increase in other types of insurance while simultaneously increasing the amount of motor insurance in the portfolio has benefitted the profitability and cost-efficiency of insurance businesses. However, providing an excessively wide range of insurance classes has a negative impact on its profitability and cost-effectiveness. Increases in gross premiums and decreases in overall operating costs help businesses become more profitable and cost-effective. In addition, non-life insurance's profitability is positively affected by GDP growth and the percentage of foreign-owned businesses in the market (Kozak, 2011) (Table 1).

3 Insurance Economics Theory

According to Doreen et al. (2014), insurance contracts can be seen as options. The person who sells an option is known as an option writer, and the premium received for the option is referred to as the option premium. A put option purchase and buying portfolio insurance are comparable, according to Doreen et al. (2014). This is because they both make it possible for investors to minimize losses while also maximizing big rewards (Murungi, 2014).

4 Variables Description

4.1 Dependent variable

All the variables used in the analysis were picked based on relevant theory and literature. In particular, the literature review portion of earlier studies on the subject was consulted by the writers. Since ROE is one of the crucial and helpful metrics for gauging business performance, it was used in the research's model as a dependent variable (Kramaric et al., 2017).

Table 1 Literature review of similar studies

Author with date	Title	Country	Industry	Method	Results
Athanasoglou et al. (2006)	Bank-specific, industry-specific and macroeconomic determinants of bank profitability	Greece	Banking	Profit persistence using a dynamic panel data estimation procedure	Defined how capital plays a key role in understanding bank profitability and how rising credit risk reduces earnings. Additionally, increasing labor productivity significantly and favorably affects profitability
Berhe and Kaur (2017)	Determinants of insurance companies profitability: an analysis of insurance sector in Ethiopia	Ethiopia	Insurance	Hausman test	According to the regression analysis's findings, the insurance company's profitability is affected by key variables: the insurance's size, capital sufficiency, liquidity ratio, and GDP growth rate
Doreen U. Murungi (2014)	Relationship between macroeconomic variables and financial performance of insurance companies in Kenya	Kenya	Insurance	The study population comprising 49 insurance firms that are registered in Kenya by the year 2015. The study utilized secondary data that was collected quarter yearly. The data was analyzed using multiple regression analysis, correlation analysis and descriptive analysis, using STATA software	The coefficients corresponding to selected macroeconomic variables; interest rates and GDP growth rates were positive, while the exchange rates, inflation rates and unemployment rates were negative
Faizulayev et al. (2021)	What drives the financial performance in the banking	CIS countries	Banking	Panel data statistics in CIS countries' banks between 1991–2017	Determined that while macroeconomic issues negatively affect financial performance,

	industry? The case of cis countries				some bank-specific factors positively and significantly boost profitability
Faizulayev et al. (2018)	Profitability and persistency in the service industry: the case of QISMUT+ 3	QISMUT+ 3	Islamic Banking	The dynamic system GMM methodology	High-profit persistency and increasing profitability of International banks' gains are high political stability can also strengthen its role
Guendouz and Ouassaf (2018)	Determinants of Saudi Takaful Insurance Companies' Profitability	Saudi Arabia	Insurance	The ordinary least squares (OLS) and Hausman test	Negative relationship between loss ratio and profitability, a positive contribution from the growth rate of written premiums, and a negative impact of risk level on profitability are all factors that positively influence profitability
Kramaric et al. (2017)	Profitability determinants of insurance markets in selected Central and Eastern European countries	Central and Eastern European countries, including Croatia, Slovenia, Hungary and Poland	Insurance	The ordinary least squares (OLS)	According to the findings, both the ROA and ROE models' performance are significantly and favorably influenced by the ln AGE variable. Real GDP per capita growth is significantly and favorably influenced, but only by the ROE model. Such a finding implies that improved insurance performance requires favorable macroeconomic circumstances. As a result, a strong

(continued)

Table 1 (continued)

Author with date	Title	Country	Industry	Method	Results
					link with profitability has macroeconomic and insurance company-specific factors
Kozak (2011)	Determinants of profitability of non-life insurance companies in Poland during integration with the European financial system	Poland	Insurance	A panel of 25 non-life insurance providers that did business in Poland between 2002 and 2009. STATA software was used for computing and the regression approach for estimate, which eliminated heteroscedasticity and autocorrelation	For robustness of results, the regression estimations were conducted for four measures of profitability and efficiency
Malik (2011)	Determinants of insurance companies profitability: an analysis of insurance sector of Pakistan	Pakistan	Insurance	Age, size, voc, leverage, and loss ratio are the variables examined in this study. Multiple regression analysis and descriptive statistics were used	The findings indicate that profitability and age of the business have no relationship, while profitability and size have a strong positive correlation. The outcome also demonstrates that profitability and volume of capital were significantly and favorably correlated
Nebolsina (2020)	The impact of demographic burden on insurance density	25 economies worldwide	Insurance	Panel vector autoregression models for the period 1980–2016 (PVAR models)	Determined that negative consequences are more enduring over time, which may be due to the economy

					being negatively impacted by the rising population burden. Short-term increases in life and non-life insurance density are caused by rising female and male old-age dependency ratios
Pan and Pan (2014)	The impact of macro factors on the profitability of China's commercial banks in the decade after WTO Accession	China	Banking	Eviews is software, Hausman test	The results of macroeconomic states that there is a substantial influence on the earning power of commercial banks. The most obvious is money supply growth

4.2 Independent variables

4.2.1 Firm-Specific Variables

Gross written insurance premiums The link between the gross written premiums and profitability of insurance companies in Kazakhstan, using the FGLS analysis method, has not been studied so far. However, it is expected to have a positive impact on profitability since the growth of insurance premiums collected by companies should increase the profitability of organizations (Kozak, 2011).

Firm size One of the most crucial factors this study considered was the size of an insurance firm. The logarithm of the total assets function is used as a proxy for insurer size because it is the way to estimate the size of insurance companies properly. Some previous studies referred to this and found that the main justification for considering an insurer's size is that larger insurers typically have a better capacity for coping with adverse market fluctuations than smaller ones, which leads to higher profitability. As a result, more empirical research is being done on the indicator of insurer size and profitability (Malik, 2011).

Capital adequacy This refers to the difference between an insurance company's asset and its liability values. It is a crucial sign of an insurer's financial performance and its capacity for long-term survival. Those companies with higher equity-to-asset ratios are viewed as having stronger financial stability and, therefore, better equipped to draw a variety of policyholders. In other words, it is generally believed that during the event of a loss or insolvency, it is best to choose insurance companies with larger capital adequacy ratios due to security. However, the risk is lower and the creditworthiness of insurers may increase if their equity-to-asset ratio is higher. As a result, insurance companies will pay less for funding. Additionally, insurance companies with stronger equity-to-asset ratios will have less need for outside funding (Malik, 2011). The equity-to-asset ratios' connection with profitability is exceedingly difficult to prove. However, this research will identify whether it has a significant or non-significant impact in both positive and negative ways.

Liquidity ratio This refers to an insurer's capacity to settle its immediate liabilities by the due date. The ratio of current assets to current liabilities is a standard way to quantify it. Additionally, it demonstrates an insurer's capacity to swiftly transform its assets into cash. A low liquidity ratio is a sign that an insurer is having trouble paying its immediate obligations. On the other side, a very high liquidity ratio could also indicate that the insurer is saving funds that could be earning money by making investments in profitable businesses. This makes the correlation between profitability and the liquidity ratio uncertain and necessitates further research, which will be covered in this study (Berhe & Kaur, 2017; Guendouz & Ouassaf, 2018; Kramaric et al., 2017).

4.2.2 Macroeconomic Variables

Growth rate of GDP It is a macroeconomic factor, and its impact on insurers' financial performance is anticipated to be favorable, given that economic growth raises people's purchasing power through raising living standards and income levels. Thus, it is anticipated that this variable will have a favorable impact on performance measurements (Murungi, 2014; Guendouz & Ouassaf, 2018; Pan & Pan, 2014).

Population growth Despite the fact that the relationship between population growth and the profitability of insurance companies has not yet been properly studied, particularly in Kazakhstan, it is anticipated to have a positive impact, given that the country's population is expanding, which should increase insurance companies' profitability. This implies that both customer numbers and insurance product sales will rise (Nebolsina, 2020).

Time dummy 2020–2021 In this particular period, the inflation was 7.3%. Food products increased in price by 10.8% over the year, non-food products by 5.7%, and paid services by 4.1%. This was all due to the COVID-19 worldwide pandemic crisis period that has also not bypassed Kazakhstan. This research will identify how this specific time period affected the financial performance of the insurance sector in Kazakhstan.

5 Hypotheses of the Study

Based on the literature above, the following hypotheses are proposed:

H1: Gross written insurance premiums are expected to have a positive effect on the profitability of insurance organizations in Kazakhstan (Kozak, 2011).
H2: Firm Size is more likely to have a significant and positive impact on the profitability of insurance organizations in Kazakhstan (Berhe & Kaur, 2017; Malik, 2011).
H3: Capital adequacy is anticipated to positively affect the profitability of insurance organizations in Kazakhstan (Malik, 2011).
H4: The liquidity ratio is expected to have a negative impact on the profitability of insurance organizations in Kazakhstan (Berhe & Kaur, 2017).
H5: The growth rate of GDP is expected to positively influence the profitability of insurance organizations in Kazakhstan (Murungi, 2014; Guendouz & Ouassaf, 2018; Pan & Pan, 2014).
H6: Population growth is more likely to affect profitability significantly and positively (Nebolsina, 2020).
H7: Time dummy is more likely to have a negative influence on the profitability of insurance organizations in Kazakhstan. However, this variable still leaves uncertainty and necessitates further research, which will be covered in this study.

6 Data and Methodology

6.1 Data

Panel data statistics from Kazakhstan insurance organizations is used in this analysis. With the exception of the ROE data, which was gathered between 2016 and 2021, all the variables were evaluated between 2011 and 2021 for the analysis. The National Bank of the Republic of Kazakhstan and The Agency of the Republic of Kazakhstan for Regulation and Development of Financial Market provided data on industry-specific variables for the study. In contrast, the macroeconomic variables were retrieved from the World Bank and The Agency for Strategic Planning and Reforms of the Republic of Kazakhstan's Bureau of National Statistics. The symbols of each variable, their proxy measurements, and the researchers' evidence are all included in the description of the variables used in this study in Table 2 (see below).

6.2 Methodology

This study's goal is to empirically evaluate the effects of macroeconomic and insurance-specific variables on the financial performance of insurance companies in Kazakhstan. To analyze the variables, the feasible generalized least square (FGLS) is employed. This model was employed according to the article by Faizulayev et al. (2021). Since nine variables were used (N) over 10 years (T) or if $N < T$ in the model, it is suggested to use FGLS to solve the autocorrelation and heteroscedasticity problems (Faizulayev et al., 2021).

The regression model for the dependent variable of ROE is displayed below:

Table 2 Summary of variables

Symbol	Variables	Proxy	Researchers
ROE	Return on equity	Net income divided by average equity (%)	Guendouz and Ouassaf (2018)
GWP	Gross written insurance premiums	Logarithm of total gross written premium	Kozak (2011)
SIZE	Firm size	Logarithm of total assets	Malik (2011)
CAP	Capital adequacy	Calculated as total capital to total assets (%)	Malik (2011)
LIQ	Liquidity ratio	Calculated as liquid assets to total assets (%)	Berhe and Kaur (2017)
GDP	Growth rate of GDP	Gross Domestic Product (%)	Guendouz and Ouassaf (2018)
POP	Population growth	Population growth (%)	Nebolsina (2020)
Time dummy	Insurance sector, crisis in Kazakhstan	1 = Insurance sector crisis, 0 = None	Faizulayev et al. (2018)

Note—compiled by the author

$$\text{ROE} = B0 + B1(\text{SIZE}) + B2(\text{GWP}) + B3(\text{CAP}) + B4(\text{LIQ}) + B5(\text{GDP}) + B6(\text{POP}) + B7(\text{Time Dummy}) + E$$

Here, ROE is the dependent variable, "B0" is the constant term, "*B*" is the coefficients and "*E*" is the error term.

7 Research Results

The descriptive statistics of the independent and dependent variables employed in the study is shown in Table 3 above. Indicators of average performance are favorable. Only two negative signals (CAP with minimum bounds of −1.282511 and GDP with minimum boundaries of −2.5) are indicated. POP has the highest mean value of 14.56636. GDP has the highest standard deviation rate, which is 2.573509. In addition, it is noticeable that there are three variables that have almost the same rate of standard deviation among the others. Moreover, those are: GWP, which is 0.5589102; SIZE, 0.5473544; and POP, 0.5245651. The LIQ mean value displays the lowest value, which is 0.0520562.

The stationarity test is necessary for unbalanced data only. However, the data in this research is strongly balanced and the stationarity test was conducted for extra precaution. According to Table 4 above, the findings of the Fisher-type unit-root test

Table 3 Descriptive statistics

Variable	Mean	Min	Max	Standard deviation (SD)
ROE	0.1385406	−0.1589225	0.8216857	0.1426938
SIZE	7.120273	5.584699	8.573484	0.5473544
GWP	6.789861	4.242492	8.113604	0.5589102
CAP	0.4649265	−1.282511	0.9740864	0.2483603
LIQ	0.0520562	0.0000404	0.7191989	0.0980243
GDP	3.536364	−2.5	7.4	2.573509
POP	14.56636	13.79	15.45	0.5245651
Time dummy	0.1818182	0	1	0.3862436

Note—compiled by the author

Table 4 Stationarity results

p-value	SIZE	GWP	CAP	LIQ	GDP	POP	Time dummy
Inverse chi-squared	0.5333	0.3041	0.0000	0.0000	0.0000	0.9978	1.0000
Inverse normal	0.9867	0.9830	0.0004	0.0000	0.0000	0.8234	1.0000
Inverse logit t	0.9857	0.9722	0.0000	0.0000	0.0000	0.7934	1.0000
Modified inv. Chi-squared	0.5563	0.3205	0.0000	0.0000	0.0000	0.9924	1.0000

Note—compiled by the author

revealed that variables that, at a significance level of 1%, are stationary. The next stage was to determine whether there was a problem with multicollinearity between independent variables once each variable's stationarity had been examined.

When attempting to explain the dependent variable, the use of multiple independent factors might result in inaccurate and inflated estimates of each independent variable's contribution. This issue may arise when there is significant collinearity between two or more independent variables. Multicollinearity can result in unreasonably high regression standard error estimates, which, in turn, might lead to incorrect conclusions about the importance of independent variables in the model under consideration (Kozak, 2011). The independent variables are inter-independent, according to the assumptions that should be used in the study.

8 Multicollinearity, Autocorrelation and Heteroscedasticity Tests

Group-wise heteroscedasticity, autocorrelation, and multicollinearity tests must be present for the feasible generalized least square (FGLS) model to be used. Tables 5, 6, 7, 8, and 9 display the findings of the diagnostic tests.

According to the correlation study, the insurance companies' financial performance drivers are dependent variables ROE and GWP, both of which have values of 43.30%. In contrast, the independent variables, such as SIZE and GWP, both have values of 74.63% and are positively correlated. These findings are consistent with the research by Kozak (2011). The relationship is, however, unfavorable, particularly between ROE and CAP (−41.92%).

The findings in Table 6 above demonstrate that Mean VIF is 3.77, greater than >1, and less than <5, and <10, which is a suitable degree of multicollinearity. This means that there is *no multicollinearity*.

Additionally, the Wooldridge test for autocorrelation in panel data indicated that the probability of f statistic (*Prob > F*) is significant and equals to *0.3677*, which is greater than >1, >5 and >10, meaning *no autocorrelation* disturbance (Table 7).

In the data provided in Table 8, the probability value of the chi2 (Prob > chi2) test for heteroscedasticity was significant (p less than <0.01, <0.05, <0.1), which showed that there is *an existence of heteroscedasticity* that must be solved and taken under control by using FGLS method. This finding aligns with (Faizulayev et al., 2021), where they researched the banking sector in CIS countries.

Table 5 Multicollinearity results

	ROE	SIZE	GWP	CAP	LIQ	GDP	POP	Time dummy
ROE	1.0000							
SIZE	0.2342	1.0000						
GWP	0.4330	0.7463	1.0000					
CAP	−0.4192	−0.0841	−0.3175	1.0000				
LIQ	−0.2224	−0.1554	−0.3268	0.3389	1.0000			
GDP	0.0595	−0.0131	−0.0158	0.1094	0.0305	1.0000		
POP	−0.1586	−0.2127	−0.1836	0.0592	0.1410	−0.0116	1.0000	1.0000
Time dummy	0.1049	0.2059	0.1849	−0.1096	−0.1477	−0.4985	−0.7922	1.0000

Note—compiled by the author

Table 6 Variance inflationary factor (VIF)

Variable	VIF	1/VIF
Time dummy	8.81	0.113480
POP	6.56	0.152546
GDP	3.28	0.304903
GWP	2.79	0.358427
SIZE	2.46	0.406583
CAP	1.27	0.788744
LIQ	1.22	0.816422
Mean VIF	**3.77**	

Note—compiled by the author

Table 7 Autocorrelation for ROE

Wooldridge test for autocorrelation in panel data
H0: no first-order autocorrelation
F(1, 27) = **0.839**
Prob > F = **0.3677**

Note—compiled by the author

Table 8 Heteroscedasticity test

Likelihood-ratio test LR chi2(104) = 181.20
(Assumption: homo nested in hetero) Prob > chi2 = 0.0000

Note—compiled by the author

Table 9 Determinants of ROE

ROE	Coef.	Std. Err.	*z*	*P* > [*z*]	[95% Conf	Interval]	Sig
SIZE	−0.0653895	0.0085734	−7.63	0	−0.082	−0.049	***
GWP	0.0771604	0.0081684	9.45	0	0.061	0.093	***
CAP	0.0026375	0.0160528	0.16	0.869	−0.029	0.034	
LIQ	0.0055282	0.0183228	0.30	0.763	−0.03	0.041	
GDP	0.0032486	0.0019338	1.68	0.093	−0.001	0.007	*
POP	−0.0041174	0.0167849	−0.25	0.806	−0.037	0.029	
Time dummy	0.0238543	0.0169682	1.41	0.16	−0.009	0.057	
Constant	0.0629784	0.2552014	0.25	0.805	−0.437	0.563	
Mean-dependent var		0.141	SD-dependent var				0.143
Number of obs		165	Chi-square				229.182
Prob > chi2		0.000	Akaike crit. (AIC)				−333.986

Note—compiled by the author
$^{***}p < 0.01$, $^{**}p < 0.05$, $^{*}p < 0.1$

9 Regression Analysis Using the FGLS Model

The same Econometric model, illustrated above in the methodology part for this study, is provided below with the results of the FGLS model:

$$\text{ROE} = \begin{array}{l} 0.0629784 - 0.0653895(\text{SIZE}) + 0.0771604(\text{GWP}) + 0.0026375(\text{CAP}) \\ + 0.0055282(\text{LIQ}) + 0.0032486(\text{GDP}) - 0.0041174(\text{POP}) \\ + 0.0238543(\text{time dummy}) + E \end{array}$$

9.1 *Cross-Sectional Time-Series FGLS Regression*

The findings of the regression analysis between dependent and independent variables are depicted in Table 9. According to the model, the insurance-specific variables such as SIZE, GWP and GDP have P-values less than <1, <5, <10, indicating a meaningful link with profitability measures.

Assuming that ceteris paribus, the size of companies operating on the insurance market has a statistically significant and detrimental impact on ROE (−0.0653895), which means that a 1% increase in SIZE will decrease the ROE by 0.065%. This finding contradicts the hypothesis theory of this research mentioned above, based on a similar study conducted by Berhe and Kaur (2017), who concluded that according to the relative market power concept, businesses with big customer bases may typically use their market power to maximize earnings by selling their products. As a result, this does not necessarily mean that a bigger company leads to higher profits and a small business leads to low profits.

Also, gross written insurance premiums of insurance organizations are statistically significant and affect profitability positively. As a result, a 1% increase in GWP will boost the financial performance of insurance businesses by 0.077%. Simply put, the increase in gross premiums enhances cost effectiveness, implying that larger businesses pay less to collect premiums and raises the profitability of the company's core insurance operations and overall profitability. This finding aligns with (Kozak, 2011), where profitability was positively affected by gross premiums of non-life insurance companies in Poland.

Regarding macro variables, the study found a substantial and positive association between the Gross Domestic Product and the insurers' profitability in Kazakhstan. Similar to this discovery, the earlier researchers who verified a substantial and positive relationship between GDP and profitability were Murungi (2014) and Pan and Pan (2014) in 2014. Therefore, the 1% increase in GDP will increase the profitability of insurance companies by 0.003%, which means that the estimated positive coefficient of the variable indicates a strong connection between economic growth and profitability. Furthermore, economic growth can help insurance companies be more profitable by boosting demand for financial services, which in turn boosts insurers' cash flows and profit margins. The need for insurance services would undoubtedly rise as the economy grows rich, which could ultimately lead to significant returns or profit margins for the insurers.

The rest of the firm (insurance)-specific variables such as CAP (0.0026375) and LIQ (0.0055282) are not statistically significant and do not exert any influence on profitability. In addition to this, macroeconomic variables such as POP (−0.0041174) do not influence profitability, as they are not statistically significant. The insurance-specific variable (LIQ), which has a positive effect and macroeconomic variable (POP), which influences negatively, reject the hypothesis theories mentioned above with regards to their authors' findings (Berhe & Kaur, 2017; Nebolsina, 2020), as they are both insignificant.

From the results of the performed regression analysis with the usage of the FGLS method, it can be seen that time dummies 2020–2021 (the pandemic crisis period) do not influence profitability as they were insignificant.

10 Conclusion

To sum up, this study investigated the effects of macroeconomic and insurance-specific factors on the financial performance of insurance businesses in Kazakhstan with data retrieved from local government sources, the World Bank and 32 listed insurance companies in Kazakhstan from 2011 to 2021. The panel data approach was employed for this study. Return on equity (ROE) was the dependent variable, while the independent factors were broken down into insurance-specific variables (gross written insurance premiums, firm size, capital adequacy and liquidity ratio) and macroeconomic variables (growth rate of GDP and population growth).

Three steps were taken in the analysis of this study. First, descriptive statistics demonstrated that a macroeconomic variable, population growth (POP), had the greatest mean. The largest standard deviation is found in GDP (GDP) growth rate. Multicollinearity, autocorrelation, and heteroscedasticity tests were conducted to run the regression model. The test depicted no multicollinearity or autocorrelation but heteroscedasticity, meaning that error or residual terms varied widely and should have been controlled by the FGLS model. Thus, to understand the impact of the independent variables on the insurance industry's financial performance, the FGLS model was employed.

The findings of this study suggest that the firms' profitability is considerably and favorably affected by the GDP growth rate and gross written insurance premiums (GWP). In contrast, the size of insurance companies (SIZE) had significantly impacted the profitability in negative way. The analysis' findings also showed that the size of the insurance company, GDP growth rate, and gross written insurance premiums were the main factors that significantly influenced the profitability of insurance companies.

The analysis's findings, as shown by R^2, showed that only *29.7%* of changes in ROE could be explained by changes in independent variables such as insurance-specific and macroeconomic variables. It can be seen that 70.3% of changes in ROE cannot be explained due to the unobserved factors affecting changes in ROE. However, the whole model is still statistically validated or best fitted.

11 Recommendations and Limitations

The following recommendations were made based on the study's findings:

- According to research, indicators particular to the insurance industry, such as gross written insurance premiums, have a large and advantageous impact on the insurance industry's profitability. Insurance companies ought to increase the insurance premiums they collect while decreasing the dividends they pay to shareholders. These could be accomplished by employing various strategies, such as developing new technology and publicizing their goods across the country.
- Insurance businesses should focus not only on the internal aspects of their organization and operations but also on the macroeconomic climate in the nation when it comes to macroeconomic variables, such as GDP growth, which has a big impact on ROE. A shift in insurers' profitability could result from an improvement in the nation's economic situation.
- The government should develop strategies to increase the country's real GDP because doing so would boost both the expansion of the economy and the insurance sector. The analysis also found that COVID-19 had caused a significant GDP issue for the entire world. The study suggests that the industry must also prepare for unfavorable outcomes such as these in the future. To prevent a decline in GDP, rising inflation, and depreciation of the local currency, which have negative effects on the economy and the insurance sector, the government must ensure that security and stability prevail throughout the nation, particularly during and after some global crises.
- There were a few issues with measurement certain statistical figures related to insurance industry in the country. There were no transparent or accessible data to examine because some data for some companies displayed zero figures or were missing. Due to the lack of certain data in some companies, a thorough empirical analysis of firm-specific variables in the insurance industry may be done in the future. This investigation may produce findings that investors, insurers, policymakers, and researchers may find useful. A firm-specific and macroeconomic variable measurement might also include the age of the company and inflation indicators, which would be more useful for future research.

References

Athanasoglou, P. P., Brissimis, S. N., & Delis, M. D. (2006). Bank-specific, industry-specific and macroeconomic determinants of bank profitability. *Journal of International Financial Markets, Institutions and Money, 18.2*(2008), 121–136. [Online] Available at: https://www.sciencedirect.com/science/article/abs/pii/S1042443106000473 (Accessed: 18 October 2022).

Berhe, T. A., & Kaur, J. (2017). Determinants of insurance companies' profitability Analysis of insurance sector in Ethiopia. *International Journal of Research in Finance and Marketing (IJRFM), 7*(4), 124–137. [Online] Available at: https://d1wqtxts1xzle7.cloudfront.net/531

60327/12FMApril-4785-with-cover-page-v2.pdf?Expires=1666160072&Signature=Y0BWRuki54-nMR4fFLLe~funVgaUYcT3OoitN0~AdJTAK5M7fqEtA9ZETvGqgStPxKZaHeql8I~8oDrPU-mV6cO5QPewZivH4-SSesLTZ4yBjnfK1WXdpBk4bMdaIpkNo6QyxtzLY0XisEbZXQN5036KM66mMXj0GidEzQ6nr37EDtufuIjA40UBRA1G0zmHKeA~i51t8IoKrDnsqTX757TGZ7aiJr0btZsl65wy6SkbLqqYBWm9jUszyRRg9pn29oJLFW-OxtCjNJsmIDHi8rv2rvSqupAnCINXs2l4u4NmxuzyHLhaTAgJfcjkcB9U4qdSBsSbo4VNXv00mWzniQ__&Key-Pair-Id=APKAJLOHF5GGSLRBV4ZA (Accessed: 18 October 2022).

Faizulayev, A., Bektas, E., & Ismail, A. G. (2018). Profitability and persistency in the service industry: The case of QISMUT+ 3. *The Service Industries Journal, 40*(3-4), 290–314. [Online] Available at: https://www.tandfonline.com/doi/abs/10.1080/02642069.2018.1461210 (Accessed: 18 October 2022).

Faizulayev, A., Dabylova, G., & Assylkhanova, A. (2021). What drives the financial performance in banking industry? The case of cis countries. *Central Asian Economic Review, 1*, 84–97. [Online] Available at: https://caer.narxoz.kz/jour/article/view/303 (Accessed: 18 October 2022).

Guendouz, A. A., & Ouassaf, S. (2018). Determinants of Saudi takaful insurance companies' profitability. *Academy of Accounting and Financial Studies Journal, 22*(5), 1–24. [Online] Available at: https://d1wqtxts1xzle7.cloudfront.net/57464108/1528-2635-22-5-280-with-cover-page-v2.pdf?Expires=1666204955&Signature=UqjasrwhBvc126hSOJe5VP90LjHSvSUfX1Wg31jUdkrDMrnlI1RqeJC1sGGVkp7Roh9Ghe36y0AhVB6~B8ZuXx8ORDJEg6NTTEgz2RCJLBGoTQsXsxEq9o7WkI5PY7cf67hgpWKGb~VAx5BCmPjcgi60Y19Yfsr8dKL1FEO4VtWIhP1VCBZD2XGjQQ5uv2qR8N2U~Zw37LX-KH2ypvMNxYVrm6DcEWFWx7ZStT4PX9QyqoldbsB6hkfD~xnW9WBNuWzGPt-rowM9NuUN-tO8GyEPf2-5DK6gP~7hqwzoDiQmq4JHx3aJ6tuwl8D8Bk0nCYCXOIj5w7IZsDIg~9MyNQ__&Key-Pair-Id=APKAJLOHF5GGSLRBV4ZA (Accessed: 19 October 2022).

Kozak, S. (2011). Determinants of profitability of non-life insurance companies in Poland during integration with the European financial system. *Electronic Journal of Polish Agricultural Universities, 14*(1), 1–9. [Online] Available at: http://www.ejpau.media.pl/articles/volume14/issue1/art-01.pdf (Accessed: 19 October 2022).

Kramaric, T. P., Miletic, M., & Pavic, I. (2017). Profitability determinants of insurance markets in selected central and eastern European countries. *International Journal of Economic Sciences, 6*(2), 100–123. [Online] Available at: https://www.researchgate.net/profile/Tomislava-Pavic-Kramaric/publication/321297370_PROFITABILITY_DETERMINANTS_OF_INSURANCE_MARKETS_IN_SELECTED_CENTRAL_AND_EASTERN_EUROPEAN_COUNTRIES/links/5a719fa60f7e9ba2e1cbb9e5/PROFITABILITY-DETERMINANTS-OF-INSURANCE-MARKETS-IN-SELECTED-CENTRAL-AND-EASTERN-EUROPEAN-COUNTRIES.pdf (Accessed: 19 October 2022).

Malik, H. (2011). Determinants of insurance companies' profitability: An analysis of insurance sector of Pakistan. *Academic Research International, 1*(3), 315. [Online] Available at: http://www.savap.org.pk/journals/ARInt./Vol.1(3)/2011(1.3-32)stop.pdf (Accessed: 18 October 2022).

Murungi, D. U. (2014). *Relationship between macroeconomic variables and financial performance of insurance companies in Kenya*. Diss. University of Nairobi, 2014. [Online] Available at: http://erepository.uonbi.ac.ke/handle/11295/74890 (Accessed: 10 December 2022).

Nebolsina, E. (2020). The impact of demographic burden on insurance density. *SAGE Open, 10*(4). [Online] Available at: https://doi.org/10.1177/2158244020983024 (Accessed: 24 November 2022).

Pan, Q., & Pan, M. (2014). The impact of macro factors on the profitability of China's commercial banks in the decade after WTO Accession. *Open Journal of Social Sciences, 2*(9), 64–69. [Online] Available at: https://file.scirp.org/pdf/JSS_2014082610400602.pdf (Accessed: 10 December 2022).

The Impact of Size and Book-to-Market Ratio on Excess Return Using Fama-French 5-Factor Model: The Case of Egypt

Nader Alber and Michael Barsoom

1 Introduction

The study of the Fama-French model (FF model) and its five factors is given a detailed theoretical and model discussion with several examinations among the factors considered to show the market explanatory power of this model to explain the expected stock returns of the Market according to the size, value, profitability, and investment patterns in at certain risk in the Egyptian stock exchange, as The Capital Asset Pricing Model (CAPM) developed by Sharpe (1964) and Lintner (1965) was designed to answer the question of how we value securities considering risk and return; this rationale for the model is derived from Developed by Harry Markowitz (1952). However, the model considers only one risk factor to reveal these excess return fluctuations: market beta, which reflects the sensitivity of the market portfolio to excess returns (the market premium). Many studies have been conducted on different stock markets to examine the effectiveness of the CAPM. However, these studies' results provide no evidence to support the validity of the CAPM model.

Fama and French (1992) and Lakonishok et al. (1994) concluded that average returns have a large value premium. Based on the results of their previous studies, Fama and French (1993) concluded that the volatility of stock returns can be described by three risk factors. These factors are market beta, company size, and book-to-market ratio. Fama and French constructed a model in the financial literature, the Fama and French three-factor model, that explained the variability in stock returns by including these three factors as explanatory variables.

The lack of theoretical basis for the empirically determined factors in the three-factor model raises questions about its generalizability and its ability to explain the

N. Alber (✉) · M. Barsoom
Ain Shams University, Faculty of Business, Cairo, Egypt

N. Ozatac et al. (eds.), *Sustainable Development in Banking and Finance*, Springer Proceedings in Business and Economics,
https://doi.org/10.1007/978-3-031-65533-3_4

relationship between risk and return across different markets and time scales. Different capital market regulations, corporate governance systems and different investor behaviors can have a significant impact on the importance of risk factors in the three-factor model. Therefore, these relationships need to be analyzed in different financial markets to understand their applicability.

Based on many empirical results, it explains stock returns better than CAPM. After that, many new factor models were developed. For example, Carhart (1997) introduced the Carhart 4-factor model (C) by extending the Fama-French 3-factor model (FF3) with the momentum factor, which accounts for the short-term persistence of expected returns. Chan and Faff (2005) advocate a liquidity-enhanced FF3 model using Australian data and find that the liquidity factor is robust to sensitivity tests.

In 2015, Fama and French proposed a five-factor model (FF5), which added profitability and investment factors to their three-factor model proposed in 1993. Since then, many studies have been done on the Fama-French 5-factor model (FF5). Therefore, the researchers seek to study the ability of the five factors model to forecast the rate of return of the most active 24 companies for EGX30, considering the most active index in the Egyptian Stock Exchange from 2015 to 2022, in addition to its 11 listed sectors.

2 Literature Review

This section discusses some of the previous work, which has been conducted in the fields of *firm size*, *book-to-market ratio* and the *Fama-French 5-factor model*. Some papers are concerned with firm size (e.g., Kurshev & Strebulaev, 2015; Dang et al., 2018; Salah & Elewa, 2018 and Hashmi et al., 2020). Others illustrate book-to-market ratio (e.g., Farooq & Muddassir, 2015; Araújo & Machado, 2018, Dash et al., 2018 and Nugroho, 2020) *regarding the Fama-french 5-factor model* (e.g., Chiah et al., 2016; Shaker & Abdeldayem, 2018; Ragab et al., 2019; Paliienko et al., 2020 and Liu, 2023).

Regarding firm size, Kurshev and Strebulaev (2015) By exploring the impact of firm size on capital structure: The case of the U.S market for 3000 firms for 152 quarters had been simulated; also the study shows that there are several straightforward reasons that can be presented regarding the capital structure, but despite this well-established pattern, no theoretical explanations have yet been put forth. So, this paper endeavors to fill this gap by utilizing a dynamic capital structure model. It is possible to elucidate the relationship between size and leverage across various industries, which show a negative impact within one refinancing cycle as Leverage can have a significant impact on small firms. These businesses often opt for increased leverage at the onset. The authors find that the correlation between firm size and capital structure has been established through empirical evidence to be significantly positive.

Dang (2018) tries to analyze the influences of employing different measurement methods of firm size in empirical corporate finance according to 100 previous studies in 20 specifications field by chosen the largest mode of firm size presence in these papers, while the total assets, total sales and market capitalization is the common and preferred used proxies to use when measuring the firm size as a key or control factor, the study concluded that the choice of firm size measures depends on both theoretical and empirical explanation and provides an empirical assessment to guide the researchers who need to use the firm size measurements in their studied, as the results show that the coefficient of firm size is robust in both sign significant across most domains of corporate finance, in case of using other measures of firm size other coefficient of regression change its sign and significant so it should pay attention to choose the appropriate size measure of firm size for each domain of study, the accuracy of coefficient of determination vary from one proxy measure to another and finally each kind of size measure concern of deferent aspect of firm size.

Salah and Elewa (2018) investigates the effect of the firm's size and leverage on the profitability of 94 firms related to the industrial sector in Malaysia over the period 2012–2016. The study shows the importance of firm size as a key element in examining profitability, and a lot of previous studies have shown the same result. In addition, the study takes into consideration other variables like assets and turnover liquidity that may affect the firm's profitability by measuring the profitability via the return on assets (ROA) and the firm size via terms of log natural of total assets and market capitalization as a proxy's variables for the firm size. It finds a positive significant relationship between the firm's size and profitability. However, a negative significant relationship according to leverage.

Hashmi (2020) shows the impact of different measures of firm size as a proxies factors on seven major elements of corporate finance (investment policy, firm performance, financial policy, diversification, dividend policy, incentives, compensation and corporate governance) by collecting secondary data from annual financial reports in five countries which are Brazil, Russia, India, China and South Africa (BRICS) during 10 years which is the period of 2006 to 2015 by choosing the non-financial sectors only for 25 firms from each country. It concludes that there is a different significance, sign and coefficient of determination between the firm size proxies and the corporate financial areas under the study, which proves the sensitivity of firm size effect on the corporate finance areas according to the selected firm size proxy (measure effect).

Regarding book-to-market ratio, Farooq and Muddassir (2015) elaborates on which of the following factors: equity debt, sales to price, book to market, and firm size have the better impact on the stock returns. The study includes 26 firms listed on the Karachi Stock Exchange (KSE) from Pakistan's chemical and pharmaceutical sector over the period 2000–2009. This study finds that the best variable among four variables to explain the stock return is the book-to-market ratio, which has a positive and significant relationship.

Araújo and Machado (2018) finds that the expected book-to-market ratio and return on equity plus its predictor factors are able to predict the Brazilian stock return by applying correlation and regression model analysis on secondary data of 89 stocks as a sample of total population of 318 stocks on average per year for Brazilian listed companies examining through a linear dynamic panel to calculate the predictor of book to market ratio and return on equity with balanced panel for each company. Also, when combined with the size and liquidity factors, it can explain a part of Brazilian stock return by examining the impact of book-to-market ratio and return on equity (ROE) combined with proxies of risk factors (systematic risk, firm size by market capitalization, momentum and liquidity on stock return for non-financial companies listed in Brazilian stock exchange over the period from first January 1995 to 30th June 2015.

Dash (2018) examines the relationship between the book-to-market ratio and stock performance for the banking sector for 18 bank stocks listed in the National Stock Exchange (NSE) for the Nifty index only in the Indian market over the period 2004–2014 by measuring the stock performance using mean returns, standard deviation of returns, systematic risk, and the Sharpe and Treynor ratios, and compute the book to market ration from the secondary data of financial reports. The results, in general, come to prove that there is a significant negative correlation between the book-to-market ratio and the stock return represented on the mean return, Sharp ratio and Treynor ratio and significant positive for the standard deviation of returns and has no significance with the beta factor except in the period of recession of the global financial disasters over the period 2008–2011.

Nugroho (2020) investigated the impact of book-to-market ratio, expected profitably represented by return on assets as a proxy factor and expected investment represented by the growth of assets as a proxy factor on stock return for a sample of non-financial companies listed in the Indonesian Stock Exchange (ISE), specially LQ-45 index which is the most active and attractive index to investors over the period of 2008–2017. A regression model approach with fixed effects in panel data by EViews software was used to indicate the ability of the model to predict the stock return. The results show that the book-to-market ratio and ROA as proxy factors for expected profitability have a significant positive effect on stock return. However, the growth in assets as a proxy factor to expected investment has no significant effect on the return assets, with a negative sign that may harm the company in case of increasing the growth of assets.

Regarding the Fama-French 5-factor model, Chiah (2016) indicates that the five-factor approach of the Fama-French model outperforms the other asset pricing models like the three-factor model, the US Carhart four-factor model, the Carhart four-factor model, etc., to explain the cross-section of stock returns which prove the superiority of the model to predict the Australian equity price over the period 1982–2013. It also shows that the book-to-market factor becomes redundant in explaining the average stock return when the profitability and investment factors are present by using the asset growth as a proxy for the investment factor and the return on equity (ROE) as a proxy for the profitability factor. In addition, the study shows the importance of practice implementation for fund formation, stock selection and portfolio behavior evaluation in the portfolio management industry.

Shaker and Abdeldayem (2018) compare the predictivity power for portfolio return among the five pricing assets models: CAPM, the Fama-French three-factor model, the Carhart four-factor model, the four-factor model of Chan and Faff (2005), which is Fama-French three-factor model plus liquidity and Fama-French Five-Factor Model which consist of Fama-French three-factor model plus momentum and liquidity for 55 listed stocks in the Egyptian Stock Exchange (EGX) over the period 2003–2007. The study finds that the best model among five models to explain the stock return in the Egyptian market for the period under study is the FF three-factor model. The alternative model showed no significant added value compared to the FF three-factor model, as it provides the highest predictability in all sex portfolios related to size and book-to-market ratio classification. Furthermore, the five-factor model does not contribute to the Fama-French three-factor model except for the S/H portfolio. Finally, the author encourages adding the profitability, investment and sales-to-price ratio to be added to Fama-French three-factor model for future research.

Ragab et al. (2019) examines the ability of the Fama and French three-factor model and the Fama and French five-factor model using the three sets of double sorting techniques to the 10 portfolios of 134 listed stocks in the Egyptian exchange from July 2005 to June 2016. The portfolios are demonstrated according to size, book-to-market ratio, size and profitability, and finally size and investment. It finds that the Fama and French three-factor and five-factor models are not reliable to use as pricing models to forecast the cross-sectional fluctuation in the stock returns in the Egyptian stock market. In contrast, the Fama and French five-factor model can provide better results than the three-factor one.

Paliienko et al. (2020) evaluates the stock portfolio behaviors according to the transformation from CAPM to the Fama-French Five-Factor Model (FF5F) and applies partial changes in RMA and CMA factors to improve the validity of fund analysis results and to analyze small and large portfolios. The results show that the model is statistically significant according to the modified approach but can only explain the yield of portfolios with negative Value of Risk (VaR) and Conditional Value of Risk (C-VaR) due to the nature of blue ships selected stock and its fewest number. It also shows that small portfolios can deliver higher returns than bigger ones due to their high kurtosis.

Liu (2023) elaborates on the reliability of using the Fama and French model and its applications to predict the return and whether any other factors could be used to influence the model's sensitivity to achieve its objective. By applying Fama and French three factors, Fama and French five factors and its application over 1970–2020, shedding light on the COVID-19 pandemic impact on Australian and U.S. markets. It finds that the Fama and French five factors model is the most appropriate to use compared to the Fama and French three factors model. Therefore, the Fama and French five-factor model is the first choice for predicting certain portfolio returns under current market conditions. Moreover, with the help of some real cases and data analysis procedures, the applicability of the Fama and French model in Australian and U.S. markets, especially after the outbreak period of the COVID-19 disease in the United States to enhance the effectiveness of all factors of two Fama and French model under study compared with their corresponding ones before the outbreak period.

Regarding the current study, compared with previous work, it's important to shed light on some differences that may clarify its importance, as follows:

1. The current paper tries to test "profitability" and "investment" factors of the Fama-French five-factor model as an independent variable versus "the stock/portfolio excess return." In contrast, most of the previous work tests these factors as a control variable only.
2. This paper tries to determine the coefficient of determination of the two models in different periods of study to indicate the most efficient model to predict the stock/portfolio excess return in the Egyptian exchange.
3. The current paper examines the 11 sectors of the EGX30 by analyzing panel set data for each one to test its significance level versus the five-factor model.

3 Measuring Variables and Developing Hypotheses

Stock/Portfolio excess return is measured by deducting the risk-free rate from the rate of return after adjusting the dividend and interest, while other independent variables are calculated according to the following:

$$\mathrm{MER} = \mathrm{R_{Mt}} - \mathrm{R_{Ft}} \tag{1}$$

where

Rit is the rate of return for stock/portfolio (i) in period (t).
RMt is the rate of return for the market in period (t).
RFt is the rate of return for the risk-free in period (t).

$$\mathrm{SMB} = \frac{\mathrm{SH} + \mathrm{SM} + \mathrm{SL}}{3} - \frac{\mathrm{BH} + \mathrm{BM} + \mathrm{BL}}{3} \tag{2}$$

$$\mathrm{HML} = \frac{\mathrm{SH} + \mathrm{BH}}{2} - \frac{\mathrm{SL} + \mathrm{BL}}{2} \tag{3}$$

where SH, SM, SL, BH, BM and BL parameters are the portfolios' average return defined in Table 1.

$$\mathrm{ROE} = \frac{\text{Net Income (quarterly)}}{\text{Shareholder's Equity}} \tag{4}$$

where

Net income is the revenue of a company minus the cost of all expenses, including interest and taxes, for a certain period.

Shareholder's equity is the total assets minus the total liabilities for a certain period.

$$\text{TAG} = \frac{\text{total assets}_2 - \text{total assets}_1}{\text{total assets}_1} \tag{5}$$

where

Total assets2 is the current total assets.

Total assets1 is the prior total assets.

The data of this study was collected through several official sources' government and non-government data as follows:

- The official site of the Egyptian Exchange (EGX) for periodic reports of stock data
  (https://www.egx.com.eg/en/Services_Reports.aspx)
- The official site of the Ministry of Finance.
- The official site of the Central Bank of Egypt for short periods treasury bills interests
  (https://www.cbe.org.eg/en/auctions/egp-t-bills)
- Decypha website of MENA region for published financial statements.
  (https://www.decypha.com)

Table 2 illustrates these variables as follows:

Table 1 Portfolios' construction definitions

Portfolio	Definition
SH	Portfolio return of stocks with small market capitalization value and high book-to-market ratio
SM	Portfolio return of stocks with small market capitalization value and medium book-to-market ratio
SL	Portfolio return of stocks with small market capitalization value and low book-to-market ratio
BH	Portfolio return of stocks with large market capitalization value and high book-to-market ratio
BM	Portfolio return of stocks with large market capitalization value and medium book-to-market ratio
BL	Portfolio return of stocks with large market capitalization value and low book-to-market ratio

Source: Author's Preparation

Table 2 Measuring research variables

Variable	Type	Sign
Stock/portfolio excess return	Dependent	SPER
Market factor by market excess return	Independent	MER
Size factor by small minus big market cap	Independent	SMB
Value factor by high minus low B/M ratio	Independent	HML
Profitability factor by return on equity	Independent	ROE
Investment factor by total asset growth	Independent	TAG

This paper investigates the effect of "size and book-to-market ratio" on "stock/portfolio excess return" according to the FF 5-factor model. So, it aims to test the following hypotheses:

1. There's no significant effect of "market factor" measured by market excess return on "stocks and portfolios excess return" measured by ROR minus risk-free rate according to the FF Five-Factor Model in the Egyptian Stock Exchange.
2. There's no significant effect of "firm size" measured by market capitalization deference SMB on "stocks and portfolios excess return" measured by ROR minus risk-free rate according to FF Five-Factor Model in the Egyptian Stock Exchange.
3. There's no significant effect of "firm value" measured by B/M ratio deference HML on "stocks and portfolios excess return" measured by ROR minus risk-free rate according to the FF Five-Factor Model in the Egyptian Stock Exchange.
4. There's no significant effect of "profitability" measured by Return on Equity ROE on "stocks and portfolios excess return" measured by ROR minus risk-free rate in Egyptian Stock Exchange.
5. There's no significant effect of "investment" measured by total assets growth on "stocks and portfolios excess return" measured by ROR minus risk-free rate in the Egyptian Stock Exchange.

   The null hypothesis H0 states that $\beta = 0$, while the alternative one H1 states that $\beta \neq 0$ where

$$\text{SPER}_t = \alpha_i + \beta 1_i \text{MER}_t + \beta 2_i \text{SMB}_t + \beta 3_i \text{HML}_t + \beta 4_i \text{ROE}_t + \beta 5_i \text{TAG}_t \tag{6}$$

4 Descriptive and Diagnostic Statistics

Table 3 illustrates descriptive statistics of the research variables using a sample of 24 listed firms in EGX30 of the Egyptian Exchange and distributed in 11 sectors illustrated in Appendix (1) over the period from 2015 to 2022 per quarter, as follows:

Regarding normality, Jarque-Bera values indicate that all variables are normally distributed at p- value of 0.05. *Regarding multicollinearity*, Table 4 illustrates the correlation coefficients between independent variables as follows:

Table 4 shows that correlation coefficients between independent variables range from −0.061952 to 0.722468, which indicates that there is no existence for multicollinearity problem.

Table 3 Descriptive statistics of research variables

Variable	SPER (Y1)	MER (X1)	SMB (X2)	HML (X3)	ROE (X4)	TAG (X5)
Mean	0.010954	–0.015010	0.017200	0.065942	7.590171	13.85580
Median	–0.040399	–0.024638	–0.022732	0.007653	13.62278	10.84267
Maximum	3.433475	0.474660	1.395149	1.283739	1740.988	176.0512
Minimum	–0.738795	–0.279407	–0.220199	–0.319899	–7215.509	–96.92430
Std. dev.	0.289278	0.157470	0.256572	0.288557	238.4284	25.41590
Skewness	3.973900	1.168546	4.477559	2.811549	–25.24195	1.322249
Kurtosis	37.74015	4.902275	24.46676	11.04130	760.4395	10.79535
Jarque-Bera	59639.22	426.4124	25405.21	4521.226	27,060,357	3181.937
Probability	0.000000	0.000000	0.000000	0.000000	0.000000	0.000000
Obs. no	1127	1127	1127	1127	1127	1127

Source: outputs of data processing using EViews 12

Table 4 Correlation coefficients between independent variables

	SPER (Y1)	MER (X1)	SMB (X2)	HML (X3)	ROE (X4)	TAG (X5)
SPER	1.00000					
P-value	–					
MER	0.596896	1.00000				
P-value	0.0000	–				
SMB	−0.041933	−0.102863	1.00000			
P-value	0.1589	0.0005	–			
HML	0.129820	0.090410	0.722468	1.00000		
P-value	0.0000	0.0024	0.0000	–		
ROE	−0.034949	−0.090864	0.013100	−0.089693	1.00000	
P-value	0.2405	0.0022	0.6604	0.0026	–	
TAG	0.090770	0.152702	0.014694	0.080450	−0.061952	1.00000
P-value	0.0023	0.0000	0.6222	0.0069	0.0375	–

Source: outputs of data processing using EViews 12

5 Testing Hypotheses

This section is dedicated to investigating the impact of each MER, SMB, HML, ROE, and TAG as independent variables on the "stock/portfolio excess return." A comparison of this model and the previous one of the three-factor is applied to measure the efficiency of the Fama-French five-factor model.

A sample of 24 companies in the Egyptian stock exchange EGX30 and its 11 impede sectors were used to explore these effects. This sample was selected quarterly from 2015 to 2022.

Table 5 Determinants comparison of stock/portfolio excess return between FF models

Variable	Excess return according to FF 5-fator			Excess return according to FF 5-fator		
	Coeff.	t-stat.	Prob.	Coeff.	t-stat.	Prob.
C	0.021471	3.688872	**0.0002**	0.016810	3.426194	**0.0006**
MER	1.007935	32.38932	**0.0000**	0.987208	33.59785	**0.0000**
SMB	−0.020599	−0.733124	0.4636	−0.018823	−0.690511	0.4900
HML	0.054054	2.859624	**0.0043**	0.051759	2.811832	**0.0050**
ROE	2.07E-05	0.766691	0.4434			
TAG	−0.000312	−1.539849	0.1239			
R^2	0.482784			0.472761		
Adjusted R^2	0.480477			0.471383		
Durbin-Watson stat	2.068609			2.092130		
F-statistic	209.2743			343.1266		
Prob(F-statistic)	0.000000			0.000000		
Obs.	1127			1152		

Source: outputs of data processing using EViews 12

Table 6 Test the equality according to the ANOVA test

Model	Df	Sum of Sq.	Mean Sq.	F value	Prob.
FF 5-factor	5	193691.4	38738.28	4.107673	0.0010
FF 3-factor	3	13.24317	4.414390	20.96030	0.0000

Source: outputs of data processing using EViews 12

A panel data analysis was conducted, which produced the following results (Table 5).

Both models support the significance of the MER & HML effect on stock/portfolio excess return in the Egyptian exchange with an explanation power of 48.27% for the model of 5-factor. Besides, the explanation power and positive sign are 47.27% for the 3-factor model. However, no significance was found for SMB, ROE and TAG, which clarifies the weakness of these models in explaining the stock/portfolio excess return in EGX. Still, the Fama-French 5-factor model is considered more powerful than the Fama-French 3-factor model according to the slightly higher of R^2.

So, for the *first* and *third* hypotheses, the null hypothesis is rejected, and the alternative one can be accepted. Signs of regression coefficients $\beta 1$ and $\beta 3$ in both models are positive, which means that stock/portfolio excess return is affected positively by market excess return and value factors So, results support several previous studies (Table 6).

The ANOVA results confirmed the statistical significance of the two models. Therefore, We can accept an alternative hypothesis that employs a modified approach of the Fama-French five-factor to assess stock and portfolio returns.

Table 7 Identification of EGX30 sectors

No.	Sector name	Sector ID	No. of firms
1	Banks (BANK)	BANK	2
2	Real estate (REAL)	REAL	6
3	Food, beverages and tobacco (FOBT)	FOBT	2
4	Industrial goods, services and automobiles (IGSA)	IGSU	2
5	Textile & durables (TEDU)	TEDU	2
6	Basic resources (BASC)	BASC	2
7	Contracting & construction engineering (COCE)	COCE	1
8	Non-bank financial services (NBFC)	NBFC	3
9	IT, media & communication services (IMCS)	IMCS	2
10	Energy & support services (ENGY)	ENGY	1
11	Travel & leisure (TRVL)	TRVL	1
	Total		24

By testing the hypotheses of the modified Fama-French five-factor model in depth for several sectors which represent the firms under study are illustrated in Table 7, including the EGX30 as follows:

To test the research hypotheses for the 11 sectors within EGX30, over the period from 2015 to 2022, a panel data analysis has been conducted and provides the following results (Table 8).

EGX30 supports the significance of MER and HML on S/P excess return with an explanation power of 43.71%. The BANK sector supports the significance of MER, SMB and ROE on S/P excess return with R^2 of 79.90%. The REAL sector supports the significance of MER and ROE on S/P excess return with R^2 of 48.62%, the FOBT sector supports the significance of MER, SMB and HML on S/P excess return with R^2 of 40.87%, the IGSU sector supports the significance of all independent variables of FF 5-factor model on S/P excess return with R^2 of 44.98%, and the TEDU sector supports the significance of MER and ROE on S/P excess return with R^2 of 44.37%.

So, for the *first* hypothesis, the null hypothesis is rejected, and the alternative hypothesis could be accepted by all sectors. Signs of regression coefficients $\beta 1$ in all panel set data are positive, which means that S/P excess return is affected positively by market excess return.

The null hypothesis is rejected for the *second* hypothesis, and the alternative one could be accepted for BANK, FOBT and IGSU sectors. Signs of regression coefficients $\beta 2$ are positive for BANK and negative for FOBT and IGSU sectors, which means that S/P excess return is affected positively or negatively by firm size.

The null hypothesis for the *third* hypothesis is rejected and the alternative one could be accepted for EGX30, FOBT and IGSU sectors. Signs of regression coefficients $\beta 3$ are positive for all these sectors, which means that S/P excess return is affected positively by firm value.

Table 8 Determinants of stock/portfolio excess return for EGX30 & 5 different sectors

Variable	Stock/portfolio excess return according to FF 5-factor					
Coeff. t-stat. prob.	EGX 30	BANK	REAL	FOBT	IGSU	TEDU
C	0.018424 2.569617 **0.0104**	−0.012411 −0.692459 0.4904	−0.001695 −0.110965 0.9117	−0.040635 −0.484529 0.6292	0.067911 1.788757 0.0771	0.040475 21.53206 **0.0021**
MER	0.992248 25.15218 **0.0000**	0.967057 20.85042 **0.0000**	0.913789 13.41428 **0.0000**	1.217061 4.381160 **0.0000**	1.139992 7.709979 **0.0000**	0.963588 12.67000 **0.0062**
SMB	−0.026392 −0.744965 0.4565	0.089009 5.284933 **0.0000**	0.013978 0.219787 0.8262	−0.975685 −3.924220 **0.0002**	−0.278984 −2.154260 **0.0339**	−0.061263 −1.112648 0.3817
HML	0.050889 2.135222 **0.0331**	0.009386 0.139575 0.8893	0.032507 0.771442 0.4413	0.769673 4.529704 **0.0000**	0.199047 2.260494 **0.0262**	0.081553 3.404337 0.0765
ROE	6.32E-06 0.201313 0.8405	0.001999 2.323352 **0.0224**	0.000807 2.015293 **0.0451**	0.002846 1.088130 0.2795	0.002412 2.442141 **0.0166**	−0.004623 −4.315262 **0.0497**
TAG	−0.000236 −1.043400 0.2971	−0.000531 −0.698278 0.4868	−0.000841 −1.821356 0.0700	0.004639 1.509351 0.1348	−0.002918 −2.566844 **0.0119**	0.001562 3.287329 0.0814
R^2	0.437101	0.799008	0.486214	0.408778	0.449838	0.443740
Adjusted R^2	0.433465	0.787842	0.474039	0.375563	0.418930	0.412489
Durbin-Watson stat.	2.09132	2.541592	2.107167	2.149096	1.568212	1.870520
F-statistic	120.2051	71.55570	39.93539	12.30712	14.55409	14.19940
Prob (F-statistic)	0.000000	0.000000	0.000000	0.000000	0.000000	0.000000
Obs.	780	96	217	95	95	95

Source: outputs of data processing using EViews 12

The null hypothesis is rejected for the *fourth* hypothesis, and the alternative one could be accepted for BANK, REAL, IGSU and TEDU sectors. Signs of regression coefficients $\beta 4$ are positive for BANK, REAL and IGSU and negative for TEDU sectors, which means that S/P excess return is affected positively or negatively by ROE.

For the *fifth* hypothesis, the null hypothesis is rejected, and the alternative one could be accepted only for the IGSU sector. Signs of regression coefficients $\beta 5$ are negative for all these sectors, which means that S/P excess return is affected positively by TAG.

To test the research hypotheses for the rest 6 sectors of BASC, COCE, NBFC, IMCS, ENGY and TRVL sectors for the period under study, a panel data analysis has been conducted and provides the following results:

Table 9 Determinants of stock/portfolio excess return for the remaining 6 sectors in EGX30

Variable	Stock/portfolio excess return according to FF 5-fator					
Coeff. t-stat. prob.	BASC	COCE	NBFC	IMCS	ENGY	TRVL
C	0.036053 2.613831 **0.0105**	−0.014305 −0.626295 0.5339	0.016216 0.660459 0.5102	0.010425 0.613885 0.5409	0.148027 1.875824 0.0657	0.034044 1.135273 0.2611
MER	1.179303 19.18177 **0.0000**	0.686323 4.021095 **0.0002**	1.041277 6.778127 **0.0000**	0.862531 10 0.19493 **0.0000**	1.756727 3.627867 **0.0006**	1.247522 6.894402 **0.0000**
SMB	0.109242 1.550529 0.1246	0.066009 0.259803 0.7960	−0.049350 −0.392752 0.6952	−0.140377 −1.908696 **0.0595**	−1.511774 −3.704965 **0.0005**	0.605805 3.918945 **0.0002**
HML	−0.091117 −1.985017 **0.0502**	−0.052987 −0.375555 0.7088	0.194724 2.257731 **0.0258**	0.117219 2.092597 **0.0392**	1.136709 4.137701 **0.0001**	−0.381008 −3.803260 **0.0004**
ROE	0.000213 2.316159 **0.0228**	0.000455 1.868087 0.0674	5.52E-06 0.147190 0.8832	−6.77E-05 −0.360202 0.7195	0.000634 0.703337 0.4847	−0.001151 −0.681451 0.4984
TAG	−0.000196 −0.341805 0.7333	−0.000373 −0.209057 0.8352	−0.000706 −1.079477 0.2826	0.000280 0.404212 0.6870	−0.001378 −0.468530 0.6412	0.001448 0.772227 0.4432
R^2	0.672198	0.337166	0.157772	0.523746	0.420965	0.503563
Adjusted R^2	0.653782	0.273432	0.122084	0.496990	0.371048	0.459238
Durbin-Watson stat.	2.135375	2.261224	2.130383	2.280058	2.586791	2.468979
F-statistic	36.50107	5.290199	4.420907	19.57502	8.433338	11.36075
Prob (F-statistic)	0.000000	0.000530	0.001001	0.000000	0.000005	0.000000
Obs.	95	58	124	95	64	62

Source: outputs of data processing using EViews 12

According to Table 9, the BASC sector supports the significance of MER, HML and ROE on S/P excess return with R^2 of 67.21%. The COCE sector supports the significance of MER on S/P excess return with R^2 of 33.71%, NBFC sector supports the significance of MER and HML on S/P excess return with low R^2 of 15.77%, IMCS, ENGY and TRVL sectors support the significance of MER, SMB and HML on S/P excess return with R^2 of 52.37%, 42.09% and 50.35% respectively.

So, for the *first* hypothesis, the null hypothesis is rejected and the alternative one could be accepted for all sectors. Signs of regression coefficients $\beta 1$ in all panel set data are positive, which means that S/P excess return is affected positively by market excess return.

For the *second* hypothesis, the null hypothesis is rejected and the alternative one could be accepted for IMCS, ENGY and TRVL sectors. Signs of regression coefficients $\beta 2$ are positive for TRVL and negative for IMCS and ENGY sectors, which means that S/P excess return is affected positively or negatively by firm size.

For the *third* hypothesis, the null hypothesis is rejected and the alternative one could be accepted for all sectors except COCE sector. Signs of regression coefficients $\beta 3$ are positive for NBFC, IMCS and ENGY sectors and negative for BASC and TRVL sectors, which means that S/P excess return is affected positively or negatively by firm value.

For the *fourth* hypothesis, the null hypothesis is rejected and the alternative one could be accepted for BASC sector only. Signs of regression coefficients $\beta 4$ are positive, which means that S/P excess return is affected positively or negatively by ROE.

For the *fifth* hypothesis, the null hypothesis is accepted and the alternative one could be rejected for all sectors. Signs of regression coefficients $\beta 5$ are positive or negative for all these sectors, which means that S/P excess return is bidirectional and not affected by TAG.

The above-shown analysis covers a sample of 24 firms in the Egyptian Exchange class into 11 sectors of BANK, REAL, FOBT, IGSA, TEDU, BASC, COCE, NBFC, IMCS, ENGY and TRVL. A robustness check was conducted on 2 sub-samples, where EGX30 plus 5 sectors and the residual 6 of 11 sectors.

Regarding the problem of autocorrelation, Durbin-Watson (DW) statistic has been conducted for the 12 data pane of the study sample concerning stock/portfolio excess return and shows that DW values range from 1.568212 to 2.586791, which means that the autocorrelation problem does not exist, as DW values are between 1 and 3.

6 Summary and Concluding Remarks

This paper attempts to investigate the effects of firm size and book-to-market ratio on stock/portfolio excess return according to the Fama-French five-factor model using a sample of 24 listed firms in the Egyptian exchange EGX30, that includes 11 sectors of different industries of banks, real state, (food, beverages and tobacco), (industrial goods, services and automobiles), textile & durables, basic resources, contracting & construction engineering, non-bank financial services, (IT, media & communication Services), energy & support services, travel & leisure Egypt over the period from 2015 to 2022.

The forecasting for stocks and portfolio returns is still a controversial topic to enhance the stock market and help investors need to identify the factors affecting these returns. According to previous studies evaluating the validity of the Fama-French five-factor model, some of these studies provide no evidence to evaluate this model. Still, others find their ability to predict yields with different significant levels and signs.

By applying the correlation and regression analysis using EViews 12 software on a dated panel data per quarter observations on the most activity and liquidity firms listed in EGX30. The study finds the efficiency of the five-factor approach of Fama-French with an explanation power of 48.27%, which overcomes the three-factor approach of 47.27% to explain the stocks and portfolios returns with differing R^2 according to the industry sector under study, as it varies from 15.77% to 79.90%. The ANOVA results confirmed the statistical significance of the models in assessing stock and portfolio returns by accepting its alternative hypothesis that employs a modified approach of the Fama-French five-factor.

The explanation power of the Fama and French models is relatively high when applied to the banking sector. This may be consistent with the high sensitivity of this sector to risk. Moreover, the development of the financial sector has been addressed in terms of profit efficiency (Alber, 2011), financial Stability (Alber, 2017), asset allocation (Alber, 2018) and financial inclusion (Alber, 2019).

For the whole sample of 24 firms listed in EGX30, results support the significance of market and value factors on the stock/portfolio excess return. Signs of regression coefficients are positive, which means that the stock and portfolio returns are affected positively by these two factors. In comparison, no significance was found for the other three factors of size, profitability and investments measured by market cap as a proxy factor, ROE and total asset growth, respectively.

The results support the significance of market factors on the stock/portfolio return for all sectors under study by testing the hypotheses for represented sectors of these firms. Signs of regression coefficients are positive, which means that the stock and portfolio returns are affected positively by the market factor for all sectors. In contrast, for the size factor it shows significance for the sectors of BANK, FOBT, IGSU, IMCS, ENGY and TRVL. Signs of regression coefficients in most cases are negative, which means that the stock and portfolio returns are affected negatively by the size factor for these sectors. Also, the value factor, it shows significance for the sectors of FOBT, IGSU, BASC, NBFC, IMCS, ENGY and TRVL. Signs of regression coefficients in most cases are positive, which means that the stock and portfolio returns are affected positively by the value factor for these sectors. Then for the profitability factor it shows significance for the sectors of BANK, REAL, IGSU, TEDU, and BASC. Signs of regression coefficients in most cases are positive, which means that the stock and portfolio returns are affected positively by the profitability factor for these sectors. Finally, for the investment factor it shows significance for the IGSU sector only. The sign of the regression coefficient is negative, meaning that the stock and portfolio returns are affected negatively by the investment factor for this sector.

To conclude, results support the significance of each of the market and value factors on stocks and portfolio return in the Egyptian market with higher explanation power for the Fama-French five-factor model than the three-factor approach, without any evidence regarding the effect of other factors in general. So, for the first and third hypotheses, the null hypothesis is rejected, and the alternative one can be accepted. Besides, for each sector it had its own significance and sign of regression coefficient toward the model's factors. Future research should attempt to recognize other factors that could better explain the returns of stocks in the Egyptian stock market.

References

Alber, N. (2011). The effect of banking expansion on profit efficiency of Saudi Banks. *Corporate Ownership and Control, 8*(2), 51–58.

Alber, N. (2017). Banking efficiency and financial stability: Which causes which? A panel analysis. *Springer Proceedings in Business and Economics*, 91–98.

Alber, N. (2018). Asset allocation, capital structure, theory of the firm and banking performance: A panel analysis. In N. Ozatac & K. K. Gökmenoglu (Eds.), *Emerging trends in banking and finance*. Springer Proceedings in Business and Economics.
Alber, N. (2019). Determinants of financial inclusion: The case of 125 countries from 2004 to 2017. *Springer Proceedings in Business and Economics*, 1–10.
Araújo, R. C. D. C., & Machado, M. A. V. (2018). Book-to-market ratio, return on equity and Brazilian stock returns. *RAUSP Management Journal, 53*, 324–344.
Carhart, M. M. (1997). On persistence in mutual fund performance. *The Journal of Finance, 52*(1), 57–82.
Chan, H. W., & Faff, R. W. (2005). Asset pricing and the illiquidity premium. *Financial Review, 40*(4), 429–458.
Chiah, M., Chai, D., Zhong, A., & Li, S. (2016). A better model? An empirical investigation of the Fama-French five-factor model in Australia: Empirical tests on the five-factor model. *International Review of Finance, 16*. https://doi.org/10.1111/irfi.12099
Dang, C., Li, Z. F., & Yang, C. (2018). Measuring firm size in empirical corporate finance. *Journal of Banking & Finance, 86*, 159–176.
Dash, M., Kantheti, S., & Teja, G. K. (2018). The book-to-market anomaly for banking stocks in the Indian stock market: A panel regression analysis. *Journal of Applied Management and Investments, 7*, 15–23.
Fama, E. F., & French, K. R. (1992). The cross-section of expected stock returns. *The Journal of Finance, 47*(2), 427–465.
Fama, E. F., & French, K. R. (1993). Common risk factors in the returns on stocks and bonds. *Journal of Financial Economics, 33*(1), 3–56.
Fama, E. F., & French, K. R. (2015). A five-factor asset pricing model. *Journal of Financial Economics, 116*, 1–22. CiteSeerX 10.1.1.645.3745. https://doi.org/10.1016/j.jfineco.2014.10.010
Farooq, S. S. U. H. S., & Muddassir, M. (2015). Stock returns indicators: Debt to equity, book to market, firm size and sales to price. *Journal of Poverty, Investment, and Development, 16*, 25–33.
Hashmi, S. D., Gulzar, S., Ghafoor, Z., et al. (2020). Sensitivity of firm size measures to practices of corporate finance: Evidence from BRICS. *Future Business Journal, 6*, 9.
Kurshev, A., & Strebulaev, I. A. (2015). Firm size and capital structure. *Quarterly Journal of Finance, 5*(03), 155–188.
Lakonishok, J., Shleifer, A., & Vishny, R. W. (1994). Contrarian investment, extrapolation, and risk. *The Journal of Finance, 49*(5), 1541–1578.
Lintner, J. (1965). The valuation of risky assets: The selection of risky investments in stock portfolios and capital budgets. *Review of Economics and Statistics*, 13–37.
Liu, Z. (2023, March 8). Reasonable conjecture and demonstration of Fama-French model and its applications in Australia and US. *BCP Business & Management*. https://doi.org/10.54691/bcpbm.v40i.4368
Markowitz, H. (1952). Portfolio selection. *Journal of Finance, 7*(1), 77–91.
Nugroho, B. Y. (2020). The effect of book to market ratio, profitability, and investment on stock return. *International Journal of Economics and Management Studies, 7*(6), 102–107.
Paliienko, O., Naumenkova, S., & Mishchenko, S. (2020). An empirical investigation of the Fama-French five-factor model. *Investment Management and Financial Innovations, 17*(1), 143–155.
Ragab, N. S., Abdou, R. K., & Sakr, A. M. (2019). A comparative study between the Fama and French Three-Factor Model and the Fama and French Five-Factor Model: Evidence from the Egyptian Stock Market. *International Journal of Economics and Finance, 12*(1), 52–69.
Salah, W., & Elewa, M. (2018). The effect of firm's size and leverage on profitability: A panel data approach. *Journal of Applied Economic Sciences, 13*(6), 1723–1732.
Shaker, M. A., & Abdeldayem, M. M. (2018). Examining asset pricing models in emerging markets: Evidence from Egypt. *Corporate Ownership and Control, 16*(1), 50–57.
Sharpe, W. F. (1964). Capital asset prices: A theory of market equilibrium under conditions of risk. *The Journal of Finance, 19*(3), 425–442.

Machine Learning for Cobalt Price Prediction

Erdem Öncü and Veclal Gündüz

1 Introduction

Cobalt is a hard, glossy, grayish-silver metallic element with low thermal and electrical conductivity, with a crustal abundance of 20–30 ppm and an abundance index of 32 (Domingo, 1989; Carr & Turekian, 1961). On Earth, Cobalt occurs in +2 and +3 compounds. However, depending on the oxidation state, this number can range between −3 and + 5. Cobalt is a crystalline, silver-gray hue, cubic element with an atomic number of 27 and an atomic mass of 58.9 (Mandeville & Fulbright, 1943). It has melting and boiling temperatures of 1495 and 2870 degrees Celsius, respectively. It can keep its resistance and magnetic qualities at high temperatures (1495 °C melting point), is one of three metals with magnetic properties in the natural environment (together with nickel and iron), and can create alloys with many other metals. Cobalt is often found in small amounts in the earth's crust (Mahey et al., 2020). There are just a few areas where it is enriched or commercially mineralized. It is manufactured in 16 countries worldwide.[1] It can only be produced from arsenic ores found in Morocco and Canada. Aside from that, it's frequently connected with copper and nickel. During the weathering of ultramafic rocks in surface circumstances, nickel and cobalt are concentrated at the lowest layers of

[1] Democratic Republic of Congo, Finland, India, Japan, Morocco, Norway, Russia, Uganda, South Africa, Zambia, South Korea, Madagascar, Australia, Brazil, Canada, China.

E. Öncü (✉)
Trakya University, Keşan Yusuf Çapraz School of Applied Sciences, Department of Banking and Insurance, Edirne, Turkey
e-mail: erdemoncu@trakya.edu.tr

V. Gündüz
Bahçeşehir Cyprus University, Faculty of Economics, Administrative and Social Sciences, Department of Banking and Finance, Nicosia, Cyprus

N. Ozatac et al. (eds.), *Sustainable Development in Banking and Finance*, Springer Proceedings in Business and Economics,
https://doi.org/10.1007/978-3-031-65533-3_5

iron-rich chemical residue-type formations. Cobalt is found in laterite as bluish-black nodules or clouds known as asbolane. Asbolan is not a mineral but rather a combination of cobalt, iron and manganese oxides, silica, and aluminum. Cobalt has been extracted from these sorts of beds for a very long time. It is known that nickel ores accounted for 44% of global cobalt output in 2003 (Aydın & Kılıç, 2012). Cobalt's and cobalt compounds' distinctive features are used in novel uses in energy storage and industrial industries. These distinctive qualities include high energy density (the amount of energy stored in a given unit mass of a material or system), the capacity to produce high-temperature-resistant alloys and ferromagnetic properties. Cobalt has a variety of essential industrial applications, making it a valuable resource for a wide range of sectors. One of the most important applications of cobalt is in the manufacturing of lithium-ion batteries, which are used in a variety of electronic devices such as cell phones, laptop computers, and electric cars. Cobalt is an important component of the cathode in these batteries, and its particular chemical characteristics make it a perfect material for this use (Shao et al., 2022). As the demand for portable electronic gadgets and electric vehicles grows, so will the need for cobalt.

Since the Bronze Age, cobalt has been used to color pottery and glass, as indicated by cobalt-containing glazes discovered in ancient Egyptian tombs (Shortland et al., 2006). The blue cobalt-colored glass piece discovered in the Bodrum Uluburun shipwreck dated from Egypt's eighteenth dynasty (1550–1292 BC). However, the source of the cobalt used was unknown (Yap, 1988). Cobalt has been found in Egyptian and Persian artifacts and jewelry, Pompeii ruins artifacts, and Chinese porcelain from the Tang (618–907 AD) and Ming dynasties (1368–1644).

Since the nineteenth century, cobalt-aluminate ($CoAl2\ O4$) has been manufactured industrially as a powerful pigment. During this time, the Norwegian cobalt mine Blaafarvevarket became the world's cobalt blue manufacturing hub. Cobalt output in Europe fell after the discovery of cobalt ores in New Caledonia in 1864. The discovery of bigger resources in the provinces of Ontario (Canada) and Katanga (Democratic Republic of the Congo, DRC) between 1904 and 1914 changed the cobalt mining production structure. Because of the clashes that began in 1978, production in Katanga's copper mines came to a halt. Cobalt was first employed for metallic applications in the early 1900s, when it was used to create Co-Cr and super alloys (Hawkins, 2001).

Cobalt is an essential component in rechargeable lithium-ion battery cathodes. As a result, it has lately become a significant mineral. Sony introduced the first lithium-ion battery in 1991. Because the lithium-cobalt oxide battery has a very high energy density, cobalt has been found to be extensively used in batteries for mobile communications devices and EV applications (Li & Lu, 2020). Cobalt has a crucial role in rising geopolitical activity to assure supply security and increasing demand for vital minerals in green investments because it is utilized in many types of electronic equipment and electric cars.

The European Union (EU) has developed a list of "essential raw materials" to ensure secure and continuous access to raw materials with high supply risk and economic importance and provide resources for future demands. Cobalt is on this list because of its great economic relevance and supply risk (Yaylali et al., 2020).

The demand for cobalt has surged recently owing to the growing consumption area. Because of this, forecasting the price of cobalt has become a significant study topic. The foundation of machine learning is found in the areas of probability, statistics, and optimization (Nacar & Erdebilli, 2021). The machine is meant to forecast the future using the created model and data from the past. In this study, machine learning will be used to forecast cobalt prices in 2023.

2 Areas of Use for Cobalt

Cobalt is used extensively in strategic, industrial, and military applications. Cobalt, which has chemical characteristics comparable to iron and nickel, dissolves only in strong acids such as nitric acid, hydrochloric acid, and sulfuric acid. It is also utilized in the production of alloys such as nickel. Important breakthroughs in the industry have been made as a consequence of research and development on ferromagnetic iron, nickel, and cobalt metals, which are in the category of magnetic alloys, with alloys of these materials with each other, aluminum, boron, or other rare earth elements (Aydın & Kılıç, 2012).

Cobalt, which has limited pure application areas, gains strategic importance when utilized as an alloying element and chemical source. Cobalt is a battery ingredient used in nickel-cadmium (NiCd), nickel metal hydride (NiMH), and lithium-ion (LI) batteries, particularly rechargeable batteries. In lithium-ion batteries, lithium cobalt oxide is a common compound. Layers of lithium and cobalt oxide make up the substance (Hawkins, 2001). Cobalt is used in nickel-cadmium and nickel metal hydride batteries to enhance nickel oxidation (Armstrong et al., 1988). Batteries are classified into two types based on their intended use. "Primary Batteries" are disposable batteries that run out of energy over time while being utilized and are subsequently discarded. Secondary Batteries are those that can be recharged and reused after they have been depleted. Many electrical equipment have become mobile as technology has advanced to meet the demands of the contemporary world. Mobile gadgets, on the other hand, need lighter and longer-lasting batteries. In addition to throwaway main batteries, mobile phones, laptop computers, and many more gadgets that we use on a daily basis now employ rechargeable secondary batteries. These secondary batteries are chosen because of their high energy density, voltage advantages, and extended cycle life. Lithium cobalt oxide is utilized as the cathodic active ingredient in 'lithium batteries,' a term used commonly among secondary batteries. Cobalt contributes to the improved performance and stability of lithium-ion batteries, making them an essential source of energy for modern technology (Julien, 2000).

Cobalt is utilized to make high-strength, lightweight alloys used in the manufacture of aviation and aerospace components (Sibley, 1979). These alloys can tolerate high temperatures and stress, making them excellent for usage in the aircraft sector.

Superalloys are alloys composed mostly of iron, nickel, or cobalt, with a high concentration of chromium and a trace of high melting molybdenum, tungsten, aluminum, or titanium. Because of their superior friction and rupture strength, high melting temperature, higher strength at high temperatures compared to iron and nickel-based superalloys, and excellent hot corrosion resistance due to their high chromium content, they are used in the compositions of equipment that will operate in the atmosphere (jet engine gas turbines). Superalloys, electric automobiles, jet engines, and rocket-specific steels all use it. Fuel cells, like batteries, are high-tech energy-generating instruments. Fuel cells generate electrical energy directly from fuel and oxygen, with no energy losses in intermediary processes and independent of the gases produced during burning (Wang, 2006).

Cobalt is essential in creating steel, one of the most widely used and required elements on the planet. Steel is primarily an alloy of iron (Fe) and carbon (C), with the addition of minerals such as chromium, magnesium, tungsten, and cobalt. Steel allows the globe to create taller structures, more durable transportation vehicles, and commodities. Cobalt is widely used in steel manufacture because of its great corrosion resistance (Yaylali et al., 2020).

Cobalt-60 was chosen as an essential source for manufacturing gamma rays because of its interaction with neutrons, and it was able to create a large number and activity (gamma rays with energy of 1.17 and 1.33 MeV) as a result of this interaction (Mandeville & Fulbright, 1943). Furthermore, it is utilized for beam radiotherapy, medical equipment and waste disinfection, cold pasteurization (Wilkinson & Gould, 1998), industrial radiography, and density assessments (concrete density measurements). Cobalt is utilized to make medical imaging devices, including computed tomography (CT) scanners and magnetic resonance imaging (MRI) machines. Radiopharmaceuticals, which are used in cancer therapy and medical imaging, are also made with it (Ravichandran & Manimegalai, 2017).

3 Literature

Many alternative approaches for estimating the price of precious metals have been investigated in the literature. In the past, forecasts were largely produced using econometric models. Predictions are now made using machine learning and artificial neural networks. According to the literature, important commodity goods for which price forecasts are made include carbon, gold, and silver.

In their study, Byun and Cho (2013) employed GARCH (Generalized Autoregressive Conditional Heteroscedasticity) models to forecast carbon prices. According to the study's findings, GJR-GARCH has a better prediction capacity than TGARCH and GARCH. It was also looked at if volatility in energy markets such as Brent oil, coal, natural gas, and electricity forecasts volatility in carbon futures. The findings may be used to assess the volatility of Brent oil, coal, and power data, as well as carbon futures.

Fan et al. (2015), one of the artificial intelligence model researchers, employed a multilayer perceptron (MLP) artificial neural network model to anticipate carbon pricing. Research has shown that the carbon pricing is chaotic. There is also evidence that linear regression forecast findings in actual carbon markets, even basic artificial neuron networks, can be deceptive. According to the authors, estimates should take into account the potentially unpredictable character of carbon pricing in carbon markets.

For carbon price estimation, Zhu and Wei (2013) employed a hybrid forecasting model that included ARIMA (Integrated Autoregressive Moving Average) and LSSVM (Least Squares Support Vector Machine). According to the results, the hybrid model is more effective than the single artificial neural network and ARIMA models.

A nonparametric technique was used to estimate carbon pricing in the Chevallier (2011) research, one of the econometric model investigations. Compared to linear autoregression models, the Diebold and Mariano test statistics show that the approach can reduce estimation error by around 15%. Furthermore, there is a large asymmetric and variable variance link between the conditional volatility functions, carbon spot returns, and futures daily returns.

Yüksel and Akkoç (2016) developed an artificial neural network model to forecast gold prices. Silver and Brent oil prices, US dollar / EUR parity, EuroNext100 index, US Dow Jones Index, 13-week US bond interest rate, and US CPI are explanatory characteristics utilized for this purpose. According to the investigation findings, ANN produced very favorable outcomes in the prediction of gold prices. When the sensitivity analysis findings were analyzed, it was shown that the most relevant variables influencing gold prices were silver and oil prices.

Hussein et al. (2011) used radial basis function neural networks to predict gold prices, a novel technique for artificial neural networks. In terms of the applicable daily closing prices, a successful prediction level of 78% has been obtained in the gold estimation. In his work in this context, Kılıç (2013) used the Markov chain to simulate gold returns and predicted the following day's return direction. Approximately 70% of the classifications in the research were successful.

In their study, Farahani and Mehralian (2013) employed Artificial Neural Network (ANN) and Adaptive Neural Fuzzy Inference System (ANFIS) approaches to forecast the gold price. In addition, a novel hybrid model is shown, which is the weighted average of the ANN and ANFIS models. The primary purpose is to forecast the price of gold in the Forex market. The standard artificial neural network model, the adaptive fuzzy artificial neural network model, and a hybrid model derived from these two models were examined in the study, and the adaptive fuzzy artificial neural network model was shown to be the most appropriate prediction model.

Alameer et al. (2019) attempted to anticipate gold prices by introducing a novel artificial neural network model based on the whale optimization technique. In estimating gold prices, the approach has been found to be superior to several other methods, including the gray wolf algorithm, genetic algorithm, and particle algorithm.

Verma et al. (2020) attempted to forecast the gold price for India. The data utilized were weekly data from January 2015 to December 2018. The data were standardized and utilized in the range of 0.1 to 0.9. The 5-week delayed gold price is utilized as input in the models. Instead of the typical quadratic error function in GDM (Gradient Descent Method), five distinct optimization functions were utilized in the study. The findings of the authors' technique were compared to the outcomes of other methods in the research. According to the findings, the algorithm based on the Cauchy error function produced better results than the authors' other approaches and traditional methods.

Risse (2019) obtained gold price forecasts using DWT-SVR, which is a mix of DWT (Discrete Wavelet Decomposition-Discrete Wavelet Decomposition) and SVR algorithms. The statistics utilized are monthly figures from January 1992 to December 2016. Nine distinct economic and financial metrics were utilized as input in the study. All variables utilized in the analyses were divided into components for distinct time periods using DWT, and the components obtained were used as inputs to the SVR. According to the data, combining all factors impacted economic and statistical performance. Inflation, trade-weighted exchange rate, GSCI and CRB commodities indexes are the input variables affecting gold prices.

In their study, Jabeur et al. (2021) tried to predict gold prices with machine learning. They began by comparing six machine learning models. The new eXtreme Gradient Boosting (XGBoost) and CatBoost methods are among these six models. The study found that the eXtreme Gradient Boosting (XGBoost) method performed better than the others. In the Yürük (2022) research, silver prices were estimated in the same way. Five significant variables for projecting silver prices are employed. The variables utilized include gold prices, the dollar index, the Nasdaq Composite Index, crude oil prices, and the S&P 500 index. The study covered weekly data from 10.01.2010 to 24.04.2022 in its scope. According to the Root Square Mean Error (RMSE) and Mean Absolute Error (MAE) performance evaluation techniques, the XGBoost algorithm is successful in calculating silver prices.

The silver price was approximated using deep learning algorithms LSTM and ARIMA in Üntez's (2022) research. The model was trained using solely silver/ounce parity data from January 1, 2018 to April 12, 2021. Following that, prediction values were generated using two methods for the dates 13.04.2021 and 21.04.2021. ARIMA surpasses the LSTM algorithm in forecasting silver prices based on performance metrics (RMSE, MAE).

The random forest approach was used in this work by Manjula and Karthikeyan (2019) to simulate gold prices for the years 2000–2018. The random forest approach outperforms the linear regression method in terms of performance metrics (RMSE, MAE). Sadorsky (2021) calculated gold prices using bagging, stochastic gradient boosting, and random forest algorithms in similar research. According to the data, the random forests technique performs best in predictions of more than 10 days.

4 Data and Method

The CBDC1 cobalt contract is traded on the Chicago Mercantile Exchange to invest in cobalt, which exhibits price volatility owing to increased consumption. CBDC1 contract prices between February 4, 2019, and February 2, 2023, were utilized as input in the training model in the study. Cobalt futures are derivative transactions whose underlying assets are standard-grade cobalt. Contracts can be exchanged on markets such as the London Metal Exchange (LME) and the Chicago Mercantile Exchange (CME). The study used machine learning methodologies such as random forest and gradient boosted trees to estimate cobalt price.

Random Forest (RF) is a sophisticated supervised machine learning technique that produces comparable classification results. The Random Forest approach combines tree estimators from the same distribution for trees in the forest, which are based on the values of random vectors collected independently of each tree in the forest. In the same way that other supervised machine learning approaches, finding out how characteristics in the dataset relate to the target variable is the goal of the random forest approach. The Random Forest design is investigated in two stages: training and evaluation. Essentially, this algorithm operates by extracting predictions from the labeled training data in order to predict the label of the fresh unlabeled input data (Cheng & Bouganis, 2013).

Random Forest is a machine learning technique that primarily employs classification and regression trees, provides huge results often, and is versatile, easy to use, and efficient. The RF algorithm belongs to the bagging-based ensemble learning methods. One of the most significant benefits of the random forest is that it can solve classification and regression issues, which are the foundations of other machine learning techniques. The random forest's decision trees are built concurrently, and these trees might include both classification trees and regression trees. Each decision tree's nodes are separated by employing the best features to find the best answer among all features (Kumral et al., 2022).

The Random Forest model is a machine learning approach that may be used for classification as well as regression issues. The Random Forest Regression model's working logic is similar to a decision tree structure. Data collection is randomly split into little bits, generating decision trees. The average of the estimations of the decision trees created from the data set is obtained during the estimation phase. Because this approach can accurately recall prior time series, it produces consistent estimates (Arslankaya & Toprak, 2021).

The Gradient Boosting Trees algorithm, like the Random Forest algorithm, uses decision trees. The primary distinction is that the final estimate is a linear sum of all trees, with each tree's objective being to reduce the residual error of prior trees (Aydın, 2018).

Boosting is a technique for creating several models that minimize a certain loss function averaged over the training data, such as a square error or an absolute error. The loss function computes the difference between the expected and actual values (Hastie et al., 2009).

5 Findings

Random forest and gradient boosted trees approaches from machine learning were used in the study to predict cobalt pricing. The data is initially randomly divided into little parts using the random forest approach. The decision tree method is then applied to these divided little bits to provide as many predictions as there are trees. In the testing phase, the required value is obtained by combining the data from all trees. The results are depicted in the graph below (Fig. 1).

The test dataset is used to assess machine learning models' ability to predict. Ground truth refers to the needed, targeted values in the test dataset. The estimations achieved using the gradient boosted trees approach in the investigation were close to the desired values (Fig. 2).

The MAPE approach was used to assess the forecast model's performance. The equation below depicts the Average Absolute Percent Error (MAPE). N is the number of samples in the equation, A^t is the actual value of the index, and F^t is the forecast value.

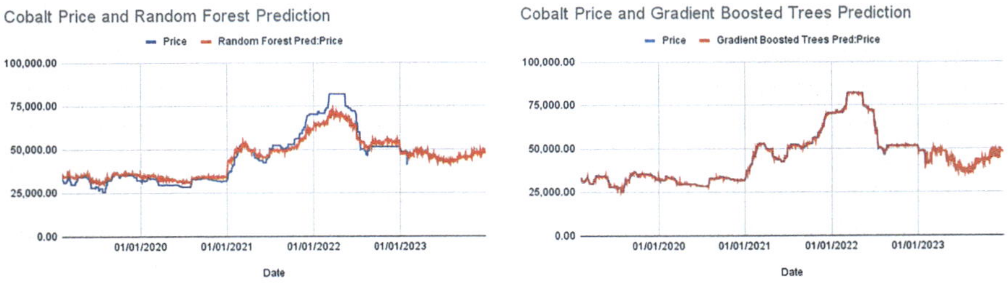

Fig. 1 Cobalt price predictions

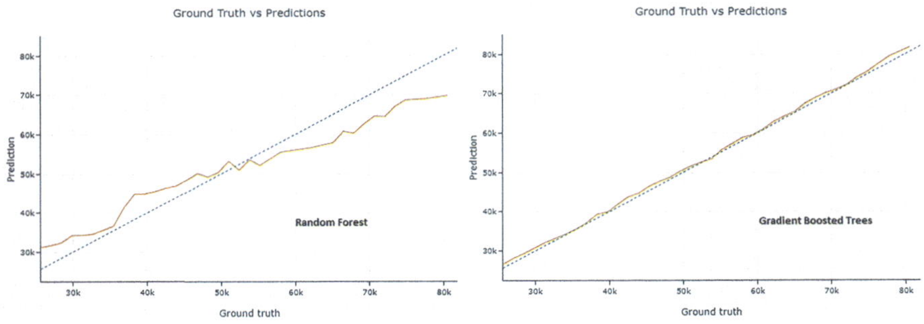

Fig. 2 Ground truth vs predictions

Table 1 Diagnostic test

	Random forest	Gradient boosted trees
MAPE	7%	0.83%

$$M = \frac{100}{n} \sum_{t=1}^{n} \left| \frac{A^t - F^t}{A^t} \right| \tag{1}$$

MAPE results are classified into four types: excellent (MAPE<10), decent (MAPE<20), acceptable (MAPE<50), and undesirable (MAPE>50) (Chang et al., 2007). The gradient boosted trees technique outperforms the price estimation match in terms of quality estimation (Table 1).

6 Conclusion

Although precious metals with significant economic worth were formerly as vital as money, they are now utilized primarily as an investment tool or for industrial uses. Gold, silver, and copper metals are the most traded commodities in global commodity markets and have a variety of applications. Because of its widespread industrial use, the commodity is significant to the entire economy when combined with complementary and replacement items. Commodity prices are determined by several factors, including supply and demand patterns, seasonality, trade policy, speculative trading, and transportation costs. Because there are a significant number of individual and institutional investors and organizations actively trading or consuming these real assets, commodities markets are supposed to establish a fair price for a specific commodity. Short-term and long-term variables influence cobalt pricing. Unlike other precious metals, cobalt supply is driven by industry needs since the quantity provided is mostly for industrial use.

The European Union (EU) has begun a collaborative effort to develop a list of "essential raw materials" to offer secure and continuous access to raw materials with high supply risk and economic importance and resources for their future requirements. Cobalt is on the list because of its significant economic relevance and supply risk. Cobalt prices skyrocketed in 2008 due to high demand from rechargeable battery producers and the aviation industry.

This research is significant in two ways. The first is an estimate of cobalt prices, which is a source of green investments. The second is that the methods utilized to create this estimation are random forest and gradient boosted trees, both of which are novel machine learning approaches. Following the analysis, it is discovered that the model performed a successful estimation in two approaches. However, the gradient boosted trees technique produced the most accurate estimates.

References

Alameer, Z., Abd Elaziz, M., Ewees, A. A., Ye, H., & Jianhua, Z. (2019). Forecasting gold price fluctuations using improved multilayer perceptron neural network and whale optimization algorithm. *Resources Policy, 61*, 250–260.

Armstrong, R. D., Briggs, G. W. D., & Charles, E. A. (1988). Some effects of the addition of cobalt to the nickel hydroxide electrode. *Journal of Applied Electrochemistry, 18*, 215–219.

Arslankaya, S., & Toprak, Ş. (2021). Using machine learning and deep learning algorithms for stock price prediction. *International Journal of Engineering Research and Development, 13*(1), 178–192.

Aydın, C. (2018). Classification of Fire Station requirement using machine learning algorithms. *The European Journal of Science and Technology, 14*, 169–175.

Aydın, O., & Kılıç, C. (2012). Cobalt from ancient times to today. *Journal of Mining Turkey, 20*, 70–75.

Byun, S. J., & Cho, H. (2013). Forecasting carbon futures volatility using GARCH models with energy volatilities. *Energy Economics, 40*, 207–221.

Carr, M. H., & Turekian, K. K. (1961). The geochemistry of cobalt. *Geochimica et Cosmochimica Acta, 23*(1–2), 9–60.

Chang, Y. F., Lin, C. J., Chyan, J. M., Chen, I. M., & Chang, J. E. (2007). Multiple regression models for the lower heating value of municipal solid waste in Taiwan. *Journal of Environmental Management, 85*(4), 891–899.

Cheng, C., & Bouganis, C. S. (2013). Accelerating random forest training process using FPGA. In *23rd International Conference on Field programmable Logic and Applications* (pp. 1–7). IEEE.

Chevallier, J. (2011). Nonparametric modeling of carbon prices. *Energy Economics, 33*(6), 1267–1282.

Domingo, J. L. (1989). Cobalt in the environment and its toxicological implications. *Reviews of Environmental Contamination and Toxicology*, 105–132.

Fan, X., Li, S., & ve Tian, L. (2015). Chaotic characteristic identification for carbon price and an multilayer perceptron network prediction model. *Expert Systems with Applications, 42*(8), 3945–3952.

Hastie, T., Tibshirani, R., Friedman, J. H., & Friedman, J. H. (2009). *The elements of statistical learning: Data mining, inference, and prediction* (Vol. 2, pp. 1–758). Springer.

Hawkins, M. (2001). Why we need cobalt. *Applied Earth Science, 110*(2), 66–70.

Hussein, S. F. M., Shah, M. B. N., Abd Jalal, M. R., & Abdullah, S. S. (2011, April). Gold price prediction using radial basis function neural network. In *2011 Fourth International Conference on Modeling, Simulation and Applied Optimization* (pp. 1–11). IEEE.

Jabeur, S. B., Mefteh-Wali, S., & Viviani, J.-L. (2021). Forecasting gold price with the XGBoost algorithm and SHAP interaction values. *Annals of Operations Research*. https://doi.org/10.1007/s10479-021-04187-w

Julien, C. (2000). Local cationic environment in lithium nickel–cobalt oxides used as cathode materials for lithium batteries. *Solid State Ionics, 136*, 887–896.

Kangarani-Farahani, M., & S. Mehralian (2013). Comparison between artificial neural network and neuro-fuzzy for gold Price prediction. In *13th Iranian Conference on Fuzzy Systems (IFSC)*. IEEE (pp. 1–5).

Kılıç, S. B. (2013). Predicting the direction of gold Price returns: Integrating composite artificial neural network models by Markov chain process. *Journal of Cukurova University Faculty of Economics and Administrative Sciences, 17*(2), 15–28.

Kumral, C. D., Topal, A., Ersoy, M., Çolak, R., & Yiğit, T. (2022). Performing performance analysis by implementing random forest algorithm on FPGA. *El-Cezeri, 9*(4), 1315–1327.

Li, M., & Lu, J. (2020). Cobalt in lithium-ion batteries. *Science, 367*(6481), 979–980.

Mahey, S., Kumar, R., Sharma, M., Kumar, V., & Bhardwaj, R. (2020). A critical review on toxicity of cobalt and its bioremediation strategies. *SN Applied Sciences, 2*, 1–12.

Mandeville, C. E., & Fulbright, H. W. (1943). The energies of the γ− R a y s from Sb 122, Cd 115, Ir 192, Mn 54, Zn 65, and Co 60. *Physical Review, 64*(9–10), 265.

Manjula, K. A., & Karthikeyan, P. (2019, April). Gold price prediction using ensemble based machine learning techniques. In *2019 3rd International Conference on Trends in Electronics and Informatics (ICOEI)* (pp. 1360–1364). IEEE.

Nacar, E. N., & Erdebilli, B. (2021). Makine Öğrenmesi Algoritmalari İle Satiş Tahmini. *Endüstri Mühendisliği, 32*(2), 307–320.

Ravichandran, R., & Manimegalai, C. (2017). Head and neck radiotherapy with tele-cobalt machine efficacy and need for tissue compensation. *International Journal of Radiology & Radiation Therapy, 2*(3), 00025.

Risse, M. (2019). Combining wavelet decomposition with machine learning to forecast gold returns. *International Journal of Forecasting, 35*(2), 601–615.

Sadorsky, P. (2021). Predicting gold and silver price direction using tree-based classifiers. *Journal of Risk and Financial Management, 14*(5), 198.

Shao, L., Kou, W., & Zhang, H. (2022). The evolution of the global cobalt and lithium trade pattern and the impacts of the low-cobalt technology of lithium batteries based on multiplex network. *Resources Policy, 76*, 102550.

Shortland, A. J., Tite, M. S., & Ewart, I. (2006). Ancient exploitation and use of cobalt alums from the Western Oases of Egypt. *Archaeometry, 48*(1), 153–168.

Sibley, S. F. (1979). *Cobalt*. US Department of the Interior.

Üntez, A. (2022). *Developing financial forecast modeling with deep learning on silver/Ons parity* (Master Thesis). Sakarya University.

Verma, S., Thampi, G. T., & ve Rao, M. (2020). ANN based method for improving gold price forecasting accuracy through modified gradient descent methods. *IAES International Journal of Artificial Intelligence, 9*(1), 46–57.

Wang, S. (2006). Cobalt—Its recovery, recycling, and application. *JOM, 58*(10), 47–50.

Wilkinson, V. M., & Gould, G. V. (1998). *Food irradiation: A reference guide*. Woodhead Publishing Ltd.

Yap, C. T. (1988). A quantitative spectrometric analysis of trace concentrations of manganese and cobalt in ceramics and the significance of AsCo and MnCo ratios. *Journal of Archaeological Science, 15*(2), 173–177.

Yaylali, B., Yazici, E. Y., Celep, O., & Deveci, H. (2020). Production of cobalt as a critical metal from primary and secondary resources. *Scientific Mining Journal, 59*(1), 35–50.

Yüksel, R., & Akkoç, S. (2016). Forecasting gold prices by using artificial neural network and an application. *Journal of Doğuş University, 17*(1), 39–50.

Yürük, M. (2022). *Estimating silver prices with Xgboost (Extreme gradient boosting) based algorithm* (pp. 227–235). ISPEC.

Zhu, B., & Wei, Y. M. (2013). Carbon price prediction with a hybrid ARIMA and least squares support vector machines methodology. *Omega, 41*(3), 517–524.

Driving Financial Performance: Exploring the Impact of ESG Policies in Telecommunication Companies Within the CIS Region

Kerim Melayev, Lyazzat Yespergenova, Aliya Dosmanbetova, Zhulduz Kupenova, and Alimshan Faizulayev

1 Introduction

The telecom industry is one of the most capital-intensive and highly productive industries in the Commonwealth of Independent States (CIS) region. Broadcast communications are dynamic and vital in the region, and they drive business development in socioeconomically advanced countries. As an instrument of a rapid growth, telecom administrations connect individuals all over the globe. The global telecommunications sector has made major advances over the past few years.

The profitability of telecom companies started booming with the development of other technologies, like the Internet of Things, fintech, and technologies in the ecommerce sector. Running a cautious test of profitability indicators is imperative because every company, whether big or small, depends on profitability. Profitability is key for measuring effectiveness, and ways of improving it are usually discussed among supervisors and researchers. Profitability, among other key factors, influences a firm's achievements. A politically stable and growing economy is necessary for developing internal sources of financing and for future development.

Although many studies are being conducted every year to understand the profitability indicators in different industries, the number of telecom companies was not high before the ecommerce era grew rapidly. In light of this, we carried out an

K. Melayev · A. Faizulayev (✉)
Bang College of Business (BCB), KIMEP University, Almaty, Republic of Kazakhstan
e-mail: a.faizulayev@kimep.kz

L. Yespergenova · A. Dosmanbetova
Almaty Management University, Almaty, Republic of Kazakhstan

Z. Kupenova
Al Farabi Kazakh National University, Almaty, Republic of Kazakhstan

N. Ozatac et al. (eds.), *Sustainable Development in Banking and Finance*, Springer Proceedings in Business and Economics,
https://doi.org/10.1007/978-3-031-65533-3_6

analysis to identify and describe the firm-specific determinants that influence the productivity of telecoms in the CIS region. Other macroeconomic components also affect such profitability, such as a financially developed market, political stability, unemployment, GDP growth, the inflation rate, digitalization, and ESG factors.

This chapter includes the following parts: In Sect. 1, we briefly explain the importance of the telecommunication industry; in Sect. 2, we conduct a literature review and present the profitability determinants for telecoms; Section 3 consists of the data on the research and presents our methodology and hypotheses; the findings of our research are provided in Sect. 4; the results are then analyzed in Sect. 5; Section 6 concludes, reporting our findings and approaches; Section 7 presents our recommendations; and Sect. 8 details the limitations of this study.

2 Literature Review

2.1 Telecom-Specific Indicators

2.1.1 Profitability

In Abdul Manaf et al.'s (2021) paper, which conducted an analysis on profitability, the authors evaluated the return on investment (ROE), stating that a positive effect on a company's effectiveness comes from a firm's size, whereas a negative effect comes from leverage. GDP and liquidity were not significant. In their study, they found that leverage and size were significant and influenced telecommunication firms in Malaysia.

Profitability was negatively associated with leverage in the Indian telecom industry, according to a study by Khan et al. (2018). Firms will be left bankrupt if they lack growth prospects, or they will be simply not profitable.

2.1.2 Size

One of the crucial variables of a firm's profitability was identified, by Sritharan (2015) and Djashan (2019), as its size, whereas Deitiana and Habibuw's (2015) study on a firm's size found that size is not an important indicator of its efficiency. In the study by Zadeh and Eskandari (2012), "quality" refers to a firm's operational excellence and customer satisfaction, while "quantity" relates to the volume of output produced. The study highlights that the influence of a firm's size on its performance varies based on these factors and the country's economic conditions. Singapurwoko and El-Wahid (2011) concluded that size is not significant to profitability. The same results were found by Endri and Fathony (2020), who reported that a firm's size is not significant for the profitability of a firm, even when it had a positive coefficient.

2.1.3 Leverage

Hossain (2020) stated in his study that leverage is a vital indicator for understanding the efficiency of using debt. The leverage formula is a debt-to-equity formula, which simply means that the total debt is divided by the equity of the firm. Endri and Fathony (2020) stated in their study that no effect on performance was produced by leverage, even though the coefficient was positive. They found that a firm that used its own funds was more likely to be profitable because it can fund its operations and activities with its own capital. Hence, a decrease or an increase in leverage is not always supported or may even reduce the profitability of a company.

2.1.4 Liquidity

Gatsi and Gadzo (2013) reported that liquidity has a negative impact on profitability. Although Ondigi and Willy (2016) reported the opposite, namely that liquidity is a major determinant of a firm's profitability, their study was conducted on the insurance industry. Here, we suggest that a firm should approach sufficient liquidity in the form of short-term assets. Unlike the preceding papers in this subsection, Abera's (2012) study discovered no significant relationship between liquidity risk and profitability.

2.1.5 Management Efficiency

In Kang's (2007) study on the Taiwan telecom industry from 1993 to 2004, which analyzed cost-efficiency and production, the results showed that profitability was highly correlated with and can be predicted by cost-efficiency and the appropriate allocation of funds.

2.2 *Macroeconomic Indicators*

2.2.1 GDP

GDP is a vital indicator that influences the profitability of a firm. Romus et al. (2020) claimed in their paper that GPD is as an indicator that shows the current economical level and business health of a country. GDP can be interpreted as having a positive effect on consumers' purchasing power and improving a company's product demand. However, the findings of Samsuri (2017) showed that GDP is not a significant indicator of the profitability of a firm.

2.2.2 Digitalization (Access to Internet)

Generally, digitalization can be understood as having access to information and communication technology (ICT), or the Internet. Nowadays, four out of five people in developed countries, as compared to one out of five in the least developed countries, have an Internet connection (Hegyes et al., 2017). Accordingly, in this study, digitalization was taken as a variable to measure the digital divide that can be caused by the nonuse of telecom services. As of 2018, only half the global population was connected to the Internet, according to the International Telecommunication Union (ITU) database (ITU, 2018). In developed countries, the Internet can be found in nearly every corner, such as in shops and cafés.

2.2.3 ESG

Environmental, social, and governance (ESG) concerns have risen dramatically over the past several years. Governments have started to pay attention to ecology and to provide new programs and funding options in light of it (Jain et al., 2016). Currently, many companies from different industries have started to focus on ESG regulations on business projects. Eventually, ESG concerns will also affect the telecom industry and can be vital indicators for determining profitability.

2.2.4 Financial Technology

Sujud and Hachem (2017) found in their study that mobile banking and hi-tech Internet penetration positively affected the profitability of banks, which are major competitors of telecoms in ecommerce, the Internet of Things, and marketplaces. These innovations increase a company's profit by keeping its funds within its system.

2.2.5 Inflation

Inflation can hamper the profitability of most firms by decreasing investment potential and lowering the value of wages, which later become key factors that affect production and economic growth. As a result of inflation, the value of money decreases, and people spend less and consume less accordingly, which causes them to also spend less on services because the prices of services also tend to increase (Riggins & Dewan, 2005; Murni, 2016) (Table 1).

Table 1 Literature review

Author	Title	Country	Period	Method	Results
Maisyarah and Sofyardi (2018)	The Impact of Internet User Growth on Profitability in Indonesia's Telecommunication Oligopoly	Indonesia	2011–2015	Generalized method of moments (GMM)	The number of Internet users has a positive impact on income. Companies must improve their service, quality, and maintenance to keep customers active and loyal to the company, which will increase profitability.
Khan et al. (2018)	Determinants of Profitability in Indian Telecom Companies: The Role of Leverage and Growth Prospects	India	2004–2017	GMM	These researchers found that leverage decreases profitability. Additionally, firms will be left bankrupt if they lack growth prospects, or they will be simply not profitable.
Abdul Manaf et al. (2021)	A Performance Analysis of Profitability Determinants in Malaysian Private Telecommunication Firms	Malaysia	2007–2016	Random effects model	This study showed that size positively affects profitability, whereas leverage decreases the profitability of a firm. GDP and liquidity were not significant.
Sahoo and Sahoo (2022)	Factors Influencing Profitability in Indian Telecommunication Industries: An Empirical Study	India	2008–2015	GMM	The results of this study showed that leverage decreases profitability, whereas advertisements and imports are significant and increase it.

3 Research Data, Methodology, and Hypotheses

3.1 Data

For our study, we decided to take panel data from telecommunication companies in CIS countries, namely Tajikistan, Azerbaijan, Kazakhstan, Uzbekistan, Moldova, the Russian Federation, the Kyrgyz Republic, Belarus, and Armenia. Descriptions of the variables that were used in this study will be provided later on. Information on the proxies of measurements and their symbols and an empirical analysis are provided. Our analysis covered the years 2010–2021 for all variables. For our research, we collected data from the telecom industry; the firm-specific and macroeconomic variables were retrieved from SP Global CapitalIq and the World Bank database.

3.2 Methodology

This study aimed to estimate the impacts of variables such as leverage (LEV), ESG, digitalization (DIG), firm size (SIZE), liquidity (LIQ), gross domestic product (GDP), management efficiency (MEF), and inflation (INFL) on the profitability of the telecom industry in the CIS region. Our study design used the quantitative method and data-collection techniques to analyze the data released by telecommunication firms for relevancy (Table 2).

To solve the autocorrelation and heteroscedasticity issue, we decided to use a feasible generalized least squares (FGLS) model because Fani et al.'s (2018) research on $N < T$ (N refers to number of variables; T refers to time period) indicated that this model can solve such issues. The following is the econometric equation model:

Table 2 Proxies for the dependent and independent variables

Dependent variable	*Definitions*
Profitability (PROF)	EBIT/total assets (ROA)
Independent variable	
Liquidity (LIQ)	Current assets/current liabilities
Firm's size (SIZE)	Log of total assets
Leverage (LEV)	Debt to assets ratio %
Management efficiency (MEF)	Operating expenses/total revenue
Macroeconomic variable	*Proxy*
GDP growth (GDPg)	GDP expected growth
Inflation (INFL)	Inflation rate
Digitalization (DIG)	Number of online users
ESG	Score of the overall ESG risks

$$\text{PROF} = \beta 0 + \beta 1 \text{ LIQ} + \beta 2 \text{ SIZ} + \beta 3 \text{ LEV} + \beta 4 \text{ MEF} + \beta 5 \text{ GDPg} + \beta 6 \text{ INFL} + \beta 7 \text{ DIG} + \beta 8 \text{ ESG} + \beta 9 \text{ DUM} + \varepsilon \quad (1)$$

where

β represents the constant variable
ROAi,t represents the return on assets (%)
GDPi,t represents gross domestic product (%)
INFLi,t represents the inflation rate (%)
DIGi,t represents the number of online users (absolute number)
ESGi,t represents the score of the ESG indicator for firms (%)
SIZEi,t represents the size of the firm (%)
MEFi,t represents management efficiency (%)
LEVi,t represents leverage (%)
LIQi,t represents liquidity (%)
DUMi,t represents COVID-19 (year)
$\varepsilon i,t$ represents the error term
βi represents the coefficients (i)

3.3 Hypotheses of This Study

H1: Liquidity negatively impacts the ROA because the company spends less money, and it doesn't increase profitability.

H2: An increase in assets, which is an increase in the share of telecommunication antennas and the coverage of the networks in cities, positively and significantly affects a company's size and its profitability.

H3: Leverage has a low negative effect on the profitability of telecom companies because most of them take out loans to invest in new technology.

H4: Management efficiency has a positive impact on the ROA because the efficient use of a company's resources reduces costs.

H5: GDP positively affects the profitability of firms. The level of economic development in a country brings with it more opportunities for people to spend money and use the services of telecom companies, which will reap profits for the telecom industry.

H6: Inflation has a negative and significant effect on the profitability of the telecom industry. As the government cannot stabilize the increase in the costs for banks, loans become expensive and profitability decreases.

H8: Digitalization has a positive effect on the telecom industry's profitability. The more online users, the more people who will spend money and consume the services of the telecommunications sector.

H9: ESG concerns have significant and has positive effects on the profitability of firms. Technological giants and other companies have switched to fostering a green economy, which has led to the reconstruction of the sector and to new practices. ESG concerns are funded by governments and are expected to be realized within the next few years.

H10: The dummy variable has a positive effect on profitability (the ROA). Because many people in the world have transitioned to remote work and distance learning, the demand for telecom services has increased rapidly. People have started to use networks more, which has brough a huge cash inflow for telecom companies.

4 Results

4.1 Descriptive Statistics

The descriptive statistics of each of the variables used in this study are represented in Table 3. According to the results, the profitability of telecom companies varies from 0.072 mln to −18.53 mln, where the standard deviation is a much larger number than that of the mean.

The standard deviation shows the volatility and stability of the variables. The lower the number, the less volatile the variable. Most of the independent variables are stable because the standard deviation is nearly the same as the mean value.

4.2 Correlation Analysis

Connections between the variables were reviewed by using the correlation matrix, which is presented in Table 4. The correlation matrix was used to determine whether the correlation between the variables was positive or negative. Additionally, a

Table 3 Descriptive statistics

Variable	Obs.	Mean	Std. Dev.	Min	Max
PROF	196	0.072	1.366	−18.53	0.719
LIQ	193	1.273	1.332	0.05	10.347
SIZE	197	0.654	0.121	0.057	0.795
LEV	196	0.598	2.71	0	28.389
MEF	193	10.246	115.988	0.482	1606.914
GDPg	216	0.021	0.028	−0.101	0.074
INFL	212	0.069	0.043	−0.002	0.487
DIG	198	0.691	0.125	0.233	0.859
ESG	180	−1.044	0.093	−1.184	−0.591
IYEAR 2019	216	0.083	0.277	0	1

Source: Calculations based on data retrieved from the STATA application, performed by the authors

Table 4 Matrix of correlations

Variables	(1)	(2)	(3)	(4)	(5)	(6)	(7)	(8)	(9)	(10)
(1) PROF	1.000									
(2) LIQ	-0.020	1.000								
(3) SIZE	0.498	-0.166	1.000							
(4) LEV	-0.977	-0.078	-0.433	1.000						
(5) MEF	-0.038	0.051	-0.202	0.012	1.000					
(6) GDPg	0.035	0.092	0.041	-0.013	-0.071	1.000				
(7) INFL	0.037	0.007	0.003	-0.067	-0.006	-0.535	1.000			
(8) DIG	-0.139	-0.059	0.055	0.133	0.040	-0.260	-0.242	1.000		
(9) ESG	0.051	-0.043	-0.091	-0.046	0.003	-0.404	0.361	-0.243	1.000	
(10) _IYEAR_2019	-0.226	-0.092	-0.045	0.236	-0.028	0.046	-0.184	0.402	-0.004	1.000

Source: Author's calculations

Table 5 VIF

Variable	VIF	1/VIF
GDPg	2.320	0.432
DIG	1.970	0.508
INFL	1.810	0.552
ESG	1.500	0.666
SIZE	1.400	0.712
LEV	1.370	0.732
IYEAR 2019	1.360	0.735
LIQ	1.080	0.924
MEF	1.060	0.942
Mean VIF	**1.540**	

Source: Authors' calculations

correlation analysis on variables can be conducted to find evidence of multicollinearity.

In Table 5, LEV has a high negative correlation with PROF, which was already described by Khan et al. (2018). Other variables don't have high correlations.

4.3 Variation Inflation Factor

A variance inflation factor test was conducted to check for multicollinearity, which showed that the mean VIF was 1.54, which is greater than 1.0 and less than 5.0. This means that the correlation between the independent variables is small, but not significant, and indicates little multicollinearity; however, some experts have noted no multicollinearity when the mean VIF was less than 10.0 (Vittinghoff et al., 2006) (Table 5).

Overall, the results in Table 5 show that the mean value of the current data does not have a multicollinearity issue.

4.4 Autocorrelation

Table 6 shows a test for autocorrelation, which indicates that the data has cross-sectional dependency.

Our study shows an autocorrelation between the variables in the analyzed data in that the *p*-value is less than 1%.

5 Statistics Estimation Results

Linear regression is depicted in Table 7. According to that table, the 97% change in the dependent variable can be attributed to the independent variables. The model is best fit with a *p*-value <0.000, which means that it's significant.

To better understand whether the data shows a normal distribution of the standard error, a heteroscedasticity test was conducted. In statistical data, variance in the error term (or heteroscedasticity) arises when a variable's standard errors are not stable throughout a predetermined period of time (Table 8).

Table 6 Autocorrelation

Wooldridge's test for determining autocorrelation in panel data
H0: no first-order autocorrelation
F (1, 16) = 2710.597
Prob > F = 0.0000

Source: Authors' calculations

Table 7 Linear regression

PROF	Coef.	St. Err.	*t*-Value	*p*-Value	[95% Conf.	Interval]	Sig.
LIQ	−0.089	0.016	−5.70	0	−0.12	−0.058	***
SIZE	1.063	0.235	4.52	0	0.598	1.528	***
LEV	−0.64	0.011	−57.70	0	−0.662	−0.618	***
MEF	0	0	−0.41	0.685	0	0	
GDPg	1.015	1.268	0.80	0.425	−1.49	3.519	
INFL	−0.998	0.601	−1.66	0.099	−2.186	0.19	*
DIG	−0.195	0.242	−0.81	0.421	−0.672	0.283	
ESG	0.391	0.265	1.48	0.142	−0.133	0.915	
_IYEAR_2019	−0.033	0.078	−0.42	0.674	−0.187	0.121	
Constant	0.387	0.297	1.30	0.195	−0.2	0.973	
Mean dependent var.		0.059	SD dependent var.			1.508	
R-squared		0.970	Number of observations			160	
F-test		545.382	Prob > F			0.000	
Akaike crit. (AIC)		41.661	Bayesian crit. (BIC)			72.413	

Source: Authors' calculations

***$p < 0.01$, **$p < 0.05$, *$p < 0.1$

Table 8 Heteroscedasticity

Heteroscedasticity test
Likelihood-ratio test LR chi^2 (104) = 342.39
(Assumption: homo nested in hetero) Prob > chi^2 = 0.0000

Source: Calculations based on data retrieved from the STATA application, performed by the authors

Table 9 Time-series FGLS regression

PROF	Coef.	St. Err.	*t*-Value	*p*-Value	[95% Conf.	Interval]	Sig.
LIQ	−0.011	0.005	−2.041	0.041	−0.022	0	**
SIZE	0.106	0.067	1.577	0.115	−0.026	0.237	
LEV	−0.079	0.035	−2.219	0.026	−0.148	−0.009	**
MEF	0	0.003	−0.057	0.955	−0.006	0.006	
GDPg	0.528	0.302	1.748	0.08	−0.064	1.12	*
INFL	0.065	0.117	0.551	0.581	−0.165	0.295	
DIG	−0.117	0.05	−2.337	0.019	−0.215	−0.019	**
ESG	0.38	0.132	2.869	0.004	0.12	0.64	***
_IYEAR_2019	0.021	0.009	2.4	0.016	0.004	0.039	**
Constant	0.604	0.136	4.453	0	0.338	0.87	***
Mean dependent var.		0.059	SD dependent var.			1.508	
Number of observations		159	Chi-square			35.372	

Source: Authors' calculations
•PROF: Dependent variable representing profitability.
•Coef.: Coefficient of the variable, indicating the expected change in the dependent variable for a one-unit change in the independent variable, holding all other variables constant.
•St. Err.: Standard Error of the coefficient, measuring the average amount that the coefficient estimates vary from the actual average value of our response variable.
•*t*-Value: A ratio obtained by dividing the difference between the sample estimate and the null hypothesis by the standard error. It is used to determine the *P*-value.
•*p*-Value: The probability of observing the data, or something more extreme, if the null hypothesis is true. A smaller *p*-value indicates stronger evidence against the null hypothesis.
•[95% Conf. Interval]: The range within which author can be 95% confident that the population parameter lies. It is calculated based on the standard error and the coefficient.
•Sig.: Significance of the coefficients, marked by asterisks: *** $p < 0.01$, ** $p < 0.05$, * $p < 0.1$.

According to Table 8, the data are heteroscedastic. Because of this, our study used the FGLS model, which eliminates autocorrelation and heteroscedasticity (Table 9).

After the FGLS (Feasible Generalized Least Square) test had been completed, coefficients were added to the variables, after which the econometric model yielded the following equation:

$$\begin{aligned} \mathrm{PROF} = 0.604 - 0.11\ \mathrm{LIQ} + 0.10\ 6\mathrm{SIZ} - 0.079\ \mathrm{LEV} + \mathrm{MEF} + 0.528\ \mathrm{GDPg} \\ +0.065\ \mathrm{INFL} - 0.117\ \mathrm{DIG} + 0.38\ \mathrm{ESG} + 0.021\ \mathrm{YEAR2019} + \varepsilon \end{aligned} \quad (2)$$

Ceteris paribus, a 1% increase in a constant variable will increase profitability by 0.604%, with significant probability.

As we assumed, liquidity (LIQ) had a statistically significant negative impact on the profitability of the telecom industry. A 1% increase in LIQ will decrease PROF by −0.011%. According to other studies, the better a company manages its current assets and liabilities, the more revenue it will gain. Ondigi and Willy (2016) reported that liquidity was significant and had a huge impact on PROF. Their paper proposed that firms need to have assets in the form of short-term liquid assets. However, according to our model, in the telecom industry, liquidity has a negative impact, which can be explained as follows: Telecom companies usually have long-term assets because their main industrial assets are concentrated in telecom infrastructure, such as cables and antennas.

Leverage (LEV), according to several studies, has been shown to have a statistically significant negative impact on the ROA of the telecom industry. A 1% increase in LEV will decrease PROF by −0.079%. Due to the trade-off theory (Hackbarth et al., 2007), firms need to pay attention to the way that they structure their businesses and need to understand the pros and cons of taking on debt. The disadvantages of leverage include the costs associated with bankruptcy and the conflict of interest between shareholders and bondholders; to reach an ideal leverage level, the marginal gain must be balanced against the cost of the debt. A strong leverage ratio will boost a company's value by influencing the public's opinion of it. According to Hackbarth et al.'s findings, leverage and firm profitability are negatively correlated, which can be explained as follows: The more debt a company takes on, the higher the risk it assumes of defaulting. This explanation is in line with the conclusions reached by Khan et al. (2018). These studies have suggested that businesses should increase their use of internal resources for growth and that profitable businesses should reduce their loans while trying to raise enough internal resources to cover their financial needs.

Gross domestic product (GDP) is often used to show the health of a country's economy. It has a statistically significant negative impact on a bank's net interest margin. A 1% increase in GDP will increase PROF by 0.528%. In other words, as GDP grows, economic expansion will accordingly ensue. In such an economic environment, companies can expand their business and, as a result, will be able to charge their customers more.

Digitalization (DIG) has a statistically significant negative impact on profitability. A 1% increase in DIG will decrease PROF by 0.117%. Digital technologies such as smartphone, cloud-based computing machines, and artificial intelligence (AI) have made economies more technological (i.e., the digital economy) and forced them to become more digitalized. The increased use of AI and changes in human behaviors have somehow positively affected the speed of decision-making processes and productivity. Digitalization has been a revolution given its obvious benefits. The overall negative effect of it, though, can be attributed to lower prices: The more users who are online, the lower the price of Internet services because the competition in the market rises, which lowers prices. Gaining new customers and increasing the prices of services are difficult because customers can change service providers; this competition will lead to a decrease in revenue.

Environment, social, and governance (ESG) concerns have been shown to have statistically significant positive impacts on the profitability of the telecom industry. A 1% increase in ESG factors will increase PROF by 0.38%. ESG factors became crucial because the problems due to global warming started to be raised by the United Nations, and governments have since enacted policies to improve ESG scores and lower emissions, policies that restrict business operations and increase business costs—according to Jain et al. (2016).

The dummy variable—YEAR2019—was time, and it used the year of the start of the COVID-19 pandemic. During this period, the world faced a dramatic boost in the usage of telecom services because people were in their homes more and because much of the world transitioned to online meetings and less personal contact. COVID-19 taught the world that the telecom industry plays a vital role in business by connecting people who are not connected physically. This led to innovations in the industry, and people still prefer to work from home; additionally, many firms decreased their costs by moving their offices online and by continuing to host meetings online even after the lockdowns ended. This factor helped to increase the profitability of telecom services, delivery services, and digital services (Samsuri, 2017; Hegyes et al., 2017; Zhao et al., 2014).

6 Conclusion

The telecom industry over the past several years has dramatically increased in importance. Internet and mobile services have become vital, no matter where the location. Moreover, the telecom industry was positively affected by COVID-19, experiencing a boost in its profitability. A lot of people still work from their homes, and meetings continue to be provided via Zoom and other digital platforms.

According to Khan et al. (2018), liquidity and leverage have detrimental impacts on a telecom company's profitability. Unexpectedly, digitalization turned out to be a decreasing factor for profitability in that the more options people have to choose from in a market, the higher demand those customers tend to have, and in response, firms decrease their prices to compete—findings that are consistent with those of Warner and Wäger (2019) and those of Zhao et al. (2014). GDP, ESG score, and the COVID-19 pandemic had positive effects on the profitability of the telecom industry. The economic growth of a country, fewer emissions, higher environmental responsibility from firms, and the early COVID-19 period were boosting factors for telecom profitability (Abera, 2012; Warner & Wäger, 2019). The model has been statistically validated; it is the best-fitting model. The 97% change in PROF can be explained by changes in independent variables, and the remaining 3% can be explained by changes in variables that were not factored into this study.

7 Recommendations

The managers of firms need to pay attention to indicators such as liquidity, leverage, digitalization, ESG concerns, and GDP when structuring their budgets for future investment or making other long-term financial decisions. Additionally, leverage level has a huge negative impact and should be considered before taking out a loan or taking on other debt. GDP was found to be a statistically significant positive factor in the firm's profitability. We recommend that managers keep fewer short-term assets, invest in their company's funds, increase sales, and produce fewer emissions, which will help their companies to acquire funding for ESG projects.

8 Limitations

Our study was limited to only those companies in the telecom industry in the CIS region. Only limited data are available on the telecom industry in the CIS region, and our study was restricted to only a few locations, such as Russia, Kazakhstan, and Ukraine, but it did not cover the remaining companies from other CIS countries, because most of them were not listed or because their data were not available from open sources. More studies are needed to explore new factors that were not studied in this research and to improve the results.

References

Abdul Manaf, S. M., Bidin, N. F., Salleh, W. A., Idris, A. R., & Mohd Yusoff, Z. Z. (2021). Profitability performance analysis: The evidence from private telecommunication firms in Malaysia. *Malaysian Management Journal, 25*, 191–212.

Abera, A. (2012). *Factors affecting profitability: An empirical study on Ethiopian banking industry*. In N. Ahmed, Z. Ahmed, & I. Ahmed (Eds.), *Determinants of capital*. Addis Ababa University.

Deitiana, T., & Habibuw, L. G. (2015). Factors affecting the financial performance of property and real estate companies listed at Indonesia stock exchange. *Asian Business Review, 5*(2), 79–88. https://doi.org/10.18034/abr.v5i2.58

Djashan, I. A. (2019). The effect of firm size and profitability on firm value with capital structure as intervening variables in Indonesia. *Journal of International Business, Economics and Entrepreneurship, 4*(2), 55–59.

Endri, E., & Fathony, M. (2020). Determinants of firm's value: Evidence from financial industry. *Management Science Letters, 10*, 111–120. https://doi.org/10.5267/j.msl.2019.8.011

Fani, K. A., Khan, V. J., Kumar, B., & Pk, B. K. (2018). Impact of internal and external factors on bank performance in Pakistan. *International and Public Affairs, 2*(4), 66–77. https://doi.org/10.11648/j.ipa.20180204.11

Gatsi, J. G., & Gadzo, S. G. (2013). Determinants of capital structure of insurance companies in Ghana. *Global Journal of Finance and Management, 5*(2), 79–86.

Hackbarth, D., Hennessy, C. A., & Leland, H. E. (2007). Can the trade-off theory explain debt structure? *The Review of Financial Studies, 20*(5), 1389–1428.

Hegyes, É. G., Csapó, I., & Farkas, M. F. (2017). Some aspects of digitalization and sustainability in the European Union. *Journal of Management, 36*(2), 37–46.

Hossain, T. (2020). Determinants of profitability: A study on manufacturing companies listed on the Dhaka Stock Exchange. *Asian Economic and Financial Review, 10*(12), 1496–1508. https://doi.org/10.18488/JOURNAL.AEFR.2020.1012.1496.1508

ITU. (2018). *Measuring the information society report (2018)*. Retrieved Nov 09, 2022, from https://www.itu.int/pub/D-IND-ICTOI

Jain, P. K., Jain, A., & Rezaee, Z. (2016). Value-relevance of corporate social performance: Evidence from short selling. *Journal Management Accounting Research, 28*, 29–52.

Kang, C. C. (2007). Measuring the production and cost efficiency in telecommunication industry: The Taiwan case. In *Proceedings of the eastern Asia Society for Transportation Studies*, vol. 6.

Khan, T., Shamim, M., & Goyal, J. (2018). Panel data analysis of profitability determinants: Evidence from Indian telecom companies. *Theoretical Economics Letters, 8*(15), 3581.

Maisyarah, R., & Sofyardi, M. (2018, January). The effect of Rice Subsidyon the expenditure of public family consumption and welfare of poor households. In *1st economics and business international conference 2017 (EBIC 2017)* (pp. 78–83). Atlantis Press.

Murni, A. (2016). *Ekonomika Makro*. PT Refika Aditama.

Ondigi, M. M., & Muturi, W. (2016). Factors affecting profitability of insurance firms: Case of firms listed on Nairobi securities exchange. *International Journal of Economics, Commerce and Management, United Kingdom, 4*(09). http://ijecm.co.uk/wp-content/uploads/2016/09/4926.pd

Riggins, F. J., & Dewan, S. (2005). The digital divide: Current and future research directions. *Journal of the Association for Information Systems, 6*(12), 298–337. https://doi.org/10.17705/1jais.00074. Available at: https://aisel.aisnet.org/jais/vol6/iss12/13

Romus, M., Anita, R., Abdillah, M. R., & Zakaria, N. B. (2020). Selected firms environmental variables: Macroeconomic variables, performance and dividend policy analysis. *International Conference on Environment and Technology, 469*, 1–7. https://doi.org/10.1088/1755-1315/469/1/012047

Sahoo, D. K., & Sahoo, P. K. (2022). Efficiency, productivity dynamics and determinants of productivity growth in Indian telecommunication industries: An empirical analysis. *Journal of Public Affairs, 22*(1), e2353.

Samsuri, N. (2017). Affin Bank performance: Relationship liuidity ratio, leverage ratio and GDP to profitability. *MPRA, 78545*, 1–11.

Singapurwoko, A., & El-Wahid, M. S. M. (2011). The impact of financial leverage to profitability study of non-financial companies listed in Indonesia stock exchange. *European Journal of Economics, Finance and Administrative Sciences, 32*(32), 136–148.

Sritharan, V. (2015). Does firm size influence on firm's profitability? Evidence from listed firms of Sri Lankan hotels and travels sector. *Research Journal of Finance and Accounting, 6*(6), 201–207.

Sujud, H., & Hachem, B. (2017). Effect of bank innovations on profitability and return on assets (ROA) of commercial banks in Lebanon. *International Journal of Economics and Finance, 9*(4), 35–50. https://doi.org/10.5539/ijef.v9n4p35

Vittinghoff, E., Glidden, D. V., Shiboski, S. C., & McCulloch, C. E. (2006). Regression methods in biostatistics: Linear, logistic, survival, and repeated measures models.

Warner, K., & Wäger, M. (2019). Building dynamic capabilities for digital transformation: An ongoing process of strategic renewal. *Long Range Planning, 52*(3), 326–349.

Zadeh, F. O., & Eskandari, A. (2012). Firm size as company's characteristic and level of risk disclosure: Review on theories and literatures. *International Journal of Business and Social Science, 3*(17), 9–17.

Zhao, F., Collier, A., & Deng, H. (2014). A multidimensional and integrative approach to study global digital divide and e-government development. *Information Technology & People, 27*, 38–62. https://doi.org/10.1108/ITP-01-2013-0022

Detecting Manipulation: Anomaly Analysis of Annual Reports of Firms Listed on Borsa Istanbul Using Benford's Law

Yavuz Selim Balcıoğlu, Abdullah Kürşat Merter, Sedat Çerez, and Gökhan Özer

1 Introduction

Today, numbers are used in many areas such as counting, reporting, accounting, measurement, mathematics, and coding and are an indispensable part of daily life. However, today, numbers can be used incorrectly and unethically through manipulative transactions while communicating the true financial status of organizations to stakeholders (Valliammai et al., 2018).

Data analytics is used as a tool to help detect and control fraud within an organization (Han, 2005; Kotsiantis & Tzelepis, 2006; Asllani & Naco, 2014). Benford's law can detect fraud in financial statements by examining the frequency of the occurrence of figures in reports (Geyer, 2010; Gorenc, 2019). However, if the frequency of occurrence of a particular number in the sample contradicts Benford's law, it does not always indicate the presence of manipulation (Valliammai et al., 2018). Instead, it guides the auditor who audits the organization on which part to conduct an in-depth examination to check for fraud (Aybars & Ataunal, 2016). Thus, instead of resorting to time-consuming methods such as physical verification and getting confirmation from employees to detect fraud in the reports, the auditor can quickly identify areas that may be fraudulent in the reports by checking the frequency of occurrence of the numbers in the steps of the financial data.

Y. S. Balcıoğlu · A. K. Merter · S. Çerez (✉)
Gebze Technical University, Faculty of Business Administration, Gebze, Turkey
e-mail: sedatcerez@gtu.edu.tr

G. Özer
Gebze Technical University, Faculty of Business Administration, Gebze, Turkey

Kyrgz-Turkish Manas University, Faculty of Economics and Administrative Sciences, Bishkek, Kyrgyzstan

N. Ozatac et al. (eds.), *Sustainable Development in Banking and Finance*, Springer Proceedings in Business and Economics,
https://doi.org/10.1007/978-3-031-65533-3_7

Table 1 Expected probability of numbers according to Benford's law

Digit (=d)	Probability of first significant digit = d	Probability of second significant digit = d	Probability of third significant digit = d	Probability of fourth significant digit = d
0	Not applicable	0.11968	0.10178	0.10018
1	0.30103	0.11389	0.10138	0.10014
2	0.17609	0.10882	0.10097	0.10010
3	0.12494	0.10433	0.10057	0.10006
4	0.09691	0.10031	0.10018	0.10002
5	0.07918	0.09668	0.09979	0.09998
6	0.06695	0.09337	0.09940	0.09994
7	0.05799	0.09035	0.09902	0.09990
8	0.05115	0.08757	0.09864	0.09986
9	0.04576	0.08500	0.09827	0.09982

Source: Nigrini (1999)

The first study on the Benford concept was conducted by Simon Newcomb in 1881 (Yanık & Samancı, 2013; Rad et al., 2021; Patel et al., 2022). Newcomb (1881), in his article titled "A note on the frequency of use of digits in natural numbers" published in the American Journal of Mathematics, mentioned that the probability of the digits in the numbers in different digits is not at the same rate. With this study, he laid the foundation of the theory that will be called Benford's law in the future. The second study on Benford's law after Simon was conducted by physicist Frank Benford. Benford (1938) published "The Law of Anomalous Numbers" in The Proceeding of the American Philosophical Society. In this study, the wear and tear on logarithm books was examined, as Simon had done, and at the end of the study, the same values were found as Simon's results. Although the same result was reached, today this law is known as Benford's law. The main reason for this is that Frank Benford attracted more attention due to the fact that he used a larger data set than Simon. For this reason, the name of the law is defined as Benford. According to Benford's law, the probabilities of each digit according to the digits are given in Table 1.

As can be seen from Table 1, the probability of each digit being seen in certain digits is not the same. The fact that 1 has the highest probabilistic value in Benford's law is due to the proportional increase of numbers. In other words, a number increasing from 1 to 2 requires a 100% increase, from 2 to 3 requires a 50% increase, from 5 to 6 requires a 20% increase, and finally from 8 to 9 requires a 12.5% increase. For this reason, numbers with low values such as 1 and 2 are used the most, while numbers such as 8 and 9 are used the least (Yanık & Samancı, 2013). As the numbers increase and the required ratio value decreases, it can be said that the most difficult threshold to overcome is the numbers with low values such as 1 and 2.

This study examines the compliance of the 2019 and 2020 annual reports of the firms operating in Borsa Istanbul with Benford's laws. Various financial institutions, such as banks, real estate investment trusts and holdings, are not included in the study as they are subject to different regulations and legislation. This study is expected to shed light on the potential of Benford's law to be an important tool for auditors and researchers for the reliability and accuracy of financial data.

Following the introduction, the second part of the study includes previous studies. The third section presents the methodology, explaining the sampling and analysis methods. The fourth section presents the results of the Benford analysis performed on the data of the firms in the sample. In the fifth section, the study is completed with a discussion where the results of the analysis are evaluated, and finally, a conclusion section with general evaluations of the study.

2 Literature Review

Möller (2009) analyzed the compliance of the annual financial statements of 1373 firms operating on the German DAX Exchange with Benford's law. As a result of the analysis of the sample of firms audited by different external auditors instead of the Big 4, it was observed that the data on financial accounts deviated significantly from Benford's law. They also stated that Benford's law can be used as an important criterion for evaluating audit quality. Yanık and Samancı (2013) examined the compliance of the 2012 general administrative expenses account of a state-owned sugar factory in Turkey with Benford's law. In the study where first and second-digit analyses were applied, they observed that the company data are most likely to comply with Benford's laws.

Uzuner (2014) examined the compliance of the balance sheets of banks traded in Borsa Istanbul with Benford's law. In the study where the first digit analysis was applied, he observed that a majority of the accounts in the balance sheet are consistent with Benford's law. Asllani and Naco (2014) tested the effectiveness of Benford's law in detecting fraud in accounting practices using data from a local hospital in Albania and presented a template for accounting auditors. Saville (2006) tested the hypothesis that Benford's laws can be used to detect misreporting or fraudulent reporting of accounting data using data from businesses listed on the Johannesburg Stock Exchange. They found that 17 listed firms that were previously reported to have misreported data were also found to have misreported data using Benford's laws. They also found that three of another group of firms that had previously received 17 compliant reports gave results inconsistent with Benford's laws, but this was a small group as it accounted for 11.2% of the sample. He also stated that Benford's law can be used as a tool by auditors to identify whether there are errors in accounting data.

Aybars and Ataunal (2016) examined manipulation in the reports of 148 firms operating in Borsa Istanbul between 2005 and 2015. They test the conformity of the numerical values in the relevant reports with Benford's law and observe that the current assets and net sales values in the reports almost perfectly match Benford's law, but the total assets and net profit values tend to deviate from Benford's law. Aris et al. (2017) examined possible fraud with the Benford's law method over 500 observation data of Malaysian public sector firms. As a result of the analysis with the first, second, first two, first three, and last two digit tests, they observed that Benford's method could be a reliable tool in identifying suspicious accounts and taking necessary measures.

Valliammai et al. (2018) examined accounting fraud with Benford's law through the quarterly reports of two companies, Satyam Computer Services Limited and Reliance Industries Limited. By making a comparative analysis of the results of both companies, they concluded that frauds in financial statements can be detected under the relevant law. Nunes et al. (2019) examined whether the financial statement headings of 27,058 companies operating in Portugal are consistent with Benford's law and whether the firms with negative results fit the distribution suggested by Benford's law. At the end of the study, they found that the turnover of the companies examined does not always follow Benford's law and shows different behaviors depending on whether the firm presents positive or negative results. Therefore, they emphasized that Benford's law can be used as a control tool by auditors.

Qu et al. (2020) applied manipulation analysis on the data of nonprofit organizations operating in the United States. In the study where Benford's law was applied, they found that although the entire sample generally complied with the law, individual organizations deviated from the law by 34%. Patel et al. (2022) examined the relationship between the violation of Benford's law and firm failure over a sample of 220,583 SME firms operating in Portugal. As a result of the study, they observed that firms that violate Benford's law have the highest failure rates. Based on this, they stated that strategic manipulation in terms of financial reporting of SME firms may lead to firm failure.

2.1 Method

In this study, we utilized the R software and Benford's law to detect potential anomalies in the annual reports of companies. Benford's law, also known as the First-Digit Law, states that the leading digit is likely to be small in many naturally occurring datasets. For example, the number 1 appears as the leading digit about 30% of the time, while 9 appears as the leading digit less than 5% of the time. By comparing the distribution of the first digits from the reports with the expected distribution according to Benford's law, we aimed to flag potential anomalies.

2.2 Data Source

We analyzed annual reports from two consecutive years:

2019: A total of 265 annual reports were examined.
2020: A total of 272 annual reports were evaluated.

2.3 *Procedure*

- Data extraction: Numbers were extracted from each report using automated scripts.
- First digit analysis: The first digit of each number was isolated.
- Comparison with Benford's law: The distribution of the first digits from the reports was compared to the expected distribution according to Benford's law.
- Anomaly detection: Deviations from the expected distribution were computed to identify potential anomalies.

By utilizing this methodology, we were able to systematically and objectively evaluate a large number of reports for potential irregularities.

3 Research Findings

3.1 *Data Extraction for 2019 Annual Reports*

The initial phase of our methodology centered on the extraction of numerical data from a comprehensive set of 265 annual reports for 2019. Given the heterogeneous format of these reports, a systematic approach was adopted. Automated scripts were developed in the R software environment to scan each report, isolate, and collate relevant numerical entries. This automation ensured consistency across the dataset and minimized manual intervention, thereby reducing potential human-induced errors. Post-extraction, the data underwent a preliminary validation process to identify and rectify any discrepancies or outliers that could adversely impact the subsequent analysis. The refined dataset, composed exclusively of the numbers extracted from the 2019 annual reports, laid the foundation for the subsequent first-digit analysis in line with Benford's law.

3.2 *First Digit Analysis for 2019 Annual Reports*

Upon successful extraction of the numerical data from the 265 annual reports of 2019, our attention shifted towards the first-digit analysis. This analysis is rooted in the premise of Benford's law, which posits that the leading digits in a wide array of datasets follow a specific logarithmic distribution. Specifically, smaller digits such as '1' are expected to appear as the leading digit more frequently than larger digits like '9'. Each extracted number was processed to isolate its leading digit to undertake this analysis, creating a distribution profile of first digits across the entire dataset.

Table 2 The key findings and expected values based on Benford's law (2019 annual reports)

Description	Value
Total annual reports	265
Leading digit '1' frequency (expected by Benford's law)	30.1%
Leading digit '2' frequency (expected by Benford's law)	17.6%
Leading digit '1' and '2' combined frequency (observed)	48%
Leading digit '1' and '2' combined frequency (expected by Benford's law)	47.7%

Table 3 The observed frequencies and their comparison with the expected values from Benford's law for the 2019 annual reports

Description	Value
Leading digit '1' frequency (observed)	29.8%
Leading digit '1' frequency (expected by Benford's law)	30.1%
Largest deviation between observed and expected frequency	<2.5%

Preliminary observations revealed that for the 2019 reports, the first digits exhibited a distribution that was largely in alignment with the predictions of Benford's law. Notably, digits '1' and '2' collectively constituted approximately 48% of the leading digits, reinforcing the law's predictions. This distribution provided a baseline against which anomalies could be detected in the subsequent phases of our study (Table 2).

3.3 Comparison with Benford's Law for 2019 Annual Reports

Having established the first-digit distribution for the 2019 annual reports, the next critical step was juxtaposing this observed distribution against the theoretical predictions of Benford's law. Benford's law provides a probabilistic framework, specifying the expected frequency of each digit as the leading number in genuine datasets. For instance, the number '1' is anticipated to appear as the leading digit approximately 30.1% of the time. Our analysis indicated that the observed frequency for the digit '1' in our 2019 reports was around 29.8%, showcasing a close alignment with Benford's expectations. Similarly, for other digits, the variances between the observed frequencies and Benford's predictions were minimal, with the largest deviation being less than 2.5%. Such a close correspondence bolstered our confidence in the authenticity of the data. However, areas where deviations did exist warranted a deeper dive to ascertain potential anomalies or peculiarities specific to the dataset (Table 3).

Table 4 The findings and the implications of the anomaly detection process for the 2019 annual reports

Description	Value
Total annual reports (2019)	265
Percentage of reports exceeding the threshold for anomalies	7%
Implicit implication of detected deviations	Not necessarily maleficence or fabrication, but areas that warrant further scrutiny

3.4 Anomaly Detection for 2019 Annual Reports

With the first-digit distributions for the 2019 reports in hand and their comparative analysis against the tenets of Benford's law completed, our methodology pivoted toward the pivotal phase of anomaly detection. The objective was to discern any significant deviations from Benford's expected distribution that could signal potential irregularities or manipulations in the reports. We employed a threshold-based approach to quantify these anomalies, where deviations exceeding a predefined percentage were flagged for further inspection. From the 265 reports, approximately 7% showcased deviations beyond our threshold. It's essential to underscore that these deviations do not necessarily imply maleficence or fabrication; instead, they spotlight areas that might benefit from further scrutiny. Factors like industry-specific financial practices, rounding off of numbers, or the nature of the data could contribute to these deviations. Nevertheless, these flagged reports became focal points for a more granular, subsequent analysis to understand the underlying causes of the anomalies (Table 4).

3.5 Data Extraction for 2020 Annual Reports

The exigencies of the COVID-19 pandemic introduced a unique set of challenges and variables into our study for the year 2020. With an expanded dataset comprising 272 annual reports, our initial task was to meticulously extract numerical data, mirroring our approach from the previous year. Utilizing automated scripts in the R software environment, each report was parsed to collate relevant numerical entries. Notably, the 2020 reports exhibited a higher degree of variability in the types and range of numbers present, potentially reflecting the tumultuous economic fluctuations induced by the pandemic. Despite the added complexities, our rigorous extraction protocol ensured consistency and precision across the dataset. The extracted data then underwent a validation phase, rectifying discrepancies and preparing it for the subsequent stages of analysis. This 2020 dataset, influenced by the unprecedented global situation, formed the basis for our comparative anomaly detection vis-à-vis the 2019 data.

3.6 First Digit Analysis for 2020 Annual Reports

For the set of 272 annual reports from 2020, the subsequent phase post data extraction was a robust first-digit analysis. Aligning with Benford's law principles, each numerical entry extracted from the reports was processed to identify its leading digit, thereby constructing a distribution profile of first digits. Intriguingly, our preliminary analysis of the 2020 data highlighted some variances from the 2019 dataset. Specifically, while digits '1' and '2' dominated the leading digit distribution in 2019, the 2020 dataset exhibited a slightly more uniform spread across the digits, although still adhering to Benford's general trend. For instance, the prevalence of the digit '1' as the leading digit was around 27.5%, a subtle decline from the previous year. This diversification of leading digits could be indicative of the erratic financial patterns and adjustments companies might have made in response to the challenges posed by the COVID-19 pandemic (Table 5).

3.7 Comparison with Benford's Law for 2020 Annual Reports

Building upon the first-digit analysis for the 2020 dataset, we embarked on a meticulous comparison of our observed distributions against the theoretical predictions set forth by Benford's law. The benchmark provided by Benford's law serves as a robust litmus test, elucidating how genuine datasets typically behave. When juxtaposing our 2020 data against this benchmark, certain nuances emerged. While the 2019 data had demonstrated close alignment with Benford's predictions, the 2020 reports exhibited subtle yet discernible shifts. The observed frequencies deviated from Benford's predictions for several digits by margins exceeding those observed in the previous year. For instance, while the digit '3' was expected to appear as the leading digit approximately 12.5% of the time, our 2020 data showcased a frequency of nearly 14.8%. Such deviations, although not inherently indicative of anomalies, underscore the unique financial landscape of 2020, shaped in part by the global reverberations of the COVID-19 pandemic (Table 6).

Table 5 The key findings and expected values based on Benford's law (2020 annual reports)

Description	Value
Total annual reports (2020)	272
Leading digit '1' frequency (2020)	27.5%
Leading digit '1' frequency (2019)	29.8%
Noted trend in 2020 dataset	More uniform spread across digits compared to 2019
Potential cause for diversification	Erratic financial patterns due to COVID-19

Table 6 The observed frequencies and their comparison with the expected values from Benford's law for the 2020 annual reports

Description	Value
Total annual reports (2020)	272
Leading digit '3' frequency (2020)	14.8%
Leading digit '3' frequency (expected by Benford's law)	12.5%
Largest deviation between 2020 and expected frequency	2.3% deviation for digit '3'
Potential cause for deviations in 2020	Unique financial landscape influenced by COVID-19

Table 7 The findings and the implications of the anomaly detection process for the 2020 annual reports

Description	Value
Total annual reports (2020)	272
Percentage of reports exceeding threshold for anomalies (2020)	12%
Percentage of reports exceeding threshold for anomalies (2019)	7%
Implication of detected deviations	Not conclusive proof of irregularities
Factors potentially contributing to deviations	Unique economic challenges due to COVID-19

3.8 Anomaly Detection for 2020 Annual Reports

With the comparative framework established against Benford's law, our attention in analyzing the 2020 dataset pivoted to the crucial task of anomaly detection. Drawing from our established threshold-based approach, we aimed to identify reports that exhibited significant deviations from the expected distribution. Interestingly, the tumultuous nature of 2020, heavily influenced by the COVID-19 pandemic, was mirrored in our findings. Approximately 12% of the 2020 reports showcased deviations surpassing our predefined threshold, a marked increase from the previous year. It's paramount to emphasize that these deviations, while indicative of potential anomalies, are not conclusive proof of irregularities. The unique economic challenges and uncertainties of 2020 could naturally lead to financial figures that diverge from traditional patterns. However, these flagged reports from 2020 warrant meticulous scrutiny to discern the intricate blend of genuine financial shifts and potential irregularities in reporting (Table 7).

4 Discussion

The analysis of annual reports from the years 2019 and 2020, using Benford's law as a heuristic tool, has surfaced some captivating insights. Central to our investigation was the scrutiny of the leading digits of numerical data extracted from these reports and the subsequent comparison against the theoretical distributions posited by Benford's law.

For the 2019 dataset, which encompassed 265 annual reports, the alignment with Benford's predictions was particularly striking. The observed frequency for the leading digit '1' was 29.8%, closely mirroring the anticipated 30.1% from Benford's law. Moreover, the combined frequency of digits '1' and '2' approximated 48%, reinforcing the law's predictions. Such findings offer a compelling validation of the authenticity of the 2019 reports. The minimal deviations from the expected frequencies, with the largest deviation being less than 2.5%, were within acceptable margins of error.

However, the narrative slightly shifts when we pivot to the 2020 dataset, which comprises 272 annual reports. The unique challenges posed by the COVID-19 pandemic manifested in financial records, as evidenced by our first-digit analysis. While the 2019 data showcased a pronounced dominance of the digits '1' and '2', the 2020 data painted a more diversified picture. The leading digit '1' had a frequency of 27.5%, marking a subtle decline from the previous year. Such diversification, particularly the observed frequency of 14.8% for the digit '3' as opposed to the expected 12.5%, can be ascribed to the tumultuous financial patterns in 2020.

Our anomaly detection for 2020 reports, leveraging a threshold-based approach, indicated that approximately 12% of the reports exceeded our predefined anomaly threshold. This was a noticeable uptick from the 7% observed in 2019. Yet, it's crucial to interpret these deviations judiciously. The global socio-economic disruptions induced by the pandemic could naturally yield financial figures that diverge from conventional patterns. These deviations, therefore, might not exclusively signal maleficence or data manipulation but could be reflective of genuine financial disruptions.

5 Conclusion

Our exploration of the annual reports of 2019 and 2020, guided by the principles of Benford's law, has furnished pivotal insights into the financial landscape of these two years. The close alignment of the 2019 reports with Benford's predictions serves as a testament to the general reliability of the data from that year. With over 265 reports analyzed, the deviations were marginal and within acceptable parameters, bolstering confidence in the authenticity of the data.

However, 2020, a year marked by unprecedented global challenges due to the COVID-19 pandemic, presented a slightly altered narrative. The subtle shifts in the leading digit distributions, especially the diversification observed in the 2020 dataset of 272 reports, echo the broader economic uncertainties and fluctuations of the year. The increased percentage of reports surpassing our anomaly threshold in 2020, compared to 2019, underscores the volatility of this period. While these deviations do hint at potential anomalies, they also serve as a reminder of the profound impact external factors, such as a global pandemic, can have on financial data.

In synthesizing these findings, it's evident that Benford's law offers a valuable lens for preliminary financial scrutiny. However, its application should always be complemented by a nuanced understanding of the contextual factors influencing the data. As we move forward, it's imperative to employ a judicious blend of statistical tools and contextual insights to ensure a holistic understanding of financial landscapes and their underlying intricacies.

References

Aris, N. A., Othman, R., Bukhori, M. M., Arif, S., & Malek, M. A. (2017). Detecting accounting anomalies using Benford's law: Evidence from the Malaysian public sector. *Management & Accounting Review, 16*(2), 1–32. https://doi.org/10.24191/MAR.V16I2.666

Asllani, A., & Naco, M. (2014). Using Benford's law for fraud detection in accounting practices. *Journal of Social Science Studies, 1*(2), 129–143. https://doi.org/10.5296/jsss.v2i1.6395

Aybars, A., & Ataunal, L. (2016). An Application of Benford's law to fundamental accounting figures reported by Borsa Istanbul (BIST) companies. *Journal of Economics, Finance and Accounting, 3*(3), 234–243. https://doi.org/10.17261/Pressacademia.2016321991

Benford, F. (1938). The law of anomalous numbers. *Proceedings of the American Philosophical Society*, 551–572.

Geyer, D. (2010). Detecting fraud in financial data sets. *Journal of Business and Economics Research, 8*(7), 75–83. https://doi.org/10.19030/jber.v8i7.744

Gorenc, M. (2019). Benford's law as a useful tool to determine fraud in financial statements. *Management, 14*(1). https://doi.org/10.26493/1854-4231.14.19-31

Han, K. (2005). *Data mining: Concept and techniques*. Morgan Koufmann.

Kotsiantis, K., & Tzelepis, T. (2006). Forecasting fraudulent financial statements using data mining. *International Journal of Computational Intelligence, 3*(2), 104–110.

Möller, M. (2009). Measuring the quality of auditing services with the help of Benford's law - An empirical analysis and discussion of this methodical approach. *SSRN Electronic Journal*. https://doi.org/10.2139/ssrn.1529307

Newcomb, S. (1881). Note on the frequency of use of the different digits in natural numbers. *American Journal of Mathematics, 4*(1–4), 39–40.

Nigrini, M. J. (1999). I've got your number: How a mathematical phenomenon can help CPAS uncover fraud and other irregularities. *Journal of Accountancy*, 1–7.

Nunes, A., Inácio, H., & Marques, R. P. (2019). Benford's law and fraud detection in Portuguese enterprises. *Iberian Conference on Information Systems and Technologies*. https://doi.org/10.23919/CISTI.2019.8760922

Patel, P. C., Tsionas, M. G., & Guedes, M. J. (2022). Benford's law, small business financial reporting, and survival. *Managerial and Decision Economics, 43*(8), 3301–3315. https://doi.org/10.1002/mde.3595

Qu, H., Steinberg, R., & Burger, R. (2020). Abiding by the law? Using Benford's law to examine the accuracy of nonprofit financial reports. *Nonprofit and Voluntary Sector Quarterly, 49*(3), 548–570. https://doi.org/10.1177/0899764019881510

Rad, M., Amiri, A., Ranjbar, M. H., & Salari, H. (2021). Predictability of financial statements fraud-risk using Benford's law. *Cogent Economics & Finance, 9*(1), 1889756. https://doi.org/10.1080/23322039.2021.1889756

Saville, A. (2006). Using Benford's law to detect data error and fraud: An Examinatıon of companies listed on the Johannesburg stock exchange. *South African Journal of Economic and Management Sciences, 9*(3), 341–354.

Uzuner, M. T. (2014). Benford Yasasının Borsa İstanbul'da İşlem Gören Bankaların Konsolide Bilançolarına Uygulanması. *Finansal Araştırmalar ve Çalışmalar Dergisi, 5*(10), 73–82. https://doi.org/10.14784/JFRS.2014104500

Valliammai, M. A., Fathima, S. S., Mastikatte, B. C., & Khan, A. (2018). Benford's law: A detailed understanding and its application in detecting accounting scams. *Journal of Emerging Technologies and Innovative Research (JETIR), 5*(11), 66–73.

Yanık, R., & Samancı, T. H. (2013). Benford Kanunu ve Muhasebe Verilerinde Uygulanmasına Ait Kamu Sektöründe Bir Uygulama. *Atatürk Üniversitesi Sosyal Bilimler Enstitüsü Dergisi, 17*(1), 335–348.

Analysis of Banking Soundness in Terms of Country Effect: A Worldwide Evidence Using the Bankers Top 1000 Banks' Database

Nader Alber and Ihab Petro

1 Introduction

There is an extended and growing literature concerning the analysis of banking soundness indicators. Besides, many global, regional, and governmental bodies have been established to investigate and elaborate on the waves of banks' collapse, especially the recent one of 2023. Regarding banking performance, Alber (2017) investigates the relationship between banking efficiency and financial stability in 15 MENA countries from 2004 to 2013. Moreover, the development of the financial sector has been addressed in terms of profit efficiency (Alber, 2011), asset allocation (Alber, 2018) and financial inclusion (Alber, 2019).

The existing research mostly covers the nexus between economic development and some aspects of banking soundness. However, to the best of our knowledge, this paper is among the first to empirically examine the effects of income level on all aspects of banking soundness according to the CAMELS approach. Moreover, unlike other studies, this paper covers a large sample for a long period, using data from 984 banks from 2002 to 2021.

In brief, this paper tries to investigate the effect of "Country Income Category according to the World Bank categorization" on "Banking Soundness Indicators according to the Bankers database." The paper is arranged as follows: after this introduction, Sect. 2 reviews research literature. Section 3 explains how to develop hypotheses and measure variables. Section 4 presents descriptive and diagnostic statistics. Section 5 is for the empirical work, presenting results, discussing how these results answer research questions with a robustness check. Section 6 summarizes the paper and provides remarks about conclusions.

N. Alber (✉) · I. Petro
Ain Shams University, Faculty of Business, Cairo, Egypt

N. Ozatac et al. (eds.), *Sustainable Development in Banking and Finance*, Springer Proceedings in Business and Economics,
https://doi.org/10.1007/978-3-031-65533-3_8

2 Literature Review

This section tries to present some of the previous work that has been conducted in the fields of the determinants of banking soundness indicators. While Arif and Anees (2012) are concerned with Pakistani banks, Kayode et al. (2015) investigate banks' performance in Nigeria and Alber and Nabil (2016) attempt to investigate the performance of Egyptian banks. In addition, Wahdan (2018) addresses banks listed on the Amman Stock Exchange.

Many scholars have analyzed the banking performance of MENA countries (e. g. Bitar et al., 2016; Caporale et al., 2017; Alber, 2022; Alber & Dabour, 2021; Alber & Ramadan, 2022). Moreover, Alber and Dabour (2021) have addressed the performance of 10 different countries during 2020, while Tomuleasa (2017) is concerned with European banks from 2005 to 2012.

Using a sample of 22 Pakistani banks from 2004 to 2009, Arif and Anees (2012) investigate liquidity risk in Pakistani banks and assess the impact on banks' profitability concerning "banking performance." To evaluate the effect of liquidity risk on banks' profitability, multiple regressions have been used. Profitability has been used to measure bank performance, while deposits, cash reserves, liquidity gaps, and provisioning for non-performing loans have been used to quantify liquidity risk. The findings demonstrate that liquidity risk substantially impacts bank profitability and that there is a positive correlation between the banking system's profitability and deposits and cash reserves. On the other hand, the banking system's profitability is negatively correlated with both the liquidity gap and the provisioning of non-performing loans.

Using a sample of six banks from 2000 to 2013, Kayode et al. (2015) examine the effect of credit risk on banks' performance in Nigeria. The ratios of non-performing loans to total loans and advances, total loans and advances to total assets, and loan-loss provisions to total loans and advances are used to quantify credit risk. In contrast, return on assets is used to measure bank performance. The results imply a substantial and negative relationship between credit risk and bank performance. This suggests that banks become less profitable when they are exposed to more credit risk. According to the results, the total loan has a good and considerable impact on bank performance. Additionally, Alber and Nabil (2016) make an effort to look into how information security affects Egyptian banks' performance. Thirteen banks out of thirty-two banks were included in the sample for this in 2013. The extent to which Egyptian banks have implemented ISO 27001 and PCI-DSS standards measures information security, while asset quality and profitability metrics gauge the performance of the banks. The findings show that while the PCI-DSS standard may impact asset quality as shown by the "Non-Performing Loan Ratio," the ISO 27001 standard may impact profitability indicators as evaluated by "Return on Capital."

Bitar et al. (2016) examine how capital requirements affect bank risk and performance in the MENA area. Between 1999 and 2013, this was implemented in 168 banks from 17 MENA nations. According to the research, banks that adhere to the Basel capital criteria are better able to manage risk and operate more profitably and efficiently. Furthermore, Caporale et al. (2017) use a sample of 76 foreign and 46 domestic banks from the 17 MENA countries between 2000 and 2012 to try and determine how the global financial crisis affected the performance of local and foreign banks in the region. Return on average equity (ROAE) and return on average assets (ROAA) are the two accounting measures used in this study to assess the performance of banks. The findings show that during the crisis, domestic institutions performed better than those of international banks. Due to their greater number of subsidiaries in developed economies, foreign banks were more exposed to risk. Regarding the factors that determine profitability, it seems that size is irrelevant, but the liquidity ratio and net interest income appear to have a positive and negative impact, respectively; GDP, on the other hand, appears to have a favorable impact on local banks.

Wahdan (2018) makes an effort to look into how financial risks affect commercial banks' financial performance. This was implemented for each of the thirteen commercial banks that were listed on the Amman Stock Exchange between 2008 and 2015. Credit risk, interest rate risk, liquidity risk, and capital adequacy risk are examples of financial hazards, and share turnover, return on equity, return on assets, and return on average (EPS) are examples of financial performance metrics. The study's conclusions demonstrate that while interest rate risk and liquidity risk have no discernible effects on the financial performance of commercial banks, credit risk and capital adequacy risk do. Additionally, Tomuleasa (2017) seeks to determine and analyze the factors that influence the performance and soundness of European banking systems, as well as to investigate the impact of various industry-specific, bank-specific, and macroeconomic factors on the development of these factors over the course of the global financial crisis. The necessary information was gathered from Bankscope for 263 commercial banks in the EU between 2005 and 2012. The variables that have a negative impact on bank performance and soundness include non-performing loans, state ownership, bank age, and global financial crises. The variables that positively impact bank performance and soundness are financial structure, management caliber, and private ownership.

The aim of Alber and Dabour (2021) is to examine the impact of social alienation and the COVID-19 epidemic on banks' asset quality. Using the GMM approach, this was carried out with a sample of 30 banks that represent 10 different countries. In 2020, information was gathered from the World Health Organization. Ten nations are included in the study: Egypt, Saudi Arabia, Indonesia, Germany, France, Russia, India, Mexico, South Korea, and Nigeria. Three banks from each of these countries have been examined. The average change of the non-performing loan ratio, which measures the banks' asset quality, appears to be sensitive to the average cases of COVID-19, which measures the spread of the virus. Additionally, Alber (2022) looks at the connection between financial stability and banking concentration using a sample of 15 MENA nations between 2008 and 2020. The Herfenhal-Hirschfield Index (HHI) and Boone Indicator of Competition (Boone) are used to quantify market concentration, and the Aggregate Banking Stability Index (ABSI) and Z-Score are used to measure financial stability. The results corroborate the importance of the Boone effect on ABSI and the HHI effect on Z-Score for the entire sample of 15 MENA countries. Regression coefficients show positive signs, indicating that banking concentration has a favorable impact on financial stability. Thus, the "stability-concentration" theory is supported by the data. The results of the investigation for African nations have confirmed these effects. Boone appears to have a considerable impact on both Z-Score and ABSI in the Near East. Furthermore, stability appears more responsive to efficiency than in African nations. The findings in Gulf nations corroborate the importance of both the HHI and Boone impacts on Z-Score with negative β1 and β2, indicating that banking concentration has a detrimental impact on financial stability. Thus, the "stability-competition" theory is supported by the data.

The goal of Alber and Ramadan (2022) is to look into how applying banking laws affects the operation of banks. This has been done annually on 19 nations in the MENA region between 2008 and 2018. The findings show that enforcing banking regulations has a major impact on each of the following: "banking efficiency," "banking stability," "credit risk," and "profitability." Panel data analysis was used, with three models (pooled regression, fixed effects, and random effects) based on static panel models (SPM).

A substantial number of studies focus on the impact of the banking and financial systems on economic growth with regard to the relationship between "banking performance" and "economic growth." Nevertheless, the impact of economic development on banking performance is rarely studied, particularly in Sub-Saharan Africa. For example, Ibrahim and Alagidede (2018) found a significant effect of financial-economic growth in their analysis of the influence of financial development on economic growth in 29 SSA nations. Using panel data for 29 sub-Saharan African nations from 1980 to 2014, this research investigates the overall economic growth effect when the growth in the finance and real sectors is unequal. The system generalized methods of moments (GMM) yield results showing that while financial development contributes to economic growth, the degree to which finance does so critically depends on the real and financial sectors growing simultaneously. Under balanced sectoral growth, the growth elasticity is stronger due to changes in the real or financial sector size. We also demonstrate how unchecked credit expansion negatively impacts economic growth, with consequences arising from the funding of hazardous and unsustainable investments and unnecessary spending that drives up inflation. On the other hand, there is a greater pass-through surplus finance–economic growth effect through the investment channel.

Between 1981 and 2018, Obiora et al. (2022) look into how economic progress affects the performance of banks in 23 SSA countries and 14 developed countries. Our findings demonstrate that, in SSA as a whole, economic development has a positive impact on commercial bank lending, raises lending rates, increases the amount of domestic credit to the private sector (DCPS), and decreases the number of non-performing loans (NPLs). We do this by using estimation models such as feasible general least squares, fixed effects estimation with Driscoll-Kraay standard errors, and system and difference generalized method of moments. Economic progress in industrialized nations has a favorable effect on DCPS, lending rates, and the quantity of non-performing loans.

In Almahadin et al. (2021), the question of whether financial development and economic growth are causally related is discussed. The acceleration of financial development can be attributed to economic expansion, as it can generate demand for financial services and products. However, when savings are combined with high diversification, risk management, and easy exchange of products and services, financial development may have an impact on growth (Camba & Camba, 2020; Kumar & Paramanik, 2020; Ngoc, 2020). Furthermore, bidirectional causation was discovered by Abu-Bader and Abu-Qarn (2008), suggesting that growth is led by finance and that the opposite is also true.

Regarding the current study, compared with previous work, it's important to pinpoint some differences that may justify its importance, as follows:

1. The existing research mostly covers the nexus between economic development and some aspects of banking soundness. However, to the best of our knowledge, this paper is among the first to empirically examine the effects of income level on all aspects of banking soundness according to the CAMELS approach.
2. Unlike other studies, this paper covers a large sample for a long period, as it uses data from 984 banks during the period from 2002 to 2021.

3 Measuring Variables and Developing Hypotheses

Table 1 illustrates the research variables as follows:

This paper investigates the effect of "Country Income Category according to the World Bank categorization" on "Banking Soundness Indicators according to the Bankers database." So, it aims to test the following hypotheses:

1. There's no significant effect of "Country Income Category" on "Bank's Capital Adequacy."
2. There's no significant effect of "Country Income Category" on "Bank's Asset Quality."
3. There's no significant effect of "Country Income Category" on "Bank's Management Quality."
4. There's no significant effect of "Country Income Category" on "Bank's Earnings."
5. There's no significant effect of "Country Income Category" on "Bank's Efficiency."
6. There's no significant effect of "Country Income Category" on "Bank's Liquidity."
7. There's no significant effect of "Country Income Category" on "Bank's Sensitivity to Risk."

Table 1 Research variables

Variable	Type	Sign	Database
BIS capital adequacy ratio (Total) %	Dependent	C	The Bankers
Non-performing loans (NPL%) %	Dependent	A	The Bankers
Staff costs to total operating expenses %	Dependent	M	The Bankers
Net interest income to average assets %	Dependent	E1	The Bankers
Asset utilisation %	Dependent	E2	The Bankers
Cash held as % total deposits %	Dependent	L	The Bankers
Allowance for loan losses to gross total loans %	Dependent	S	World Bank
Income category according to the World Bank categorization[a]	Independent	INC	The Bankers
Natural logarithm of banks' assets in $ (bn.)	Independent	Size	The Bankers
Number of banks' branches	Independent	Branches	The Bankers
Natural logarithm of banks' ATMs numbers	Independent	ATMs	The Bankers

[a]INC = 1 for low-income countries, = 2 for lower-middle-income countries, = 3 for upper-middle-income countries, and = 4 for high-income ones

The research hypotheses *could be tested* using *panel data analysis* according to the following models:

$$C_{i,t} = \alpha + \beta_1 INC_{i,t} + \beta_2 Size_{i,t} + \beta_3 Branches_{i,t} + \beta_4 ATMs_{i,t} \quad (1)$$

$$A_{i,t} = \alpha + \beta_1 INC_{i,t} + \beta_2 Size_{i,t} + \beta_3 Branches_{i,t} + \beta_4 ATMs_{i,t} \quad (2)$$

$$M_{i,t} = \alpha + \beta_1 INC_{i,t} + \beta_2 Size_{i,t} + \beta_3 Branches_{i,t} + \beta_4 ATMs_{i,t} \quad (3)$$

$$E1_{i,t} = \alpha + \beta_1 INC_{i,t} + \beta_2 Size_{i,t} + \beta_3 Branches_{i,t} + \beta_4 ATMs_{i,t} \quad (4)$$

$$E2_{i,t} = \alpha + \beta_1 INC_{i,t} + \beta_2 Size_{i,t} + \beta_3 Branches_{i,t} + \beta_4 ATMs_{i,t} \quad (5)$$

$$L_{i,t} = \alpha + \beta_1 INC_{i,t} + \beta_2 Size_{i,t} + \beta_3 Branches_{i,t} + \beta_4 ATMs_{i,t} \quad (6)$$

$$S_{i,t} = \alpha + \beta_1 INC_{i,t} + \beta_2 Size_{i,t} + \beta_3 Branches_{i,t} + \beta_4 ATMs_{i,t} \quad (7)$$

4 Descriptive Statistics and Diagnostic Statistics

Table 2 illustrates descriptive statistics of the independent and control variables using all banks data (984 banks), over the period from the 2002 to 2021, as follows:

Table 2 Descriptive statistics of independent and control variables

	Inc	Size	Branches	ATM
Mean	3.411908	10.31027	5.244776	2254.221
Median	4.000000	10.15385	5.225747	37.00000
Maximum	4.000000	16.06614	10.59801	171300.0
Minimum	1.000000	0.505939	0.000000	0.000000
Std. dev.	0.758020	1.713825	1.792720	9621.088
Skewness	−0.878462	−0.199387	−0.073193	8.876888
Kurtosis	2.393640	5.703980	3.137236	101.5425
Jarque-Bera	945.2251	2044.123	11.01690	2743314.
Probability	0.000000	0.000000	0.004052	0.000000
Observations	6567	6567	6567	6567

Source: Outputs of data processing using EViews 10

Regarding normality, Jarque-Bera values indicate that all variables are normally distributed at p-value of 0.01. Regarding multicollinearity, Table 3 illustrates the correlation coefficients between the study variables as follows:

Table 4 shows that correlation coefficients between independent variables fail within the range ± 0.6; thus, the multicollinearity problem does not exist.

5 Testing Hypotheses

This section investigates the effects of income level on each of banks' soundness indicators using data from 984 banks during the period from 2002 to 2021, where a panel data analysis has been conducted using the GMM technique and provides the following results:

According to Table 5, model (2) supports the significance of income effect on asset quality with an explanation power of 1.81%. Besides, model (5) supports the significance of income on asset utilization with an explanation power of 1.48%. So, for the second and fifth hypotheses, the null hypothesis is rejected, and the alternative one can be accepted. Signs of regression coefficients β_1 in model (2) and β_1 in model (5) are negative, which means that banks' asset quality is affected negatively by the country's income level. So, results indicate that banks of low-income countries may have a better performance—in terms of asset quality and profitability—than banks of high-income countries. However, the explanation power—for each model—is relatively low. Regarding the problem of autocorrelation, Durbin-Watson (DW) indicates that the autocorrelation problem exists, while the Breusch-Pagan LM test shows that the problem of heteroskedasticity does not exist. Controlling for size, branches and ATMs, Table 6 provides the following results:

Table 6 indicates that model (2) supports the significance of income effect on asset quality with an explanation power of 5.33% while model (3) supports this significance on management quality with an explanation power of 4.31%. Besides,

Table 3 Descriptive statistics of dependent variables

	C	A	M	E1	E2	L	S
Mean	14.12169	2.444380	31.90293	2.519179	2.156344	7.184359	1.021536
Median	13.73000	1.075000	43.32889	1.824747	1.268756	0.032258	0.000000
Maximum	260.7400	74.10000	591.4942	2800.789	83.30912	9047.826	127.5323
Minimum	−17.56000	0.000000	0.000000	−49.84878	−17.59137	0.000000	0.000000
Std. dev.	9.729042	4.436067	31.29224	32.83409	3.232688	90.16096	2.693918
Skewness	5.332074	4.819498	1.822644	80.84860	4.984181	89.65030	11.71958
Kurtosis	77.39666	37.83699	25.42523	6608.872	61.01116	8505.216	364.3751
Jarque-Bera	4628782.	1070644.	422987.3	3.58E+10	2839147.	5.93E+10	1.07E+08
Probability	0.000000	0.000000	0.000000	0.000000	0.000000	0.000000	0.000000
Observations	19667	19667	19667	19667	19667	19667	19667

Source: Outputs of data processing using EViews 10

Table 4 Correlation coefficients between independent variables

	Inc	Size	Branches	ATM
Inc	1.000000			
Size	0.150972	1.000000		
Branches	−0.314439	0.595587	1.000000	
ATM	−0.086921	0.327823	0.396074	1.000000

Source: Outputs of data processing using EViews 10

Table 5 Determinants of banking soundness in terms of country effect without control variables

	Model (1)	Model (2)	Model (3)	Model (4)	Model (5)	Model (6)	Model (7)
Variable	C	A	M	E1	E2	L	S
C		**5.463135 (0.44675)***			**4.153762 (0.2695)***		
Income		**−0.854553 (0.12252)***			**−0.565424 (0.0722)***		
R^2		0.018069			0.014896		
Adjusted R^2		0.018019			0.014846		
DW statistic		0.483041			0.443381		
Breusch-Pagan LM Prob.		0.0000			0.0000		
Periods included		19			19		
Cross-sections		537			537		
Obs.		3617			3617		

Source: outputs of data processing using EViews 10
*** denotes p-value of 1%.

models (4) and (5) support the significance of income on earnings indicators E1 and E2 with explanation power of 19.51% and 19.345 respectively while model (7) supports the significance of income effect on sensitivity to risk with explanation power of 4.58%. So, for the *second*, *third*, *fourth* and *fifth* hypotheses, the null hypothesis is rejected, and the alternative one could be accepted. Signs of regression coefficients in models (2) and (3) are positive. In contrast, these signs are negative in models (5) and (6), which means that banks' asset quality and management are affected positively by country's income level. In contrast, earnings and efficiency indicators E1 and E2 are affected negatively. So, results indicate that banks of low-income countries may have a better performance—in terms of profitability—than banks of high-income countries, while banks of high-income countries may have a better performance in asset quality and management—than banks of low-income countries. However, models (4) and (5) provide higher explanation powers compared with the models without control variables. Regarding the problem of autocorrelation, Durbin-Watson (DW) indicates that the autocorrelation problem exists, while the Breusch-Pagan LM test shows that the problem of heteroskedasticity does not exist.

Table 6 Determinants of banking soundness in terms of country effect with all control variables

	Model (1)	Model (2)	Model (3)	Model (4)	Model (5)	Model (6)	Model (7)
Variable	C	A	M	E1	E2	L	S
C		**4.549531 (1.02134) *****	**57.45239 (12.883) *****	**6.896465 (0.4581)*****	**9.878246 (0.6819)*****		**3.663661 (0.6373)*****
Income		**0.430075 (0.22294)***	**6.450017 (1.6661) *****	**−0.642255 (0.0831)*****	**−0.860246 (0.1164)*****		0.129566 (0.143938)
Assets		**−0.710961 (0.11080) *****	−2.708728 (1.829836)	**−0.400139 (0.0664)*****	**−0.582449 (0.0930)*****		**−0.474479 (0.0783)*****
Branches		**0.903094 (0.12500) *****	0.644992 (0.415534)	**0.338457 (0.0583)*****	**0.494257 (0.07998) *****		**0.551692 (0.0758)*****
ATMs		**−2.96E-05 (7.59E-6) *****	−1.519486 (7.34E-05)	**7.60E-06 (4.33E-06)***	8.39E-06 (6.80E-06)		−5.62E-06 (5.14E-06)
R^2		0.053253	0.043095	0.195060	0.193426		0.045755
Adjusted R^2		0.052676	0.042511	1.906414	0.192934		0.045173
DW statistic		0.308401	0.372753	0.220532	0.229096		0.434281
Breusch-Pagan LM Prob.		0.0000	0.0000	0.0000	0.0000		0.0000
Periods included		19	19	19	19		19
Cross-sections		537	537	537	537		537
Obs.		3617	3617	3617	3617		3617

Source: outputs of data processing using EViews 10

* denotes p-value of 10% and *** denotes p-value of 1%.

Robustness checks have been conducted, controlling for each size, branch and ATM separately, as shown in Tables 7, 8 and 9:

Tables 7, 8 and 9 indicate the following:

1. Results have not supported any significant effects of income level on each of banks' capital adequacy and liquidity.
2. Findings show significant positive effects on each asset quality and management when controlling for size. However, when controlling for branches and ATMs, these significant positive effects have been supported only by management.
3. Models (4) and (5) support the significant negative effects of income on earnings and efficiency indicators E1 and E2 when controlling for branches. However, when controlling for branches or size, these effects have been supported only by efficiency.

Table 7 Determinants of banking soundness in terms of country effect controlling for size

	Model (1)	Model (2)	Model (3)	Model (4)	Model (5)	Model (6)	Model (7)
Variable	C	A	M	E1	E2	L	S
C		**5.625999 (0.58676)*** **	7.554056 (4.8932)		**3.629186 (0.3792)*** **		
Income		**−0.851353 (0.12176)*** **	**3.680503 (0.7712) *** **		**−0.597612 (0.0733)*** **		
Assets		−0.017297 (0.038155)	**1.159118 (0.598662) * **		**0.065304 (0.0286)** **		
R^2		0.018291	0.012761		0.016278		
Adjusted R^2		0.018191	0.012661		0.016177		
DW statistic		0.483309	0.376458		0.444163		
Breusch-Pagan LM Prob.		0.0000	0.0000		0.0000		
Periods included		19	19		19		
Cross-sections		537	537		537		
Obs.		3617	3617		3617		

Source: outputs of data processing using EViews 10

* denotes p-value of 10%, ** denotes p-value of 5% and *** denotes p-value of 1%.

Table 8 Determinants of banking soundness in terms of country effect controlling for branches

	Model (1)	Model (2)	Model (3)	Model (4)	Model (5)	Model (6)	Model (7)
Variable	C	A	M	E1	E2	L	S
C		**2.143301 (0.90418) *** **	**46.26201 (5.5139) *** **	**5.274845 (0.3408)*** **	**7.547582 (0.5060)*** **		**1.905810 (0.5486)*** **
Income		−0.187887 (0.196151)	**4.187422 (0.6179) *** **	**−0.977394 (0.0712)*** **	**−1.349526 (0.1035)*** **		**−0.276155 (0.12268) ** **
Branches		**0.000119 (1.2E-08) *** **	−1.042178 (0.858893)	**0.082234 (0.0293)*** **	**0.115408 (0.0424)*** **		**0.215654 (0.0456)*** **
R^2		0.018588	0.026259	0.141691	0.136482		0.018740
Adjusted R^2		0.018289	0.025963	0.141430	0.136219		0.018441
DW statistic		0.280122	0.361701	0.178959	0.184997		0.409737
Breusch-Pagan LM Prob.		0.0000	0.0000	0.0000	0.0000		0.0000
Periods included		19	19	19	19		19
Cross-sections		537	537	537	537		537
Obs.		3617	3617	10.64536 (0.1278)***	3617		3617

Source: outputs of data processing using EViews 10

** denotes p-value of 5% and *** denotes p-value of 1%.

Table 9 Determinants of banking soundness in terms of country effect controlling for ATMs

	Model (1)	Model (2)	Model (3)	Model (4)	Model (5)	Model (6)	Model (7)
Variable	C	A	M	E1	E2	L	S
C		**5.446131 (0.45087) *** **	**15.61629 (2.1694) *** **		**4.033606 (0.2699)*** **		**2.135051 (0.1961)*** **
Income		**−0.851124 (0.12324) *** **	**4.506545 (0.6417) *** **		**−0.540812 (0.0722)*** **		**−0.321326 (0.0555)*** **
ATMs		6.53E-06 (6.68E-06)	**0.000431 (8.25E-5) *** **		**3.98E-05 (1.03E-5) *** **		**2.57E-05 (5.16E-6) *** **
R^2		0.018163	0.015271		0.019937		0.010649
Adjusted R^2		0.018063	0.015171		0.019838		0.010549
DW statistic		0.483278	0.377768		0.445369		0.686722
Breusch-Pagan LM Prob.		0.0000	0.0000		0.0000		0.0000
Periods included		19	19		19		19
Cross-sections		537	537		537		537
Obs.		3617	3617		3617		3617

Source: outputs of data processing using EViews 10
*** denotes p-value of 1%

So, robustness checks indicate that for the second, third, fourth and fifth hypotheses, the null hypothesis is rejected and the alternative one could be accepted. Regarding the problem of autocorrelation, Durbin-Watson (DW) indicates that the autocorrelation problem exists, while the Breusch-Pagan LM test shows that the problem of heteroskedasticity does not exist.

6 Summary and Concluding Remarks

This paper attempts to investigate banking soundness indicators using the Bankers Top 1000 banks' database, which includes 638 high-income countries, 233 upper-middle-income countries, 111 lower-middle-income countries and the remaining two low-income countries. This study was conducted using data from 984 banks during the period from 2002 to 2021, during which banking soundness was measured mainly using the CAMELS approach.

The income-performance relationship is still a controversial topic. According to the traditional view, banks of high-income countries may enhance profits and reduce financial fragility by maintaining higher levels of capital that protect them from external economic and liquidity shocks. On the contrary, the proponents of the other view argue that rich banks are more likely to take on risky investments with the knowledge of being protected, resulting in a solid economic position. Investments may be inefficiently managed due to moral hazard problems, lowering the banking soundness indicators.

Using panel data analysis according to the GMM model, the results have not supported any significant effects of income level on each of banks' capital adequacy and liquidity. Besides, findings indicate significant positive effects on each asset quality and management, which means that banks of high-income countries seem to have high non-performing loans and staff costs ratios. In addition, these countries seem to have lower profitability and sensitivity to risk indicators. Robustness checks have been conducted and results have been supported.

Appendix 1 Distribution of banks included according to their countries

No.	Country	No. of banks	No.	Country	No. of banks
1	US	177	48	Greece	4
2	China	139	49	Luxembourg	4
3	Japan	85	50	Pakistan	4
4	Switzerland	32	51	Panama	4
5	Taiwan	30	52	Poland	4
6	India	25	53	Singapore	4
7	UK	25	54	Sri Lanka	4
8	Germany	23	55	Angola	3
9	Italy	21	56	Bangladesh	3
10	Vietnam	18	57	Costa Rica	3
11	Austria	15	58	Czech Republic	3
12	Spain	15	59	Dominican Republic	3
13	Canada	13	60	Finland	3
14	United Arab Emirates	13	61	Guatemala	3
15	Malaysia	12	62	Iceland	3
16	Netherlands	12	63	Jordan	3
17	Brazil	11	64	Liechtenstein	3
18	South Korea	11	65	Puerto Rico	3
19	Australia	10	66	Bulgaria	2
20	Indonesia	10	67	Cyprus	2
21	Norway	10	68	Ecuador	2
22	Philippines	10	69	Georgia	2
23	Saudi Arabia	10	70	Hungary	2
24	Thailand	9	71	Ireland	2
25	Bahrain	8	72	Kazakhstan	2
26	Denmark	8	73	Lebanon	2

(continued)

No.	Country	No. of banks	No.	Country	No. of banks
27	Qatar	8	74	Peru	2
28	Sweden	8	75	Romania	2
29	Argentina	7	76	Slovenia	2
30	Chile	7	77	Trinidad and Tobago	2
31	Colombia	7	78	Tunisia	2
32	Egypt	7	79	Uruguay	2
33	Kuwait	7	80	USA	2
34	South Africa	7	81	Azerbaijan	1
35	Belgium	6	82	Belarus	1
36	France	6	83	Bermuda	1
37	Mexico	6	84	Brunei	1
38	Russia	6	85	Cambodia	1
39	Turkey	6	86	Estonia	1
40	Hong Kong	5	87	Ethiopia	1
41	Iran	5	88	Malta	1
42	Israel	5	89	Mauritius	1
43	Kenya	5	90	New Zealand	1
44	Morocco	5	91	Papua New Guinea	1
45	Nigeria	5	92	Togo	1
46	Oman	5	93	Uzbekistan	1
47	Portugal	5	*Total*		*984*

References

Abu-Bader, S., & Abu-Qarn, A. S. (2008). Financial development and economic growth: empirical evidence from six MENA countries. *Review of Development Economics, 12*(4), 803–817.

Alber, N. (2011). The Effect of Banking Expansion on Profit Efficiency of Saudi Banks. *Corporate Ownership and Control, 8*(2), 51–58.

Alber, N. (2017). Banking efficiency and financial stability: Which causes which? A panel analysis. Springer Proceedings in Business and Economics (pp. 91–98).

Alber, N. (2018). Asset allocation, capital structure, theory of the firm and banking performance: A panel analysis. In N. Ozatac & K. K. Gökmenoglu (Eds.), *Emerging trends in banking and finance*. Springer Proceedings in Business and Economics.

Alber, N. (2019). Determinants of financial inclusion: The case of 125 countries from 2004 to 2017. *Springer Proceedings in Business and Economics*, 1–10.

Alber, N. (2022). The controversy of concentration-stability in banking industry: Evidence from the MENA countries (October 29, 2022). Available at SSRN: https://ssrn.com/abstract=4262075 or https://doi.org/10.2139/ssrn.4262075

Alber, N., & Dabour, M. (2021). The impact of Covid-19 pandemic and social distancing on banks' asset quality: An international evidence. *European Journal of Business and Management Research, 6*(6), 12–16. https://doi.org/10.24018/ejbmr.2021.6.6.1122

Alber, N., & Nabil, M. (2016). The impact of information security on Banks' performance in Egypt. Available at SSRN: https://ssrn.com/abstract=2752070.

Alber, N., & Ramadan, H. (2022). The effect of applying banking regulations on banking performance of MENA region countries. *European Journal of Business and Management Research, 7*(1), 170–185. https://doi.org/10.24018/ejbmr.2022.7.1.1258

Almahadin, H., Al-Gasaymeh, A., Alrawashdeh, N., & Abu Siam, Y. (2021). The effect of banking industry development on economic growth: An empirical study in Jordan. *The Journal of Asian Finance, Economics and Business, 8*(5), 325–334.

Arif, A., & Anees, A. (2012). Liquidity risk and performance of banking system. *Journal of Financial Regulation and Compliance, 20*(2), 182–195.

Bitar, M., Saad, W., & Benlemlih, M. (2016). Bank risk and performance in the MENA region: The importance of capital requirements. *Economic Systems, 40*(3), 398–421.

Camba, A., & Camba, A. (2020). The dynamic relationship of domestic credit and stock market liquidity on the economic growth of the Philippines. *Journal of Asian Finance, Economics and Business, 7*(1), 37–46. https://doi.org/10.13106/jafeb.2020.vol7.no1.37

Caporale, G., Lodh, S. & Nandy, M. (2017). The performance of banks in the MENA region during the global financial crisis. *Research in International Business and Finance, 42*, 583–590. Retrieved from: https://doi.org/10.1016/j.ribaf.2017.07.003

Ibrahim, M., & Alagidede, P. (2018). Effect of financial development on economic growth in Sub-Saharan Africa. *Journal of Policy Modeling, 40*(6), 1104–1125. https://doi.org/10.1016/j.jpolmod.2018.08.001

Kayode, O., Obamuyi, T. M., Owoputi, J. A., & Adeyefa, F. A. (2015). Credit risk and bank performance in Nigeria. *IOSR Journal of Economics and Finance, (IOSR-JEF)*, e-ISSN: 2321-5933, p-ISSN: 2321-5925, *6*(2). Ver. II, 21–28. Retrieved from: www.iosrjournals.org

Kumar, A., & Paramanik, R. (2020). Nexus between Indian economic growth and financial development: A non-linear ARDL approach. *Journal of Asian Finance, Economics and Business, 7*(6), 109–116. 10.13106/jafeb.2020.vol7.no6.109.

Ngoc, B. (2020). The asymmetric effect of inflation on economic growth in Vietnam: Evidence by nonlinear ARDL approach. *Journal of Asian Finance, Economics and Business, 7*(2), 143–149. https://doi.org/10.13106/jafeb.2020.vol7.no2.143

Obiora, S., Zeng, Y., Li, Q., Liu, H., Adjei, P., & Csordas, T. (2022). The effect of economic growth on banking system performance: An interregional and comparative study of Sub-Saharan Africa and developed economies. *Economic Systems, 46*(1), 100939.

Tomuleasa, I. (2017). *Performance and soundness of European banking systems. Economics and finance* (Doctoral dissertation). University Clermont Auvergne. NNT: 2017CLFAD005. tel-02067868.

Wahdan, T. (2018). *"The effect of financial risks on the financial performance for commercial banks": An empirical study on commercial banks listed in Amman Stock Exchange* (Master's thesis), Zarqa University.

Does Renewable Energy Innovation a Key to Reduce Ecological Footprint? Empirical Evidence from the United States

Seyeddanyal Hosseini, Merve Coşkun, and Nigar Taşpınar

1 Introduction

One of the most important challenges that humanity has been facing for many years is undoubtedly climate change. Human activities such as burning fossil fuels, cutting forests for agriculture, and farming livestock are increasingly affecting the climate and the temperature of the earth (European Comission, 2021). As a result of all these activities, greenhouse gases (i.e., carbon dioxide, methane, nitrous oxide, fluorinated gases), which are the main cause of climate change, are increasing significantly (European Comission, 2021). Among these greenhouse gases, carbon dioxide (CO_2) is the primary reason for human-induced climate change since it has a longer impact by staying in the atmosphere for a long time (Government of Canada, 2021). According to GEO6 (2019), the main drivers of CO_2 emissions are and will continue to be economic growth and population because of burning fossil fuels. In this regard, a significant body of research investigated various variables that may affect CO_2 emissions to understand the driving forces of environmental degradation. For instance, affluence (Bekhet et al., 2017; Pao & Tsai, 2011; Saidi & Hammami, 2015), population (Liddle & Lung, 2010; Wang et al., 2012; He et al., 2017; Zhang & Tan, 2016), and technology (Shuai et al., 2017; Wang et al., 2016a; Wen & Li, 2019) are the most tested determinants of environmental degradation. Moreover, scholars have also examined the role of urbanization (Yao et al., 2018; Liu & Liu, 2019), foreign direct investment (Behera & Dash, 2017; Marques & Caetano, 2020), energy consumption (Pata, 2018; Apergis & Payne, 2010), energy structure (Wang

S. Hosseini (✉)
Western Sydney University, Business School, Sydney, NSW, Australia
e-mail: 22053143@student.westernsydney.edu.au; Hosseinidanyal@gmail.com

M. Coşkun · N. Taşpınar
Department of Banking and Finance, Eastern Mediterranean University, Famagusta, Cyprus

N. Ozatac et al. (eds.), *Sustainable Development in Banking and Finance*, Springer Proceedings in Business and Economics,
https://doi.org/10.1007/978-3-031-65533-3_9

et al., 2016a, b), (Sun et al., 2018), and Kyoto protocol obligations (Bargaoui et al., 2014) on environment. To do this, the IPAT (Integrated Population, Affluence, and Technology) model developed by Ehrlich and Holdren (1971) is adopted for investigating the impacts of human activities on environmental quality, however, the model has faced a lot of criticism. Therefore, (Dietz & Rosa, 1994) proposed the STIRPAT model with some modifications (Stochastic Impact by Regression on Population, Affluence, and Technology), such as allowing decomposition of the driving factors and empirical hypothesis tests. After that, earlier studies (Dietz & Rosa, 1997; Cramer, 1998; Soulé & DeHart, 1998; Shi, 2003; Fang et al., 2006; Lin et al., 2009; Li et al., 2011), and some recent researches, (Shahbaz et al., 2016; Shuai et al., 2018; He & Hu, Analysis and Prediction of the Influencing Factors of China's Secondary Industry Carbon Emission under the New Normal, 2018; Xiong et al., Extended STIRPAT model-based driving factor analysis of energy-related CO_2 emissions in Kazakhstan, 2019; Chekouri et al., 2020; Wu et al., 2021) analyzed the human-environment relationship by performing the STIRPAT model. Based on these studies, it is clear that the existing literature has focused on investigating the impacts of several driving factors on the environment, mainly using carbon emissions as a measure of environmental degradation. Although carbon emissions have been considered a major representative of greenhouse gas emissions in the literature, as it represents approximately 70% of greenhouse gas emissions globally (Yilanci & Pata, 2020), CO_2 may be a weak and insufficient measure since environmental quality is not only limited to the atmosphere (Khalid et al., 2021; Yang et al., 2021; Usman & Makhdum, What abates ecological footprint in BRICS-T region? Exploring the influence of renewable energy, non-renewable energy, agriculture, forest area and financial development, 2021; Usman & Hammar, 2021; Usman et al., 2021). In other words, CO_2 does not include the other most important factors of nature such as water, oil, forests, soil, mineral resources, etc. (Bartelmus, 2008; Destek & Sinha, Renewable, non-renewable energy consumption, economic growth, trade openness and ecological footprint: Evidence from organisation for economic Co-operation and development countries, 2020; Usman & Makhdum, 2021). Based on these arguments, we adopt the ecological footprint (EF) proxy as a measure of environmental degradation to have a more comprehensive picture within the STIRPAT approach.

The ecological footprint (EF) measures how fast humanity consumes resources and generates waste (Global Footprint Network, 2021). It is also a significant measure to understand the consumption of individuals and its impact on the environment. Today, the world's average ecological footprint is calculated as 2.75 hectares per person or 22.6 billion in total. Furthermore, the average biocapacity is measured as 1.63 global hectares, meaning that there is a worldwide deficit of 1.1 hectares per person globally (World Population Review, 2021). When this is the case, it is inevitable to examine the primary drivers of EF, especially from the energy perspective, since it is crucial for the environment. The energy sector consists of six sub-sectors: transportation, electricity and heat, manufacturing and construction, buildings, fugitive emissions, and other types of fuel combustion. Moreover, the consumption of energy is the main contributor to global greenhouse gas (GHG) emissions, which is approximately 76% worldwide (Ge et al., 2021). On the other hand, energy plays a significant role in reducing climate change's impact by accelerating innovation and enabling the transition from conventional energy technologies to sustainable energy technologies (World Economic Forum, 2018). For instance, solar-powered PV and onshore wind, energy storage, and electric vehicles are the most mature resources and have the greatest potential to be commercially competitive against conventional energy sources and achieve climate targets (World Economic Forum, 2018). In this regard, several studies found that the consumption of renewable energy (RE) mitigate the detrimental effects of human activities on the environment and improves environmental quality (Ozcan et al., A revisit of the environmental Kuznets curve hypothesis for Turkey: new evidence from bootstrap rolling window causality, 2018), (Destek & Sinha, Renewable, non-renewable energy consumption, economic growth, trade openness and ecological footprint: Evidence from organisation for economic Co-operation and development countries, 2020; Baloch et al., 2019; Dogan et al., 2019; Nathaniel & Iheonu, 2019). It is also examined that innovation is a significant factor for the environment since it may have an improving (Huang et al., 2020; Churchill et al., 2019) or detrimental effect (Ganda, 2019; Dauda et al., 2019) on the environment. Therefore, the question arises here: what if we consider renewable energy and innovation together and examine the impact of renewable energy innovation (REI) on environmental degradation (proxied by ecological footprint) based on the STIRPAT model.

Our study attempts to examine the United States as the sample country. According to Global Footprint Network (2021), the United States has one of the highest ecological footprints in terms of total global hectares around the world, which ranks second (See Fig. 1) with 2,610,000,000 (in global hectares), and the average ecological footprint of the U.S. is approximately 50% greater than the average person in most European countries. Therefore, the U.S. is a significant representation of a high ecological footprint since it uses more energy and water per person, whereas less public transportation compared to other developed countries Global Footprint Network (2021).

To the best of our knowledge, numerous studies mentioned above have explored factors that affect the environment from a CO_2 emissions perspective; however, very few studies have examined the ecological footprint as a measure of environmental degradation. For this reason, we adopt ecological footprint as a measure instead of CO_2 emissions. As mentioned, previous studies have investigated the impacts of several driving factors on the environment. For instance, innovation has been considered technological improvements without focusing on renewable technologies, and the impact of renewable energy has been considered mainly based on energy consumption in the current literature. Therefore, the potentially significant environmental effect of innovations, specifically in the field of renewable energy, has been largely ignored in the existing literature, and these two factors are considered separately. In other words, the renewable energy innovation index (REI) has never been included in the STIRPAT model. For this purpose, we will expand the STIRPAT model by adding the novel REI index for the United States between 1996 and 2015 by employing Fourier methods.

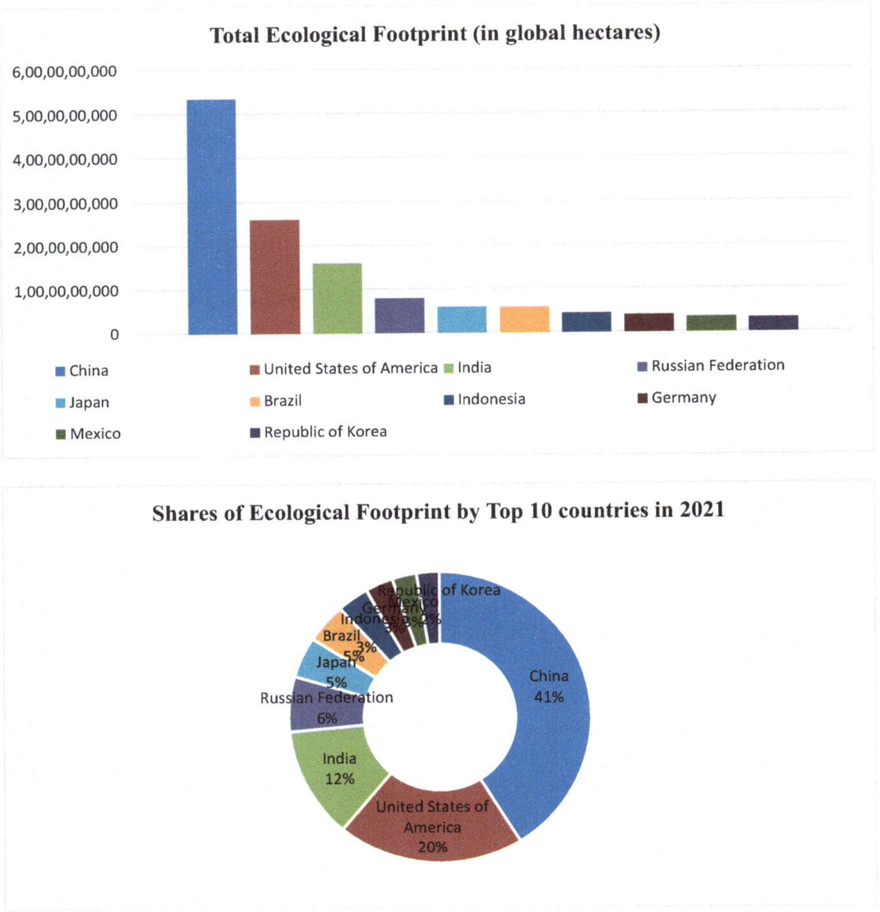

Fig. 1 Top 10 countries ranked by total ecological footprint (in global hectares)

This paper is structured as follows: Section 2 provides a review of the existing literature based on the STIRPAT model, and Sect. 3 explains the data and methodology. Section 4 discusses empirical findings. Section 5 concludes by suggesting significant implications for sustainable development.

2 Literature Review

Many studies have been carried out in the literature using the STIRPAT model on the relationship between environmental degradation and several driving factors affecting it. For instance (Fang et al., 2006) measure the impacts of affluence, population, and technology on the total CO_2 emissions and conclude that economic growth has the strongest effect on environmental degradation. In contrast, the population aged 15 to 64 has the least effect. Similarly, Shahbaz et al. (2016) found that economic growth is the primary driver of increasing CO_2 emissions. Using the STIRPAT model, the association between population and environmental degradation has also been examined in previous studies (Dietz & Rosa, 1997; Shi, 2003; York et al., 2003; Martínez-Zarzoso, 2009; Sanglimsuwan, 2012) by obtaining carbon dioxide emission as an ecological impact proxy. For example, Martínez-Zarzoso (2009) concluded that the impact of population growth on the environment varies according to different income levels of countries. Another study explains that an increase in population and proportion of working-age (i.e., those aged between 15–64) population has a positive impact on CO_2 emissions Sanglimsuwan (2012). From the perspective of the technology-environmental impact relationship, York et al. (2003) are one of the first researchers to consider technology as an explanatory variable, and they found that industrialization has an increasing impact on CO_2 emissions. Furthermore, Shuai et al. (2017) investigated the effects of population, affluence, and technology on carbon emission for a sample of 125 countries and concluded that technology (affluence) has the strongest impact factor on carbon emission for the high-income (low-income) level countries, whereas affluence (technology) has the least impact on carbon emission. In some recent studies, it has been concluded that the technology has an emission-reducing effect (Cui et al., 2018; He & Hu, Analysis and Prediction of the Influencing Factors of China's Secondary Industry Carbon Emission under the New Normal, 2018; Hong, 2017), however, some other studies found that technological progress may lead to higher carbon emissions (Xiong et al., Extended STIRPAT model-based driving factor analysis of energy-related CO_2 emissions in Kazakhstan, 2019). As seen from those mentioned above and some other research (Han et al., 2020; Sinha et al., 2020), the current literature has focused on the determinants of environmental degradation mainly using the proxy of carbon emissions. Since ecological footprint includes CO_2 emissions and represents a more complete picture of environmental quality, EF will be used in this study.

In recent years, with the understanding of the importance of ecological footprint in measuring environmental degradation, the effect of various variables such as innovation (Huang et al., 2020; Churchill et al., 2019; Ganda, 2019; Dauda et al., 2019; Sinha et al., 2020; Khattak et al., 2020) and renewable energy (Ozcan et al., A revisit of the environmental Kuznets curve hypothesis for Turkey: new evidence from bootstrap rolling window causality, 2018; Destek et al., Analyzing the environmental Kuznets curve for the EU countries: the role of ecological footprint, 2018; Dogan et al., 2019; Baloch et al., 2019) on EF has begun to be examined. For instance, Huang et al. (2020) revealed that innovation activities enhance the quality of the environment, whereas Ganda (2019) concluded that innovation activities might deteriorate the environmental quality. Although data availability is limited in measuring innovation, the most used variable in the literature is research and development (R&D) activities (Greenhalgh & Rogers, 2010). In the context of the STIRPAT model, (Usman & Hammar, Dynamic relationship between technological innovations, financial development, renewable energy, and ecological footprint: fresh insights based on the STIRPAT model for Asia Pacific Economic Cooperation countries, 2021) investigate the effects of technological innovations, renewable energy, and other variables on the ecological footprint for Asian Pacific Economic Cooperation (APEC) countries, and concluded that renewable energy consumption leads to higher environmental quality, while technological innovations have a detrimental influence on the ecological footprint in the long-run. Another study (Nathaniel & Khan, 2020) found a decreasing impact of renewable energy on ecological footprint using the STIRPAT model. Examining the 14 Sub-Saharan African countries, (Wang & Dong, 2019) indicated that renewable energy has an environmental quality-enhancing effect. Likewise, Destek and Sinha (2020) analyzed the impact of renewable energy on environmental degradation using an ecological footprint proxy for the sample of OECD members. They found that renewable energy has an improving impact on EF. When all these studies are taken into account, it is seen that innovation and renewable energy have important effects on the ecological footprint. Considering the impact of innovation activities, specifically in the field of renewable energy, on the environment is a significant issue to investigate. In this study, we will analyze this association based on the STIRPAT model. Therefore, our paper is broadly related to the linkage between renewable energy innovation and environmental degradation literature (Table 1).

3 Data and Methodology

The United States annual data from 1975 to 2015 is employed in this study. Ecological footprint as an index for 6 variables: built-up land, carbon emission, cropland, fishing grounds, forestry product and grazing land taken from Global Footprint Network (Global Footprint Network, 2021). The total value of research and development in renewable energy sources used as a proxy for renewable energy innovation in this study (IEA, 2023). Other variables are taken from the World Bank data set (World Development Indicators, 2023). Growth domestic product constant 2010 was used as a proxy for economic growth. The total population shows the population of the United States, and energy use (kg of oil equivalent per capita) is the primary energy before transformation is used as a proxy for energy use in the United States.

To determine whether a series is stationary or non-stationary, the Augmented Dickey-Fuller and Phillips-Perron unit root tests are used (Dickey and Fuller, 1981; Phillips and Perron, 1988). These tests look at the potential of cointegration and the amount of variable integration. In the general framework with the intercept and trend, the ADF test model is as follows:

Table 1 Summary of literature that used ecological footprint as a measure of environmental degradation based on the STIRPAT model

Author(s)	Sample structure	Dependent variable	Independent variables	Methodology	Main findings
Yang et al. (2021)	10 countries, 1995–2018	Ecological footprint, Healthcare expenditures	Industrial value-added,Per capita economic growth, Globalization,Urban population	Panel Unit Root Test,Panel Westerlund Cointegration Test,Augmented Mean Group Test,Dumitrescu & Hurlin Causality Test	Healthcare expenditures, economic growth, industrilization increases environmental degradation, while globalization and urbanizations decreases Unidirectional causality exists from economic growth and globalization to the ecological footprint
Usman and Hammar (2021)	APEC countries, 1990–2017	Ecological footprint	Technological innovation, Financial development,Economic growth,Renewable energy consumption, Population	Panel Unit Root Tests,Panel Westerlund Cointegration Test,Feasible Generalized Least Square,Augmented Mean Group EstimatorCommon Correlated Effect Mean Group Estimator,Panel Dumitrescu & Hurlin Non-causality Test	Financial development and renewable energy utilization improve environmental quality, however, technological innovation activities, economic growth and population reduce it Bidirectional causality exists between all variables and ecological footprint
Li et al. (2021)	Shandong province of China, 2018–2030	Ecological footprint	Population,Per capita economic growth,Urbanization, Output value of the industrial department,In-house expenditure/GDP,Patent number	Partial east quares,Back ropagation eural etwork	Total population, urbanization rate, and per capita economic growth lead to higher ecological footprint, but technological progress may have a negative effect on ecological footprint in the short-run

(continued)

Table 1 (continued)

Author(s)	Sample structure	Dependent variable	Independent variables	Methodology	Main findings
Kihombo et al. (2021)	West Asia and Middle Eastcountries, 1990–2017	Ecological footprint	Financial development,Per capita economic growth, Urbanization,Technological innovation	Panel Unit Root,Panel Westerlund Cointegration, Pedroni and Kao Cointegration,CUP-FM and CUP-BC methods	Technological innovation decreases EF, whereasFinancial development, and urbanization increases EF Unidirectional causality exists from financial development to EF Bidirectional causality exists between technological innovation and EF
Zuo et al. (2020)	G20 countries, 1999–2016	Ecological footprint	Per capita GDP,Population, Energy intensity,Energy consumption,Urbanization rate	EF-Path-STIRPAT Model	Developing members of G20 have higher EF than developed members In developed countries, the primary driving factor of EF is technology (energy intensity) In developing countries, the most important factor is GDP
Kilbourne and Thyroff (2020)	113 countries, 2011	Ecological footprint	Population,GDP,Consumer spending,Consumer spending pn material goods, Energy consumption,Carbon emissions	Ordinary Least Squares	All driving forces of EF are significant and good predictor

Wu (2020)	30 provinces of China, 2004–2012	Ecological footprint	Population,Per capita GDP, Technology,Per capita consumption,Urbanization, Non-tertiary GDP,Openness	Geographically Weighted Regression Model,Ordinary Least Squares	Population and GDP are the main influencing factors of EFDevelopments in technology may mitigate EF growth,Technology has the primary role among other factors on EF
Guo and Wang (2019)	China, 2006–2016	Ecological footprint	GDP per capita,% of secondary industry ,The year-end resident population, Urbanization rate,The unit GDP energy consumption	Principal Component Analysis	The most dominant driving factors of EF are GDP per capita and proportion of secondary industry
Bello et al. (2018)	Malaysia, 1971–2016	Ecological footprint, Carbon footprint,Water footprint,CO_2 emission	Hydroelectricity consumption,Real GDP per capita, Square of GDP,Urbanization	ARDL Bounds Testing Cointegration,VECM Granger-causality analysis	An inverted U-shaped linkage exists between real GDP-environmental degradation Hydroelectricity consumption decreases environmental degradation Unidirectional causality exists from hydroelectricity and fossil fuel consumption to environmental degradation and real GDP, Bidirectional causality exists between real GDP and environmental degradation measures

(continued)

Table 1 (continued)

Author(s)	Sample structure	Dependent variable	Independent variables	Methodology	Main findings
Uddin et al. (2016)	Australia, 1960–2014	Ecological footprint	Total population,GDP per capita,Quadratic term of GDP per capita,Urbanization,% of GDP from industry sector,Energy use per capita, Non-dependent population ratio,Energy intensity,CO_2 emissions per capita	Ordinary Least Squares, Ridge Regression	Population is found the most dominant driving factor on EF, followed by GDP per capita and urbanization
Teixidó-Figueras and Duro (2015)	1993–2017	International ecological footprint inequality	GDP per capita,Industrial GDP share (%),Urbanization share (%), Non-dependent population share (aged from 15 to 65), Average minimum temperature (daily)	Ordimary Least Squares	Economic growth has an increasing impact on ecological inequality, and demographic factors are important for differences in international EF
Marquart-Pyatt (2015)	5 Western African countries, 1961–2006	Ecological footprint	GDP per capita,Total population,Urbanization (%),Age dependency ratio,Rural population density,Land area, Arable land	Prais-Winsten Regression Model	Demographic factors have the most significant role on EF
Wei et al. (2011)	Sichuan Province of China, 1995–2008	Ecological footprint	Population size,GDP per capita,Quadratic term of GDP per capita,% of GDP,% of GDP from industry, Urbanization rate	Ridge Regression	Population is the primary driving factor on EF, urbanization and industrialization also affect EF positively
Wang & Wang (2011)	China, 2006–2016	Ecological footprint	Total population,GDP per capita,% of the urban population	Ridge Regression, EKC	GDP per capita is the primary driving factor of EF

Wang et al. (2010)	Jilin Province of China, 1986–2006	Ecological footprint of consumption (EFc),Ecological footprint of production (EFp)	Population,GDP per capita, Quadratic term of GDP per capita,Urbanization,Quadratic term of urbanization,% of economy (in primary industry)	Ordinary Least Squares	(1) Urbanization and quadratic term of urbanization are the most important driving factors of EFc (2) GDP per capita, quadratic term of GDP per capita are the most crucial driving factors for EFp
Jia et al. (2009)	Hennan Province of China, 1983–2006	Ecological footprint	Population,GDP per capita, Quadratic term of GDP per capita,% of GDP (except service sector),% of Urban population	Partial Least Squares	Population, GDP per capita, quadratic term of GDP per capita, and % of urban population are main drivers of EF
Heyden and Shandra (2009)	45 countries, 2000	Ecological footprint	GDP per capita,Annual hours worked (per employee),Output per hour of work,Employment/Population,Total population size, Urbanization,Service production,Military expenditures,Trade balance	Multivariate Regression Analysis	Hours of work lead to higher ecological footprint

$$\Delta Y_t = \alpha_0 + \alpha_2 t + \delta Y_{t-1} + \sum_{i=2}^{p} \beta_j \Delta Y_{t-i-1} + \in_t \quad (1)$$

Where y shows the variable; α is showing intercept; t is indicated trend; $\in_t$ is the white noise, and p shows the lag level.

The Phillips and Perron test (Phillips & Perron, 1988) uses nonparametric techniques to discover serial correlation in errors without adding lag. The widely used method estimate is Newey-West and is as follows:

$$\omega^2 = \gamma_0 + 2\sum_{j=1}^{q}\left(1 - \frac{j}{\alpha + 1}\right)\gamma_j \quad (2)$$

$$\gamma_j = \frac{1}{T}\sum_{t=j+1}^{T} \in_t \in_{t-j} \quad (3)$$

Where q = the truncation lag, γ_j is showing the estimated residuals covariance j-lag apart and T in the model.

Three alternative models on Zivot and Andrews are utilized in the model, which may be stated as follows. According to Zivot and Andrews (2002), the unit root test is another test used in this study to examine the likelihood of structural breaks and stability. Model B displays a break in both trend and drift, followed by Model T, which only displays trend, and Model I, which only displays drift. All of these models are displayed as follows:

$$\text{Model B}: \Delta Y_t = \beta_1 + \beta_2 t + \delta Y_{t-1} + \theta \mathrm{DU}_t + \gamma \mathrm{DU}_t + \sum_{i=1}^{m} \alpha i \Delta Y_{t-1} + \in_t \quad (4)$$

$$\text{Model T}: \Delta Y_t = \beta_1 + \beta_2 t + \delta Y_{t-1} + \gamma \mathrm{DU}_t + \sum_{i=1}^{m} \alpha i \Delta Y_{t-1} + \in_t \quad (5)$$

$$\text{Model I}: \Delta Y_t = \beta_1 + \beta_2 t + \delta Y_{t-1} + \theta \mathrm{DU}_t + \sum_{i=1}^{m} \alpha i \Delta Y_{t-1} + \in_t \quad (6)$$

where DUt = 1 and DTt = t − Tb if t > Tb and 0 otherwise. Tb is an abbreviation used to show possible breakpoints.

The ARDL model used for the first time by Pesaran et al. (2001) may be accepted regardless of whether the explanatory variables are I(0), I(1), or mutually cointegrated in order. There are a lot of benefits to the ARDL technique. Still, the two main ones are as follows: first, it does not suffer from the serial correlation and endogeneity issues that other cointegration approaches do. Additionally, variables should not be used as pretests since they are non-stationary, which is also a prerequisite for using other approaches (Narayan, 2004). Following error correction models is suggested by the ARDL technique;

$$\begin{aligned}\Delta\ln\mathrm{ECO}_t = {} & \alpha_{0_Y} + \sum_{i=1}^{n} b_{i_Y}\Delta\ln\mathrm{ECO}_{t-i} + \sum_{i=0}^{n} c_{i_Y}\Delta\ln\mathrm{GDP}_{t-i} \\ & + \sum_{i=0}^{n} c_{i_Y}\Delta\ln\mathrm{POP}_{t-i} + \sum_{i=0}^{n} c_{i_Y}\Delta\ln\mathrm{EU}_{t-i} + \sum_{i=0}^{n} c_{i_Y}\Delta\ln\mathrm{REI}_{t-i} \\ & +\lambda_{1_Y}\ln\mathrm{ECO}_{t-1} + \lambda_{2_Y}\ln\mathrm{GDP}_{t-1} + \lambda_{3_Y}\ln\mathrm{POP}_{t-1} \\ & +\lambda_{4_Y}\ln EU_{t-1} + \lambda_{5_Y}\ln REI_{t-1} + \in_t\end{aligned} \tag{7}$$

where α_{0_Y} is the drift and $\in_t$ is the error. The model's first section demonstrates error-correction dynamics, while the second section represents the long-term relationship. The null hypothesis for the bounds test is $\lambda_{1_Y}=\lambda_{2_Y}=\lambda_{3_Y}=\lambda_{4_Y}=0$ and the alternative hypothesis is $\lambda_{1_Y}\neq\lambda_{2_Y}\neq\lambda_{3_Y}\neq\lambda_{4_Y}\neq 0$. The Narayan (2005) critical values are used to assess the calculated F-statistic.

Once the long-run linkage has been established, the short-run association and error correction term are estimated using the error correction model. ECM is described as follows:

$$\begin{aligned}\Delta\ln ECO_t = {} & \alpha_{0_Y} + \sum_{i=1}^{n} b_{i_Y}\Delta\ln\mathrm{ECO}_{t-i} + \sum_{i=0}^{n} c_{i_Y}\Delta\ln\mathrm{GDP}_{t-i} \\ & + \sum_{i=0}^{n} c_{i_Y}\Delta\ln\mathrm{POP}_{t-i} + \sum_{i=0}^{n} c_{i_Y}\Delta\ln\mathrm{EU}_{t-i} + \sum_{i=0}^{n} c_{i_Y}\Delta\ln\mathrm{REI}_{t-i} + \in_t\end{aligned} \tag{8}$$

where ECT_{t-1} shows the error correction term that explains the speed of adjustment to the long-run equilibrium level.

To demonstrate a casual relationship between variables, the Toda and Yamamoto (1995) test is used. The main benefit of this test is that it may be performed regardless of the variables integrated. Toda and Yamamoto (1995) proposed a modified Wald statistic to identify the causal links between variables. In this model, the information criteria proposed by Hacker and Hatemi (2012) are employed to determine the best lag selection. The greatest integration order is denoted by dmax in this equation, while k is the ideal VAR order. Following is the calculated VAR (k + dmax):

$$\begin{aligned}\ln\mathrm{ECO} = {} & \alpha_0 + \sum_{i=1}^{k}\alpha_{1\mathrm{i}}\ln\mathrm{ECO}_{t-i} + \sum_{j=k+1}^{d_{\max}}\alpha_{2\mathrm{j}}\ln\mathrm{ECO}_{t-j} + \sum_{i=1}^{k}\beta_{1\mathrm{i}}\ln\mathrm{GDP}_{t-i} \\ & + \sum_{j=k+1}^{d_{\max}}\beta_{2\mathrm{j}}\ln\mathrm{GDP}_{t-j} + \sum_{i=1}^{k}\gamma_{1\mathrm{i}}\ln\mathrm{POP}_{t-i} + \sum_{j=k+1}^{d_{\max}}\gamma_{2\mathrm{j}}\ln\mathrm{POP}_{t-j} \\ & + \sum_{i=1}^{k}\delta_{1\mathrm{i}}\ln\mathrm{EU}_{t-i} + \sum_{j=k+1}^{d_{\max}}\delta_{2\mathrm{j}}\ln\mathrm{EU}_{t-j} + \sum_{i=1}^{k}\theta_{1\mathrm{i}}\ln\mathrm{REI}_{t-i} \\ & + \sum_{j=k+1}^{d_{\max}}\theta_{2\mathrm{j}}\ln\mathrm{REI}_{t-j} + \in_{1t}\end{aligned}$$

$$\ln \mathrm{GDP} = \beta_0 + \sum_{i=1}^{k} \beta_{1i} \ln \mathrm{GDP}_{t-i} + \sum_{j=k+1}^{d_{\max}} \beta_{2j} \ln \mathrm{GDP}_{t-j} + \sum_{i=1}^{k} \alpha_{1i} \ln \mathrm{ECO}_{t-i} + \sum_{j=k+1}^{d_{\max}} \alpha_{2j} \ln \mathrm{ECO}_{t-j} + \sum_{i=1}^{k} \gamma_{1i} \ln \mathrm{POP}_{t-i} + \sum_{j=k+1}^{d_{\max}} \gamma_{2j} \ln \mathrm{POP}_{t-j} + \sum_{i=1}^{k} \delta_{1i} \ln \mathrm{EU}_{t-i} + \sum_{j=k+1}^{d_{\max}} \delta_{2j} \ln \mathrm{EU}_{t-j} + \sum_{i=1}^{k} \theta_{1i} \ln \mathrm{REI}_{t-i} + \sum_{j=k+1}^{d_{\max}} \theta_{2j} \ln \mathrm{REI}_{t-j} + \in_{2t}$$

$$\ln \mathrm{POP} = \gamma_0 + \sum_{i=1}^{k} \gamma_{1i} \ln \mathrm{POP}_{t-i} + \sum_{j=k+1}^{d_{\max}} \gamma_{2j} \ln \mathrm{POP}_{t-j} + \sum_{i=1}^{k} \beta_{1i} \ln \mathrm{GDP}_{t-i} + \sum_{j=k+1}^{d_{\max}} \beta_{2j} \ln \mathrm{GDP}_{t-j} + \sum_{i=1}^{k} \alpha_{1i} \ln \mathrm{ECO}_{t-i} + \sum_{j=k+1}^{d_{\max}} \alpha_{2j} \ln \mathrm{FD}_{t-j} + \sum_{i=1}^{k} \delta_{1i} \ln \mathrm{EU}_{t-i} + \sum_{j=k+1}^{d_{\max}} \delta_{2j} \ln \mathrm{EU}_{t-j} + \sum_{i=1}^{k} \theta_{1i} \ln \mathrm{REI}_{t-i} + \sum_{j=k+1}^{d_{\max}} \theta_{2j} \ln \mathrm{REI}_{t-j} + \in_{3t}$$

$$\ln \mathrm{EU} = \delta_0 + \sum_{i=1}^{k} \delta_{1i} \ln \mathrm{EU}_{t-i} + \sum_{j=k+1}^{d_{\max}} \delta_{2j} \ln \mathrm{EU}_{t-j} + \sum_{i=1}^{k} \beta_{1i} \ln \mathrm{GDP}_{t-i} + \sum_{j=k+1}^{d_{\max}} \beta_{2j} \ln \mathrm{GDP}_{t-j} + \sum_{i=1}^{k} \gamma_{1i} \ln \mathrm{POP}_{t-i} + \sum_{j=k+1}^{d_{\max}} \gamma_{2j} \ln \mathrm{POP}_{t-j} + \sum_{i=1}^{k} \alpha_{1i} \ln \mathrm{ECO}_{t-i} + \sum_{j=k+1}^{d_{\max}} \alpha_{2j} \ln \mathrm{ECO}_{t-j} + \sum_{i=1}^{k} \theta_{1i} \ln \mathrm{REI}_{t-i} + \sum_{j=k+1}^{d_{\max}} \theta_{2j} \ln \mathrm{REI}_{t-j} + \in_{4t}$$

$$\ln \mathrm{REI} = \theta_0 + \sum_{i=1}^{k} \theta_{1i} \ln \mathrm{REI}_{t-i} + \sum_{j=k+1}^{d_{\max}} \theta_{2j} \ln \mathrm{REI}_{t-j} + \sum_{i=1}^{k} \beta_{1i} \ln \mathrm{GDP}_{t-i} + \sum_{j=k+1}^{d_{\max}} \beta_{2j} \ln \mathrm{GDP}_{t-j} + \sum_{i=1}^{k} \gamma_{1i} \ln \mathrm{POP}_{t-i} + \sum_{j=k+1}^{d_{\max}} \gamma_{2j} \ln \mathrm{POP}_{t-j} + \sum_{i=1}^{k} \delta_{1i} \ln \mathrm{EU}_{t-i} + \sum_{j=k+1}^{d_{\max}} \delta_{2j} \ln \mathrm{EU}_{t-j} + \sum_{i=1}^{k} \alpha_{1i} \ln \mathrm{ECO}_{t-i} + \sum_{j=k+1}^{d_{\max}} \alpha_{2j} \ln \mathrm{ECO}_{t-j} + \in_{5t} \tag{9}$$

4 Empirical Results

The Augmented Dickey-Fuller (ADF) and Phillips-Perron(PP) as formal unit root tests were conducted for one of the most important assumptions to check whether the series is stationary or not. Moreover, the Kwiatkowski–Phillips–Schmidt–Shin (KPSS) as a stationary test was applied in this study to confirm the findings of the ADF and PP tests. Table 2 illustrates the result of the ADF and PP unit root test and the KPSS stationarity test.

ADF, PP, and KPSS tests are applied as formal unit root tests to check the integration order of variables. In Table 3, Zivot and Andrews (2002) unit root test was used to support the previous finding of the integration order for variables under the one structural break as well. All the variables stationarity in level form was checked. As a result ecological footprint, GDP, and energy use are not stationary in level, so the first difference form was applied and all tests support that they are all stationary in the first difference level. Concisely, Ln Eco, Ln GDP, Ln EU are I(1), and Ln POP, Ln REI are I(0).

In this study as we found all variables are integrated as I(0) and I(1) and we are sure there is no I(2) variable so as Pesaran et al. (2001) suggested in their study we applied bounds test under the Autoregressive Distributed Lag (ARDL) cointegration test. Figure 2 shows the top 20 models' lag order selection between 162 evaluated models. The maximum lag for dependent variables and regressors is 2. The best order of lag selection under the Schwarz criteria is based on model 135: ARDL (1,1,0,0,0).

Table 4 shows the bounds test result according to the best-selected order of the lag for the model. The result is based on the third model, namely, unrestricted constant and no trend developed by Pesaran et al. (2001). F-statistic is 5.889 and lies above the upper bound criteria (Narayan, 2005), and all 1, 5, and 10 percent levels of significant null hypothesis were rejected. The null hypothesis explains that there is no level relationship, and the rejected and bound test results show a level relationship between variables. Moreover, the t-statistic for the bound test is also greater than I (0) and I(1) of t-bound criteria and the null hypothesis, which is nonsensical cointegration rejected, and both tests robustly showed that there is a level relationship between variables.

Asymptotic: $n = 1000$.

Table 5 shows the coefficients in the level form in the long-run relationship between explanatory variables and ecological footprint and conditional error correction term. A model based on the STIRPAT model having a positive and significant coefficient in the long run for GDP, population and energy use is expected, as discussed in the literature before. The GDP is 0.157 and has an inelastic significant positive effect on ecological footprint. Previous studies of WU (2020), Szigeti and Tóth (2017). Molaei and Basharat (2015) study results support our finding that an increase in GDP has a positive impact on the ecological footprint. Population, same as GDP, has a positive and significant effect on ecological footprint, and one percent increase in Population in the case of the United States will lead to increase the

Table 2 The ADF, PP, and KPSS tests

Statistics (level)	Ln ECO	Lag	Ln GDP	Lag	Ln POP	Lag	Ln EU	Lag	Ln REI	Lag
τ_T (ADF)	−1.545	(0)	−1.715	(1)	−3.316***	(1)	−1.453	(0)	−3.020	(0)
τ_μ (ADF)	−1.567	(0)	−1.845	(1)	−0.801	(2)	−0.757	(0)	−3.241**	(0)
τ (ADF)	0.526	(0)	4.003	(1)	2.029	(2)	−0.966	(0)	0.637	(0)
τ_T (PP)	−1.671	(3)	−1.153	(2)	−2.427	(5)	−1.739	(2)	−3.327***	(4)
τ_μ (PP)	−1.548	(2)	−1.434	(3)	0.476	(5)	−1.015	(1)	−3.445**	(4)
τ (PP)	0.547	(1)	7.949	(1)	4.991	(5)	−0.966	(0)	0.436	(3)
τ_T (KPSS)	0.126***	(5)	0.171**	(4)	0.117	(5)	0.128***	(4)	0.126***	(4)
τ_μ (KPSS)	0.585**	(5)	0.806*	(5)	0.789*	(5)	0.355*	(5)	0.197	(4)
Statistics (first difference)	Ln ECO	Lag	Ln GDP	Lag	Ln POP	Lag	Ln EU	Lag	Ln REI	Lag
τ_T (ADF)	−6.825*	(0)	−5.135*	(0)	−1.843	(1)	−4.435*	(1)	−6.354*	(0)
τ_μ (ADF)	−6.723*	(0)	−4.776*	(0)	−2.095	(1)	−5.038*	(0)	−6.483*	(0)
τ (ADF)	−6.725*	(0)	−2.151**	(0)	−0.354	(0)	−5.045*	(0)	−6.538*	(0)
τ_T (PP)	−6.813*	(1)	−5.157*	(3)	−1.372	(0)	−5.156*	(0)	−6.351*	(2)
τ_μ (PP)	−6.710*	(2)	−4.827*	(1)	−1.813	(1)	−5.105*	(1)	−6.483*	(2)
τ (PP)	−6.712*	(2)	−2.018**	(1)	−0.506	(2)	−5.111*	(1)	−6.548*	(2)
τ_T (KPSS)	0.086	(1)	0.083	(4)	0.173**	(5)	0.078	(0)	0.112	(4)
τ_μ (KPSS)	0.142	(1)	0.240	(1)	0.231	(5)	0.156	(0)	0.144	(3)

Note: ECO represents ecological footprint; GDP indicates gross domestic product; POP shows urban population (% of the total population); EU is energy use (kg of oil equivalent per capita); and REI is renewable energy innovation. All of the data in each series is used in logarithmic forms. τT indicates the general model with trend and intercept; $\tau\mu$ is the model with intercept and without the trend; τ is the limited model without trend and intercept. Lag lengths were used to remove the effect of serial correlation and are shown in the brackets. In the PP test, numbers in brackets indicate Newey-West Bandwidth (as determined by Bartlett-Kernel). In KPSS, the null-hypothesis series is stationary. Both in ADF and PP tests, unit root tests were performed from the general to the least limited model by removing intercept and trend from the models. *, **, and *** respectively show rejection of the null hypothesis at the 1 percent, 5 percent, and 10 percent levels. Tests for unit roots have been carried out in E-VIEWS 12

Table 3 Unit root test—Zivot and Andrews (2002)

	Statistics (level)			Statistics (first D)			
	ZA_B	ZA_T	ZA_I	ZA_B	ZA_T	ZA_I	Conclusion
Ln ECO	−3.309	−3.258	−3.404	−8.812*	−6.961*	−7.729*	I(1)
Break year	1996	2005	2008	1984	1998	1984	
Lag length	0	0	0	0	0	0	
Ln GDP	−4.356	−4.450**	−4.190	−6.511*	−5.087*	−5.573*	I(1)
Break year	2004	2006	2008	1983	1998	1983	
Lag length	1	1	1	0	0	0	
Ln POP	−5.477**	−3.556	−7.058*	−4.517	−3.539	−3.517	I(0)
Break year	1991	1999	1991	1991	1992	2000	
Lag length	1	1	1	1	1	1	
Ln EU	−3.509	−3.183	−3.385	−8.256*	−4.767**	−5.650*	I(1)
Break year	1987	2005	2008	1983	1989	1984	
Lag length	1	1	1	0	2	0	
Ln REI	−4.924***	−5.263*	−5.346*	−8.749*	−8.517*	−3.645	I(0)
Break year	1984	1991	2007	1984	1983	1991	
Lag length	0	0	0	0	0	2	

Notes: ECO represents ecological footprint; GDP indicates gross domestic product; POP shows urban population (% of the total population); EU is energy use (kg of oil equivalent per capita); and REI is renewable energy innovation. All of the data in each series is used in logarithmic forms. ZA_B represents the model with a break in both the intercept and trend; ZA_T is the model with a break in the trend; ZA_I is the model with a break in the intercept. *, **, and *** respectively show the null hypothesis rejection at 1%, 5%, and 10% levels. Tests for unit roots have been carried out in E-VIEWS 12

Ecological footprint by 1.52%. This result is supported in the literature by many studies, such as Chen et al. (2022), and Jie et al. (2023). Energy use as a third part of the STIRPAT model is significant in our study. One percent increase in energy use, which is primary energy used, will increase the Ecological footprint by 1.08%, which is elastic like the population in our study. Results supported in the literature are almost the same as GDP and population and explain the positive impact on Ecological footprint (Rehman et al., 2021; Nathaniel, 2021). Renewable energy innovation, which contributes to this study, also has a significant t statistic for the

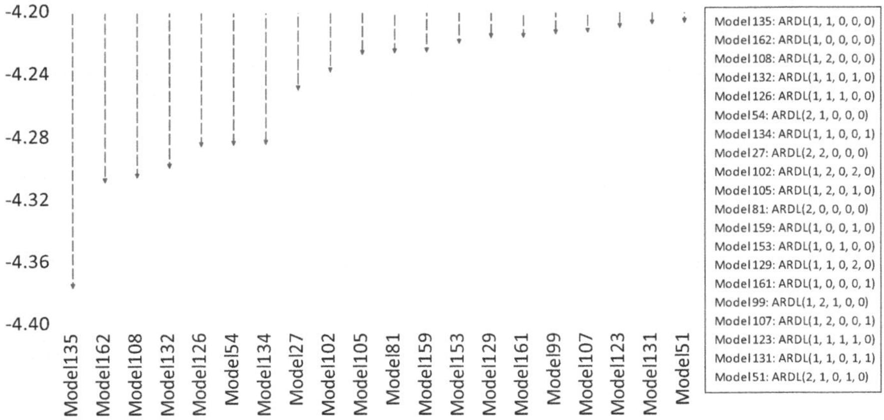

Fig. 2 Best top 20 models of lag order selection according to Schwarz Criteria

Table 4 Bounds tests for the level relationship

Variables	*F-statistic*	*Level of significance*	*I(0)*	*I(1)*	*Conclusion*
F LnECO (LnGDP, LnPOP, LnEU, LnREI)	5.889	10%	2.45	3.52	H0 Rejected
		5%	2.86	4.01	H0 Rejected
		1%	3.74	5.06	H0 Rejected
Variables	*T-statistic*	*Level of significance*	*I(0)*	*I(1)*	*Conclusion*
F LnECO (LnGDP, LnPOP, LnEU, LnREI)	−5.110	10%	−2.57	−3.66	H0 Rejected
		5%	−2.86	−3.99	H0 Rejected
		1%	−3.43	−4.6	H0 Rejected

Notes: Schwarz criteria (SC) were used to select the number of lags. F-statistic and T-statistic are in the model with unrestricted constant and no trend

coefficient. The result is that one percent increase in renewable energy innovation will decrease the ecological footprint inelastic by 0.014%. The outputs of this model show that the error correction term (ECT) of this model is equal to −0.669. Based on GDP, Population, Energy Use, and the Contribution of Renewable Energy Innovation in the United States, the ECT of the model shows that the Ecological footprint converges to the long-run equilibrium level every year with a 66.9% speed of adjustment. Only short-term terms, according to the lag selection of the ARDL model, are valid for GDP, with one significant lag supporting the long-term results as well.

Table 5 Level coefficients in the long-term model and conditional error correction model

Long term	*Dependent variable*	*Ln GDP*	*Ln POP*	*Ln EU*	*Ln REI*
	Ln ECO	0.157***	1.523***	1.082*	−0.014***
		(1.843)	(1.883)	(9.863)	(−1.791)
Conditional error correction	*Dependent variable*	*Regressor*	*Coefficient*	*Standard error*	*T-Statistic*
	Ln ECO [1, 1, 0, 0, 0]	$\hat{U}_{t-1}$	−0.669*	0.131	(−5.110)
		ΔLn GDP	0.749*	0.240	(3.123)

Notes: The numbers in parentheses are t-statistics for variables. *, **, and *** significance level at 1%, 5%, and10% levels, respectively. The numbers in brackets indicate p-lag structures in the model

Table 6 Diagnostic tests

Test statistics	F-Version	Prob
Serial correlation (LM Test)	1.7159	0.196
Functional form	1.7611	0.194
Heteroskedasticity (White Test)	1.1348	0.376
Normality	2.263*	0.322

Notes: * indicates LM-version of the test

The stability of the model must be checked, and diagnostic tests must be used to confirm model validity, once the ARDL technique has been used to estimate the coefficients for explanatory variables in the long- and short-term. The outcomes of the four diagnostic tests are presented in Table 6. The results of these tests support the validity and reliability of the ARDL approach used in this study.

The ecological footprint and explanatory factors were shown to be causally linked with time using the Toda Yamamoto (1995) test and vice versa. Table 7 provides a summary of the results. The Toda Yamamoto causality test shows that there is unidirectional causality between renewable energy innovation and ecological footprint. This supports our model and the important contribution of renewable energy innovation in this model. Results show there is no causality from ecological footprint to any explanatory variables that are meaningful and acceptable.

Figure 3 shows the results of the CUSUM test, while Fig. 4 shows the results of the CUSUMSQ test in the model. The crucial lines in Figs. 3 and 4 are the green and red lines in the up and down directions, respectively. The blue line between the critical lines displays the statistical value of CUSUM and CUSUMSQ. They claimed that, both in the long and short periods, the ARDL model used in this study was stable.

Table 7 Toda Yamamoto (1995) causality test

Hypothesis	Chi-square P-value	Decision
lnEU does not cause lnECO	0.033	Reject
lECO does not cause lnEU	0.338	Fail to reject
lnGDP does not cause lnECO	0.046	Reject
lnECO does not cause lnGDP	0.438	Fail to reject
lnPOP does not cause lnECO	0.132	Fail to reject
lnECO does not cause lnPOP	0.627	Fail to reject
lnREI does not cause lnECO	0.015	Reject
lnECO does not cause lnREI	0.969	Fail to reject

Notes: 5000 simulations are used to compute bootstrapped critical values. For the optimum lag length, the HJC criteria are used in this model

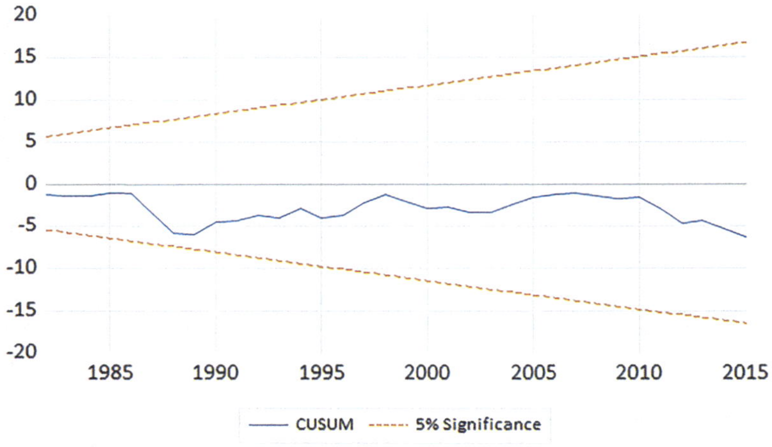

Fig. 3 CUSUM test

5 Conclusion

This study demonstrates the effects of long-term renewable energy innovation on ecological footprint between 1975 and 2015 in the US. Unit root tests led to the discovery of mixed-order integration for the variables, and bounds tests carried out using the ARDL technique verified a long-run linkage of the variables. The model's error correction shows that the presence of other explanatory factors causes the short values of ecological footprint to converge to the long-run equilibrium level annually with a 66.9% speed of adjustment. This finding demonstrates the importance of GDP, population, energy usage, and renewable energy innovation in determining ecological footprint.

In this study results based on the STIRPAT model show that GDP, energy use and population have positive effects on ecological footprint. The contribution of this

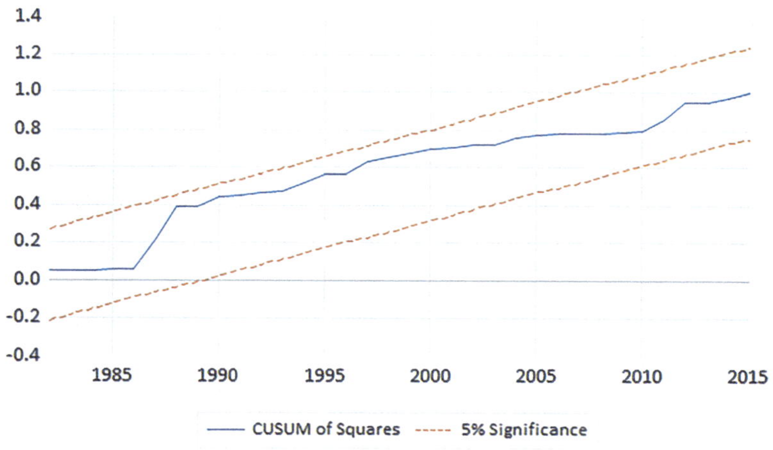

Fig. 4 CUSUMSQ test

study, which is renewable energy innovation, can be the key to reducing the ecological footprint in the united states. The results of this study show that increase in research and development in renewable energy that is used as a proxy for renewable energy innovation will lead to a decrease in the ecological footprint in the long term. The greatest strategy for addressing environmental concerns is using renewable energy sources, such as bioenergy, hydropower, geothermal, solar, wind, and ocean (tide and wave) (Owusu and Asumadu-Sarkodie, 2016). Economic growth and environmental quality have traditionally been seen as mutually exclusive. Yet, there is a need to address the rising energy demand in a way that promotes both environmentally friendly economic growth and protects the environment. Our model and the significant role that renewable energy innovation plays in this model are supported by the Toda Yamamoto causality test, which demonstrates a one-way causal relationship from renewable energy innovation, to ecological footprint.

Research and development investments in renewable energy should be prioritized by policymakers, who should also enhance this spending. This involves providing funds for creative initiatives, aiding research organizations, and providing incentives to commercial businesses engaged in renewable energy studies. Continuous financial assistance may accelerate the creation of affordable and efficient renewable energy alternatives.

Encourage the adoption of renewable energy technology by implementing policies that offer incentives. This may include tax credits, subsidies, and grants for businesses and people that invest in renewable energy systems. The adoption rate of renewable energy is anticipated to rise as it becomes more financially appealing, which will reduce its total ecological footprint. The expansion of renewable energy innovation may be facilitated by policymakers, resulting in a lower ecological footprint and a more sustainable future.

References

Apergis, N., & Payne, J. E. (2010). On the causal dynamics between emissions, nuclear energy, renewable energy, and economic growth. *Ecological Economics, 69*(11), 2255–2260. https://doi.org/10.1016/j.ecolecon.2010.06.014

Baloch, M. A., Zhang, J., Iqbal, K., & Iqbal, Z. (2019). The effect of financial development on ecological footprint in BRI countries: Evidence from panel data estimation. *Environmental Science and Pollution Research, 26*, 6199–6208. https://doi.org/10.1007/s11356-018-3992-9

Bargaoui, S. A., Liouane, N., & Nouri, F. Z. (2014). Environmental impact determinants: An empirical analysis based on the STIRPAT model. *Procedia - Social and Behavioral Sciences, 108*, 449–458. https://doi.org/10.1016/j.sbspro.2013.12.489

Bartelmus, P. (2008). How sustainable are our economies? *Quantitative Economics*. https://doi.org/10.1007/978-1-4020-6966-6

Behera, S. R., & Dash, D. P. (2017). The effect of urbanization, energy consumption, and foreign direct investment on the carbon dioxide emission in the SSEA (South and Southeast Asian) region. *Renewable and Sustainable Energy Reviews, 70*, 96–106. Retrieved from 10.1016/j.rser.2016.11.201.

Bekhet, H. A., Matar, A., & Yasmin, T. (2017). CO2 emissions, energy consumption, economic growth, and financial development in GCC countries: Dynamic simultaneous equation models. *Renewable and Sustainable Energy Reviews, 70*, 117–132. Retrieved from 10.1016/j.rser.2016.11.089.

Bello, M. O., Solarin, S. A., & Yen, Y. Y. (2018). The impact of electricity consumption on CO2 emission, carbon footprint, water footprint and ecological footprint: The role of hydropower in an emerging economy.*Journal of Environmental Management, 219*, 218–230.

Chekouri, S. M., Chibi, A., & Benbouziane, M. (2020). Examining the driving factors of CO2 emissions using the STIRPAT model: The case of Algeria. *International Journal of Sustainable Energy, 39*(10), 927–940. https://doi.org/10.1080/14786451.2020.1770758

Chen, Y., Lee, C. C., & Chen, M. (2022). Ecological footprint, human capital, and urbanization. *Energy & Environment, 33*(3), 487–510.

Churchill, S. A., Inekwe, J., Smyth, R., & Zhang, X. (2019). R&D intensity and carbon emissions in the G7: 1870–2014. *Energy Economics, 80*, 30–37. https://doi.org/10.1016/j.eneco.2018.12.020

Cramer, J. C. (1998). Population growth and air quality in California. *Demography, 35*, 45–56.

Cui, H., Wu, R., & Zhao, T. (2018). Decomposition and forecasting of CO2 emissions in China's power sector based on STIRPAT model with selected PLS model and a novel hybrid PLS-Grey-Markov model. *Energies, 11*(11), 2985. https://doi.org/10.3390/en11112985

Dauda, L., Long, X., Mensah, C. N., & Salman, M. (2019). The effects of economic growth and innovation on CO2 emissions in different regions. *Environmental Science and Pollution Research, 26*, 15028–15038. https://doi.org/10.1007/s11356-019-04891-y

Destek, M. A., & Sinha, A. (2020). Renewable, non-renewable energy consumption, economic growth, trade openness and ecological footprint: Evidence from organisation for economic co-operation and development countries. *Journal of Cleaner Production, 242*, 118537. https://doi.org/10.1016/j.jclepro.2019.118537

Destek, M. A., Ulucak, R., & Dogan, E. (2018). Analyzing the environmental Kuznets curve for the EU countries: The role of ecological footprint. *Environmental Science and Pollution Research*, 29387–29396. https://doi.org/10.1007/s11356-018-2911-4

Dickey, D. A., & Fuller, W. A. (1981). Likelihood ratio statistics for autoregressive time series with a unit root.*Econometrica: Journal of the Econometric Society*, 1057–1072.

Dietz, T., & Rosa, E. A. (1994). Rethinking the environmental impacts of population, affluence, and technology. *Human Ecology Review, 1*(2), 277–300. Retrieved from https://www.jstor.org/stable/24706840

Dietz, T., & Rosa, E. A. (1997). Effects of population and affluence on CO2 emissions. *Proceedings of the National Academy of Sciences, 94*, 175–179. https://doi.org/10.1073/pnas.94.1

Dogan, E., Taspinar, N., & Gokmenoglu, K. K. (2019). Determinants of ecological footprint in MINT countries. *Energy & Environment*. https://doi.org/10.1177/0958305X19834279
Ehrlich, P. R., & Holdren, J. P. (1971). Impact of population growth. *Science New Series, 171*(3977), 1212–1217. Retrieved from https://www.jstor.org/stable/1731166
European Comission. (2021). Retrieved from Climate Action: https://ec.europa.eu/clima/climate-change/causes-climate-change_en
Fang, Y., Liu, L.-C., Wu, G., & Wei, Y.-M. (2006). Analyzing impact factors of CO2 emissions using the STIRPAT model. *Environmental Impact Assessment Review, 26*(4), 377–395. https://doi.org/10.1016/j.eiar.2005.11.007
Ganda, F. (2019). The impact of innovation and technology investments on carbon emissions in selected organisation for economic co-operation and development countries. *Journal of Cleaner Production, 217*, 469–483. https://doi.org/10.1016/j.jclepro.2019.01.235
Ge, M., Friedrich, J., & Vigna, L. (2021). Retrieved from World Resources Institute: https://www.wri.org/insights/4-charts-explain-greenhouse-gas-emissions-countries-and-sectors
GEO6. (2019). *Global environment outlook GEO-6 summary for policymakers*. United Nations Environment Programme.
Global Footprint Network. (2021). Retrieved from Global Footprint Network Advancing the Science of Sustainability: https://www.footprintnetwork.org/our-work/ecological-footprint/
Government of Canada. (2021). *Causes of Climate Change*. Retrieved from Environment and natural resources: https://www.canada.ca/en/environment-climate-change/services/climate-change/causes.html
Greenhalgh, C., & Rogers, M. (2010). *Innovation, intellectual property, and economic growth*. Princeton University Press.
Guo, S., & Wang, Y. (2019). Ecological security assessment based on ecological footprint approach in Hulunbeir grassland, China. *International Journal of Environmental Research and Public Health, 16*(23), 4805.
Hacker, S., & Hatemi-J, A. (2012). A bootstrap test for causality with endogenous lag length choice: Theory and application in finance. *Journal of Economic Studies, 39*(2), 144–160.
Han, D., Li, T., Feng, S., & Shi, Z. (2020). Application of threshold regression analysis to study the impact of clean energy development on China's carbon productivity. *International Journal of Environmental Research and Public Health, 17*(3), 1060. https://doi.org/10.3390/ijerph17031060
He, Y., & Hu, S. (2018). Analysis and prediction of the influencing factors of China's secondary industry carbon emission under the new Normal. *IOP Conference Series: Materials Science and Engineering, 452*(3).
He, Z., Xu, S., Shen, W., Long, R., & Chen, H. (2017). Impact of urbanization on energy related CO2 emission at different development levels: Regional difference in China based on panel estimation. *Journal of Cleaner Production, 140*(Part 3), 1719–1730. Retrieved from 10.1016/j.jclepro.2016.08.155.
Hong, Y. (2017). The impact of Chongqing population size and structure on carbon emissions: A study base on STIRPAT model. In*Advances in Social Science, Education and Humanities Research (ASSEHR). 156*. 2nd International Seminar on Education Innovation and Economic Management.
Huang, J., Luan, B., Cai, X., & Zou, H. (2020). The role of domestic R&D activities played in carbon intensity: Evidence from China. *Science of the Total Environment, 708*, 135033. https://doi.org/10.1016/j.scitotenv.2019.135033
International Energy Agency (2023). World Energy Outlook 2023, IEA. *Licence: Creative Commons Attribution CC BY-NC-SA 4.0.*
Jia, J., Deng, H., Duan, J., & Zhao, J. (2009). Analysis of the major drivers of the ecological footprint using the STIRPAT model and the PLS method—A case study in Henan Province. *China. Ecological Economics, 68*(11), 2818–2824.

Jie, H., Khan, I., Alharthi, M., Zafar, M. W., & Saeed, A. (2023). Sustainable energy policy, socio-economic development, and ecological footprint: The economic significance of natural resources, population growth, and industrial development.*Utilities Policy, 81*, 101490.

Khalid, K., Usman, M., & Mehdi, M. A. (2021). The determinants of environmental quality in the SAARC region: A spatial heterogeneous panel data approach. *Environmental Science and Pollution Research, 28*, 6422–6436. https://doi.org/10.1007/s11356-020-10896-9

Khattak, S. I., Ahmad, M., Khan, Z. U., & Khan, A. (2020). Exploring the impact of innovation, renewable energy consumption, and income on CO2 emissions: New evidence from the BRICS economies. *Environmental Science and Pollution Research, 27*, 13866–13881. https://doi.org/10.1007/s11356-020-07876-4

Kihombo, S., Ahmed, Z., Chen, S., Adebayo, T. S., & Kirikkaleli, D. (2021). Linking financial development, economic growth, and ecological footprint: What is the role of technological innovation?*Environmental Science and Pollution Research, 28*(43), 61235–61245.

Kilbourne, W. E., & Thyroff, A. (2020). STIRPAT for marketing: An introduction, expansion, and suggestions for future use.*Journal of Business Research, 108*, 351–361.

Li, H., Mu, H., Zhang, M., & Li, N. (2011). Analysis on influence factors of China's CO2 emissions based on path–STIRPAT model. *Energy Policy, 39*(11), 6906–6911. https://doi.org/10.1016/j.enpol.2011.08.056

Li, Y., Wang, Z., & Wei, Y. (2021). Pathways to progress sustainability: An accurate ecological footprint analysis and prediction for Shandong in China based on integration of STIRPAT model, PLS, and BPNN.*Environmental Science and Pollution Research, 28*(39), 54695–54718.

Liddle, B., & Lung, S. (2010). Age-structure, urbanization, and climate change in developed countries: Revisiting STIRPAT for disaggregated population and consumption-related environmental impacts. *Population and Environment, 31*, 317–343. https://doi.org/10.1007/s11111-010-0101-5

Lin, S., Zhao, D., & Marinova, D. (2009). Analysis of the environmental impact of China based on STIRPAT model. *Environmental Impact Assessment Review, 29*(6), 341–347. https://doi.org/10.1016/j.eiar.2009.01.009

Liu, F., & Liu, C. (2019). Regional disparity, spatial spillover effects of urbanisation and carbon emissions in China. *Journal of Cleaner Production, 241*, 118226. https://doi.org/10.1016/j.jclepro.2019.118226

Marquart-Pyatt, S. T. (2015). Environmental sustainability: The ecological footprint in West Africa. *Human Ecology Review, 22*(1), 73–92.

Marques, A. C., & Caetano, R. (2020). The impact of foreign direct investment on emission reduction targets: Evidence from high- and middle-income countries. *Structural Change and Economic Dynamics, 55*, 107–118. https://doi.org/10.1016/j.strueco.2020.08.005

Martínez-Zarzoso, I. (2009). *A general framework for estimating CO2 emissions*. IAI Discussion Papers, 180.

Molaei, M., & Basharat, E. (2015). Investigating relationship between gross domestic product and ecological footprint as an environmental degradation index.*Journal of economic research (tahghighat-e-eghtesadi), 50*(4), 1017–1033.

Narayan, P. K. (2004). Fiji's tourism demand: The ARDL approach to cointegration.*Tourism Economics, 10*(2), 193–206.

Narayan, P. K. (2005). The saving and investment nexus for China: Evidence from cointegration tests.*Applied Economics, 37*(17), 1979–1990.

Nathaniel, S. P., & Iheonu, C. O. (2019). Carbon dioxide abatement in Africa: The role of renewable and non-renewable energy consumption. *Science of the Total Environment, 679*, 337–345. https://doi.org/10.1016/j.scitotenv.2019.05.011

Nathaniel, S., & Khan, S. A. (2020). The nexus between urbanization, renewable energy, trade, and ecological footprint in ASEAN countries. *Journal of Cleaner Production, 272*, 122709. https://doi.org/10.1016/j.jclepro.2020.122709

Nathaniel, S. P. (2021). Economic complexity versus ecological footprint in the era of globalization: Evidence from ASEAN countries.*Environmental Science and Pollution Research, 28*(45), 64871–64881.

Owusu, P. A., & Asumadu-Sarkodie, S. (2016). A review of renewable energy sources, sustainability issues and climate change mitigation.*Cogent Engineering, 3*(1), 1167990.

Ozcan, B., Apergis, N., & Shahbaz, M. (2018). A revisit of the environmental Kuznets curve hypothesis for Turkey: New evidence from bootstrap rolling window causality. *Environmental Science and Pollution Research, 25*, 32381–32394. https://doi.org/10.1007/s11356-018-3165-x

Pao, H.-T., & Tsai, C.-M. (2011). Multivariate Granger causality between CO2 emissions, energy consumption, FDI (foreign direct investment) and GDP (gross domestic product): Evidence from a panel of BRIC (Brazil, Russian Federation, India, and China) countries. *Energy, 36*(1), 685–693. https://doi.org/10.1016/j.energy.2010.09.041

Pata, U. K. (2018). Renewable energy consumption, urbanization, financial development, income and CO2 emissions in Turkey: Testing EKC hypothesis with structural breaks. *Journal of Cleaner Production, 187*, 770–779. https://doi.org/10.1016/j.jclepro.2018.03.236

Pesaran, M. H., Shin, Y., & Smith, R. J. (2001). Bounds testing approaches to the analysis of level relationships.*Journal of Applied Econometrics, 16*(3), 289–326.

Phillips, P. C., & Perron, P. (1988). Testing for a unit root in time series regression.*Biometrika, 75* (2), 335–346.

Rehman, A., Radulescu, M., Ma, H., Dagar, V., Hussain, I., & Khan, M. K. (2021). The impact of globalization, energy use, and trade on ecological footprint in Pakistan: Does environmental sustainability exist?*Energies, 14*(17), 5234.

Saidi, K., & Hammami, S. (2015). The impact of CO2 emissions and economic growth on energy consumption in 58 countries. *Energy Reports, 1*, 62–70. https://doi.org/10.1016/j.egyr.2015.01.003

Sanglimsuwan, K. (2012). The impact of population pressure on carbon dioxide emissions: Evidence from a panel-econometric analysis. *International Research Journal of Finance and Economics, 82*, 89–94.

Shahbaz, M., Loganathan, N., Muzaffar, A. T., Ahmed, K., & Jabran, M. A. (2016). How urbanization affects CO2 emissions in Malaysia? The application of STIRPAT model. *Renewable and Sustainable Energy Reviews, 57*, 83–93. https://doi.org/10.1016/j.rser.2015.12.096

Shi, A. (2003). The impact of population pressure on global carbon dioxide emissions, 1975–1996: Evidence from pooled cross-country data. *Ecological Economics, 44*(1), 29–42. https://doi.org/10.1016/S0921-8009(02)00223-9

Shuai, C., Shen, L., Jiao, L., Wu, Y., & Tan, Y. (2017). Identifying key impact factors on carbon emission: Evidences from panel and time-series data of 125 countries from 1990 to 2011. *Applied Energy, 187*, 310–325. https://doi.org/10.1016/j.apenergy.2016.11.029

Shuai, C., Chen, X., Wu, Y., Tan, Y., Zhang, Y., & Shen, L. (2018). Identifying the key impact factors of carbon emission in China: Results from a largely expanded pool of potential impact factors. *Journal of Cleaner Production, 175*, 612–623. https://doi.org/10.1016/j.jclepro.2017.12.097

Sinha, A., Sengupta, T., & Alvarado, R. (2020). Interplay between technological innovation and environmental quality: Formulating the SDG policies for next 11 economies. *Journal of Cleaner Production, 242*, 118549. https://doi.org/10.1016/j.jclepro.2019.118549

Soulé, P. T., & DeHart, J. L. (1998). Assessing IPAT using production- and consumption-based measures of I. *Social Science Quarterly*, 754–765. Retrieved from https://www.jstor.org/stable/42863845

Sun, J., Li, G., & Wang, Z. (2018). Optimizing China's energy consumption structure under energy and carbon constraints. *Structural Change and Economic Dynamics, 47*, 57–72. https://doi.org/10.1016/j.strueco.2018.07.007

Szigeti, C., Toth, G., & Szabo, D. R. (2017). Decoupling–shifts in ecological footprint intensity of nations in the last decade.*Ecological Indicators, 72*, 111–117.

Teixidó-Figueras, J., & Duro, J. A. (2015). International ecological footprint inequality: A methodological review and some results.*Environmental and Resource Economics, 60*(4), 607–631.

Toda, H. Y., & Yamamoto, T. (1995). Statistical inference in vector autoregressions with possibly integrated processes.*Journal of Econometrics, 66*(1–2), 225–250.

Uddin, G. A., Alam, K., & Gow, G. (2016). Estimating the major contributors to environmental impacts in Australia.*International Journal of Ecological Economics and Statistics, 37*(1), 1–14.

Usman, M., & Hammar, N. (2021). Dynamic relationship between technological innovations, financial development, renewable energy, and ecological footprint: Fresh insights based on the STIRPAT model for Asia Pacific Economic Cooperation countries. *Environmental Science and Pollution Research, 28*, 15519–15536. https://doi.org/10.1007/s11356-020-11640-z

Usman, M., & Makhdum, M. S. (2021). What abates ecological footprint in BRICS-T region? Exploring the influence of renewable energy, non-renewable energy, agriculture, forest area and financial development. *Renewable Energy, 179*, 12–28. https://doi.org/10.1016/j.renene.2021.07.014

Usman, M., Anwar, S., Yaseen, M. R., Makhdum, M. S., Kousar, R., & Jahanger, A. (2021). Unveiling the dynamic relationship between agriculture value addition, energy utilization, tourism and environmental degradation in South Asia. *Journal of Public Affairs*, 1–15. https://doi.org/10.1002/pa.2712

Wang, J., & Dong, K. (2019). What drives environmental degradation? Evidence from 14 Sub-Saharan African countries. *Science of the Total Environment, 656*, 165–173. https://doi.org/10.1016/j.scitotenv.2018.11.354

Wang, M., Liu, J., Wang, J., & Zhao, G. (2010). Ecological footprint and major driving forces in West Jilin Province, Northeast China.*Chinese Geographical Science, 20*, 434–441.

Wang, P., & Wang, X. (2011). Spatiotemporal change of ecological footprint and sustainability analysis for Yangtze Delta region.*Journal of Geographical Sciences, 21*, 859–868.

Wang, Z., Yin, F., Zhang, Y., & Zhang, X. (2012). An empirical research on the influencing factors of regional CO2 emissions: Evidence from Beijing city, China. *Applied Energy, 100*, 277–284. https://doi.org/10.1016/j.apenergy.2012.05.038

Wang, S., Fang, C., & Wang, Y. (2016a). Spatiotemporal variations of energy-related CO2 emissions in China and its influencing factors: An empirical analysis based on provincial panel data. *Renewable and Sustainable Energy Reviews, 55*, 505–515. https://doi.org/10.1016/j.rser.2015.10.140

Wang, H., Yang, Y., Keller, A. A., Li, X., Feng, S., Dong, Y.-N., & Li, F. (2016b). Comparative analysis of energy intensity and carbon emissions in wastewater treatment in USA, Germany, China and South Africa. *Applied Energy, 184*, 873–881. https://doi.org/10.1016/j.apenergy.2016.07.061

Wen, L., & Li, Z. (2019). Driving forces of national and regional CO2 emissions in China combined IPAT-E and PLS-SEM model. *Science of the Total Environment, 690*, 237–247. https://doi.org/10.1016/j.scitotenv.2019.06.370

World Economic Forum. (2018). *Accelerating sustainable energy innovation.* White Paper. Retrieved from https://www3.weforum.org/docs/Accelerating_sustainable_energy_innovation_2018.pdf

World Population Review. (2021). Retrieved from Ecological Footprint By Country 2021. https://worldpopulationreview.com/country-rankings/ecological-footprint-by-country

Wu, D. (2020). Spatially and temporally varying relationships between ecological footprint and influencing factors in China's provinces using geographically weighted regression (GWR). *Journal of Cleaner Production, 261*, 121089.

Wu, R., Wang, J., Wang, S., & Feng, K. (2021). The drivers of declining CO2 emissions trends in developed nations using an extended STIRPAT model: A historical and prospective analysis. *Renewable and Sustainable Energy Reviews, 149*, 111328. https://doi.org/10.1016/j.rser.2021.111328

Xiong, C., Chen, S., & Huang, R. (2019). Extended STIRPAT model-based driving factor analysis of energy-related CO2 emissions in Kazakhstan. *Environmental Science and Pollution Research, 26*, 15920–15930. https://doi.org/10.1007/s11356-019-04951-3

Yang, B., Usman, M., & jahanger, A. (2021). Do industrialization, economic growth and globalization processes influence the ecological footprint and healthcare expenditures? Fresh insights based on the STIRPAT model for countries with the highest healthcare expenditures. *Sustainable Production and Consumption, 28*, 893–910. https://doi.org/10.1016/j.spc.2021.07.020

Yao, X., Kou, D., Shao, S., Li, X., Wang, W., & Zhang, C. (2018). Can urbanization process and carbon emission abatement be harmonious? New evidence from China. *Environmental Impact Assessment Review, 71*, 70–83.

Yilanci, V., & Pata, U. K. (2020). Convergence of per capita ecological footprint among the ASEAN-5 countries: Evidence from a non-linear panel unit root test. *Ecological Indicators, 113*, 106178. https://doi.org/10.1016/j.ecolind.2020.106178

York, R., Rosa, E. A., & Dietz, T. (2003). STIRPAT, IPAT and ImPACT: Analytic tools for unpacking the driving forces of environmental impacts. *Ecological Economics, 46*(3), 351–365. https://doi.org/10.1016/S0921-8009(03)00188-5

Zhang, C., & Tan, Z. (2016). The relationships between population factors and China's carbon emissions: Does population aging matter? *Renewable and Sustainable Energy Reviews, 65*, 1018–1025. https://doi.org/10.1016/j.rser.2016.06.083

Zivot, E., & Andrews, D. W. K. (2002). Further evidence on the great crash, the oil-price shock, and the unit-root hypothesis.*Journal of Business & Economic Statistics, 20*(1), 25–44.

Zuo, Z., Guo, H., Cheng, J., & Li, S. (2020). Ecological security assessment of the G20 and its drivers: EF-path-STIRPAT modeling.*Natural Resources Research, 29*, 4161–4174.

Behavioral Black Swan Investment Strategy and Global Stock Market Contagion Dynamics

Asil Azimli and Amin Shakourloo

1 Introduction

This research is the continuation of Rhee and Wu (2020), Gilboa et al. (2020) and Goodell (2020) in terms of black swan investment (Bhatti et al., 2021) and Hannafey (2021) about the application of game theory in the stock market.

Many empirical studies have emphasized the importance of the financial market's role, especially the stock market, and the positive relationship between financial development and economic growth (Enisan, 2009; Wu et al., 2010; Jalil et al. 2011; Alhassan, 2016). The active participation of people in the stock market guarantees the capital market's sustainability and affects the country's economy (Cole & Shastry, 2009; Cocco et al., 2015). Today, the effort to improve stock analysis, where many companies are presented, has led to new solutions, which, along with the previous techniques, try to maximize investors' gains (Serletis & Rosenberg, 2009). Furthermore, financial crises emerge due to the acceptance of hidden and abundant risks and can have vast and widespread consequences (Taleb, 2008). Accordingly, this research tried to identify and turn existing black swan events into white swans in the game theory-based black swan investment strategy.

Investigating the behavior of stock returns is an important matter (Hassan et al., 2007). People are investing in the stock market to increase their wealth and consume more in the future, which requires having the correct information about the stock market and being able to predict its future direction. Therefore, investors need robust and reliable models to analyze stock prices (Enke & Thawornwong, 2005). According to Cornell and Paté (2019), it is not easy to predict events that significantly disrupt the movement of asset prices. Moreover, due to their restrictive

A. Azimli · A. Shakourloo (✉)
Cyprus International University, Department of Accounting and Finance, Nicosia, Cyprus
e-mail: ashakourloo@ciu.edu.tr

N. Ozatac et al. (eds.), *Sustainable Development in Banking and Finance*, Springer Proceedings in Business and Economics,
https://doi.org/10.1007/978-3-031-65533-3_10

assumptions, current models may not be able to fully capture such shocks in asset prices (Taleb, 2008). International capital markets have been experiencing sharp fluctuations, either positive or negative, on different trading days, which have caused irreparable losses to investors' wealth. Investors always seek to maximize the return on their investments in proportion to the risk they take. Appropriate investment strategies and methods should be selected to achieve this, and a relevant criterion to measure the risk taken must be used (Grinblatt & Titman, 1989).

Recently, global economies have been harmed by an undetectable adversary: the coronavirus (COVID-19) and the global financial markets have been disrupted abnormally. The coronavirus has caused enormous damage to international capital markets. Several researchers believe that such a sickness phenomenon can have sustainable negative consequences for economic activities (e.g., Fogli & Veldkamp, 2021; Goodell, 2020). Despite the wealth of existing literature on this subject, there is an essential gap concerning the impact of COVID-19 on investing patterns. This study examines whether the black swan investing strategy is profitable during such times. Previous crises, such as the global financial crisis of 2007–2008 and the technology bubble in 2002, have introduced new perspectives on active portfolio management. One of them is the "black swan theory." According to Nicholas Taleb, intense and influential events in market trends that can cause high positive or negative returns in the index are called the "black swan events"; these are events that deviate significantly from what is usually expected for a given situation. In financial markets, black swan events also refer to the risk of end-distribution of probability. According to Taleb, since predicting and avoiding black swan events is not easy, investors must benefit from them. As a result, the author introduced a black swan investment strategy (Taleb, 2008).

One way to realize abnormal returns is to identify price patterns during market inefficiencies (Fama, 1970; French, 1980; Shiller, 1981). In this regard, when a market experiences severe fluctuation or the so-called black swan event, it would be possible to achieve abnormal returns by timing the market (Taleb, 2007). In the first level, this research has examined the historical incidence of black swan events in global financial markets and the impact of these events on investment performance. Moreover, providing a rigorous framework for modeling and analyzing the behavior of different market participants through game theory promotes risk management in the extreme market black swan events incidence.

Before Europeans discovered Australia, there was no evidence that the swans could be any color other than white. However, with the discovery, black swans were seen for the first time, and human beliefs were revised. The idea of Nicholas Taleb, the author of the black swan theory, is to encourage people to think about the unknown and its power. He believes that the application of many methods and models of investment and decision-making, in itself, has exacerbated the financial crisis and misled investors in their financial decisions. Taleb (2008) identifies three main characteristics of the black swan events: (i). The data of these events are the outlier; for example, in the capital market return's data distribution curve, a black swan event is placed at tails, (ii) such events have severe effects; for example, they can cause a sharp fall or rise in the capital market index on a trading day, and (iii) although significant event data are black and have very little predictability, by using past black events, criteria can be defined to identify them (e.g., Burnie & De Ridder, 2010; Estrada & Vargas, 2012).

In the context of a black swan strategy, it is assumed that markets are inefficient or that the index returns distribution is not normal. In other words, the efficiency distribution is in the form of a "Fat tail." As a result, the data moves away from the normal form. The black swan strategy emphasizes that if the distribution of returns is mistakenly considered normal, investors will be less likely to consider their actual risk. As a result, they will be exposed to unexpected and severe losses (Taleb, 2008). The black swan investing strategy calls for investing in shares with the highest price changes amid an adverse black swan event and investing in shares with the lowest price change amid a positive black swan event (Jonas & Jakob, 2017). In other words, stocks selected in adverse events have experienced the maximum price decline because it is assumed that such stocks are priced below their fundamental value due to the overreaction of loss-averse investors (Jonas & Jakob, 2017). On the other hand, stocks considered positive in any black swan event have had the lowest price increase, which is assumed that investors underreact to these stocks as an initial reaction to a positive black swan event (Estrada & Vargas, 2012).

The primary purpose of this study is to form an investment strategy based on the black swan approach of Taleb (2008) in international stock markets from 2006 to 2021. Thus, the effectiveness of the black swan investing strategy is examined for periods that cover critical fluctuations, such as the global financial crisis, European credit crunch, oil market crashes, and pandemics. Then, formed portfolios are optimized based on superiority over the market index and risk-free returns. The black swan, investment model optimization, is used based on the game theory. It does not consider the balance between risk and return but the best response of the actor to the market conditions examined. Consequently, this paper provides a new portfolio optimization method during black swan events. Finally, the contagion effect of different players' interaction with various proportions in stock markets during the application of the black swan strategy was analyzed through scenarios and the Monte Carlo simulation method. Through different scenarios, this research shed light on the dynamics of different stock market investors' behavior and the contagion effect during stock market black swan events and corresponding strategies.

There are several notable results from the empirical analysis. First, in terms of investment time horizon, the portfolio analysis according to a six-month investment horizon shows that the black swan investment strategy had superior returns in developing financial markets, including Argentina (44.27), Brazil (22.41), China (3.95), India (22.29), Russia (24.59), and Turkey (14.02). However, in developed countries, stock markets include Australia, France, Germany, Italy, Japan, South Korea, the United States, and the United Kingdom. The black swan investment strategy's excessive return is accompanied by a higher degree of risk in the same investing time horizon. Moreover, the black swan investing strategy on a one-year horizon generates a higher average return in both developing and developed countries' stock markets. Second, the black swan events have lower persistence in developing stock markets. Consequently, unexpected positive black swan event occurrences have lower costs and can generate a higher return in developing markets during short-time investing horizons. Finally, based on the findings of this research, the application of the cooperative game theory to promote black swan strategy performance has led to outperforming this strategy over market index strategy performance in most periods except one month. Finally, the research found that developing stock markets experienced more contagion effects during the black swan events than developed markets, especially during negative events on a short time horizon.

Investors in the capital market always seek maximum returns and avoid accepting huge losses from their investments in proportion to the risk they have accepted (Baker & Haslem, 1974). To achieve these goals, one should choose the appropriate investment strategy and method according to the prevailing market conditions and use accurate and precise criteria to measure risk. So this study aims to form an optimal index portfolio based on the black swan investment strategy. In this way, the capability of this investment method to obtain returns is examined. Our paper contributes to the existing literature by offering a new way of managing investment portfolios. Thus, current results are essential for investors. Investors can benefit from the results of this paper for their portfolio optimization decisions during turbulent times.

The remainder of the paper is organized as follows. Section 2 is the literature review, Section 3 explains the methods, Section 4 reports and discusses the results of the empirical analysis and Sect. 5 concludes the paper.

2 Literature Review

The intertwined financial system and new channels of shock transmission have emerged due to mutual communication and institutions (Krygier, 2014). Today, whatever is experienced in one market affects other markets (Arago & Fernandez, 2007). Much evidence shows fluctuations across the price of financial assets, spread to other assets, and financial markets in times of crisis move much closer together because of the conditional correlation between assets over the financial crisis period (Ang, 2006). Financial crises have been a common phenomenon during the economic life of countries. However, properly dealing with the crisis and reducing its negative consequences have been critical concerns for countries in crisis (Darrat & Benkato, 2003).

In this context, systemic risk is defined as the probability of the collapse of the entire market system against the crash of each part or component. This is evident in the directional movements among most or all of the parts (Kaufman & Scott, 2003). To analyze the impact of an event on other parts of the system, dynamic changes that take place over a distinct period must be monitored in the relationship between various asset markets (Szpunar & Glogowski, 2012).

Estrada (2009) examined the effect of black swan events on the Dow Jones Industrial Average from 1900 to 2006 and 1990 to 2006 through the Jarqua-Berra test and the kurtosis and skewness criteria. The study's findings imply that trading days with black swan events are widely seen in the market index, and these events significantly impact returns. Estrada and Vargas (2012) examined the possibility of market dominance using a black swan strategy and the performance of the beta benchmark during black swan events. The most critical assumption in this research was that the selected stocks have the property of returning to the average. Finally, Estrada and Vargas (2012) concluded that a higher return over the benchmark could be achieved based on a black swan investment strategy. The beta criterion was good for predicting risk in market conditions during high volatility. Brunaker and Nordqvist (2013) examined the strategy of investing in ten selected stocks out of 30 traded stocks in the Swedish stock market to assess the effect of black swans and unpredictable events on the value of the selected portfolio. The researcher selected stocks with an average return property and a high liquidity rating to form a portfolio. The results showed that this strategy can overcome the market and achieve excess efficiency. Nihlén & Malm (2014) examined the acquisition of excess returns through a black swan investment strategy in the international market of the Indian Stock Exchange. They considered black swan events as positive and negative daily fluctuations of 2%, 5%, and 6%, and the study period was considered from 2014 to 2020. They formed an investment portfolio based on a black swan strategy and the beta criterion. The researchers concluded that the return was 558% higher than the market index over the period under review and the result not previously seen in previous research.

This paper applies game theory to analyze the complex dynamics of the stock market in the occurrence of black swan events. By modeling the behavior of different agents and examining their incentives and strategies, game theory can provide insights into the functioning of the market. Portfolio optimization based on game theory is an exciting and rapidly evolving research area that has the potential to generate new insights into the behavior of financial markets. (Li & Zhao, 2015, Zhang et al., 2018, Chen & Wang, 2019). In recent years, there has been a growing interest in using game theory to model and predict the behavior of investors and other market participants; Eisenbach and Schmalz (2016) review the use of game theory in modeling the behavior of agents in the stock market. Their paper discusses the limitations of traditional models and the potential benefits of game theory in capturing more realistic investor behavior. Nofsinger & Sias (1999) apply game theory to the study of behavioral finance, which is concerned with the psychological factors influencing investor decision-making between rational and irrational investors. Bertrand & Mullainathan (2000) applies game theory to the analysis of insider trading, which is the practice of buying or selling stock based on non-public information. The authors model the incentives of insiders and outsiders in a game-theoretic framework and analyze the impact of insider trading on market efficiency. Game theory can be used to analyze the impact of market structure on collusion in the stock market (Philipp et al., 2015). In this way, Philipp et al., (2015) modeled the behavior of traders in different market structures and examined the conditions under which collusion is more likely to occur.

In this research, we apply the Monte Carlo method to estimate the different scenarios. The Monte Carlo simulation method was used by Xiong et al. (2023) to estimate the continuation values of America. It is established that the suggested method is more accurate and effective than conventional Monte Carlo techniques. The use of parallel computing to speed up the least-squares Monte Carlo method is also covered in the paper. The potential of distributed least-squares Monte Carlo methods for option pricing and risk management is generally highlighted in this paper. Thach (2023), exemplifies the benefit of the Bayesian approach in addressing the issue of economic growth during the COVID-19 pandemic. To determine the probability distribution of the model parameters, Monte Carlo simulations are used in the case study of ASEAN economic growth. The findings demonstrate that, compared to conventional approaches, the Bayesian approach can provide more precise estimates of the model parameters and better economic growth predictions.

In the first phase, the current study aims to form the optimal index portfolio based on the black swan investment strategy in countries with different economic development conditions, especially when international stock markets have experienced unstable behavior in their index. Thus, the efficiency of this investment method is investigated. In this way, instead of looking at different investment scenarios and forecasts, discussed how unstable the return of the investment portfolio is through evaluating the risk and return of the black swan's investment strategy to determine if the black swan's unexpected events investment risk proportionate with the return earned by investors?

In this paper, before examining the central hypothesis, two preliminary conditions are considered that are necessary for the black swan investment strategy application (Taleb, 2008; Taleb, 2011; Narayan & Smyth, 2017; Brubaker & Nordqvist, 2013). First, the return distribution of the stock exchanges' index is not normal, and second, there is a lack of information efficiency in the stock exchanges. After the normality and market efficiency tests, it can be concluded that there have been black swan events in the stock exchange markets. So the research's normality test and stock market efficiency test methods are explained with the method of determining the black swan fluctuation degree for each stock market in the research method section and, in the following research data analysis, the black swan investment strategy evaluation takes place to examine the efficiency of this method in the international stock markets. The game theory is applied to promote the black swan strategy in the next step. The model has been optimized based on superiority over the market index and risk-free returns. However, optimization is used in the investment model based on the game theory and superiority over the market index performance and risk-free returns. The mentioned optimization is not about the balance between risk and return; it seeks to examine the best response of the individual actor to the market conditions.

3 Research Method

In the first stage of the empirical analysis, this research examines whether the black swan strategy provides commensurate gains from January 2006 to December 2021. For this purpose, the markets' index portfolio that was formed based on the positive black swan event is sold, and after the adverse black swan event, the portfolio is purchased. Finally, the portfolio's performance is calculated. As a result, a black swan method of managing and covering the risk of investment portfolio performance can be examined by investors and capital market activists. Furthermore, through this method, it is possible to identify the right investing time horizons to enter and exit the international stock market in developed and developing countries.

The two preliminary research hypotheses are related to proving and identifying a black swan event in the international stock exchanges from developed and developing countries and examining the return-to-average feature in the indices. First, a preliminary hypothesis, namely the presence of black swans in the international capital markets during the pandemic and economic shocks, is examined. In the presence of black swan events, the assumption of a normalized return of the market index returns is disrupted, and the return distribution of the sequence index widens. Thus, the Jaque-Bera test is used in the first step to determine the abnormality and prove the existence of sharp events in the international stock exchanges. The formula of the Jaque-Bera test takes the following form:

$$n = \left[\frac{\text{skewness}^2}{6} + \frac{\text{kurtosis} - 3^2}{24} \right] \tag{1}$$

In addition to the lack of normality in market return distribution, the inefficiency of the market at a weak level also confirms the existence of black swan events in the market, So the black swan investment method is a solution to avoid portfolio vulnerability (Narayan & Smyth, 2017; Brubaker & Nordqvist, 2013). Moreover, based on Taleb (2011), when there are continuous black swan events in the financial markets, the capital market index does not have a normal return distribution, the market loses its efficiency, and the prices lose the random walk feature. So, for the black swan investment strategy, it is necessary to examine the efficiency of the stock market and the normality in the return distribution of the market index.

It should be noted that if hypothesis 2 is confirmed, the market inefficiency at a weak level will also be proven. To examine Hypothesis 2, based on the article by Brunaker and Nordqvist (2013), the total index of international stock exchanges is tested for the property of returning to the average. The Dickey–Fuller, unit Root test will be used to examine the return on average stock price:

$$y_t = \alpha y_{t-1} + \in_t \tag{2}$$

In the black swan investment strategy, fluctuations are less frequent and are not normal market index behavior. When markets experience high fluctuations and unstable behavior in their index, they are suitable for determining the level of black swan events (Estrada & Javier, 2009). Although the stock market's historical highest fluctuation levels selection for evaluating the black swan investment strategy performance is more suitable in terms of the research's validity and is closer to this study's goal. To maintain the reliability of the results, it is necessary to find an appropriate level of deviation from the mean, which could identify a black swan event. For this purpose, to determine positive and negative deviations as black swan events, this study follows Estrada and Vargas's (2012) research method, which takes place over 47 countries through index funds and exchange-traded funds (ETFs) Estrada and Vargas (2012) used ±5% level to identify a black swan event. However, this may not be appropriate for international stock markets. We examine each market index used in the sample to identify an appropriate level and use different fluctuation levels according to each market average return volatility level.

So, this issue is examined for each market separately at this research level. Finally, the fluctuation level has been adjusted with a risk-free rate of return for each country.

We start with the calculation of index returns for each market over the 2006–2021 period as follows:

$$R_M = \mathrm{Ln}\left(\frac{P_t}{P_{t-29}}\right) \tag{3}$$

Then, we proceed to determine an appropriate threshold level of volatility to identify the black swan event. As shown in Table 3, different levels of index return are reported, and the fluctuations in the categories of 1 to 3.9%, 4% to 7.9%, 8% to 11.9%, 12% to 15.9%, and 16% to 19.9% are classified. According to the frequency distributions for each return fluctuation group, the 4% to 7.9% class in which black swan events are expected to occur is determined, and this research used a minimum of 4 percent and a maximum of 7.9% fluctuation to determine the exact level of black swan event. It was found that the 1 to 3.9 percent level indicates the expected behavior of the markets, given that this range hosts the highest frequency of occurrences. Moreover, other high fluctuation levels, such as 8.9 to 11%, 12 to 15.9%, and 16 to 19.9%, are inappropriate due to a negligible number of observations.

In the later stage, we assume that when a market fluctuates below 4%, the minimum rate of expected return is the risk-free rate of return. Thus, the return obtained by the black swan investment strategy should be adjusted to each country's risk-free rate of return and the average market return reported in Table 1. As a result, the minimum and maximum fluctuation range that leads to the nearest black swan event is considered for each country as a black swan fluctuation range.

Since consecutive positive and negative changes in a similar fluctuation range tend to neutralize each other, usually, if sharp negative or positive events occur several times in a row in the stock market, the portfolio composition will not change. At the end of the portfolio formation process, the formed portfolio is sold in each black swan event after the next intense negative or positive event. Then the

Table 1 Countries' stock market black swan fluctuation range determination

N	Country	Countries' risk-free rate of return	Countries' average market return	1–3.9% frequency	4–7.9% frequency	8–11.9% frequency	12–15.9% frequency	16–19.9% frequency	BS scenario return	BS fluctuation range
1	Argentina	49.25	35.65	4097	42	30	4	2	118.86	−7, 7
2	Australia	3.2	3.6	4125	48	2	0	0	9.52	−4, 4
3	Brazil	12.31	10.17	4116	37	17	5	0	43.71	−6, 5
4	China	2.7	15.11	4130	38	7	0	0	20.13	−6, 5
5	France	1.4	7.7	4125	38	11	1	0	11.7	−5, 5
6	Germany	0.8	4.9	4131	38	5	1	0	8.7	−5, 5
7	India	7.3	13.92	4109	57	6	2	1	23.62	−4, 5
8	Italy	3.04	0.22	4119	47	9	0	0	5.46	−5, 5
9	Japan	0.16	2.41	4108	55	12	0	0	5.07	−5, 4
10	Russia	9.04	10.41	4076	51	29	12	7	22.87	−7, 6
11	South Korea	3.17	7.91	4120	50	5	0	0	13.28	−4, 4
12	Turkey	16.28	14.73	4125	40	9	1	0	33.76	−6, 5
13	UK	1.9	7.5	4126	42	7	0	0	12.42	−4, 4
14	US	2.7	10	4115	53	6	1	0	15.2	−4, 4

performance of the black swan portfolio relative to the market portfolio is calculated. Risk and return metrics are generally used to calculate portfolio performance and compare it to market index returns (Estrada & Vargas, 2012). The geometric average calculates the average monthly return, strategy portfolio, and market index return.

$$\mathrm{GM} = \left[\prod_{i=1}^{n} (1+r)_i\right]^{1/n - 1} \tag{4}$$

The criterion for measuring portfolio risk is standard deviation and is calculated as follows.

$$\mathrm{SD} = \sqrt{\frac{\sum_{i=1}^{N} (x_i - \overline{x})^2}{N}} \tag{5}$$

Because out-of-range data and abnormal returns are likely, the efficiency distribution is expected to be wide-ranged and skewed. The deviation criterion calculates the adjusted return criterion for the strategy and market portfolio to estimate the exchange of risk and return for conditions where the distribution of returns is not normal.

$$\mathrm{RAR} = \frac{\mathrm{GM}}{\mathrm{SD}} \tag{6}$$

Finally, the following benchmarks are calculated between the strategy and market portfolios. Performance evaluation criteria include average annual return, average monthly return, the total return over the period, minimum and maximum returns over the period, standard deviation, and risk-adjusted returns. Criteria for assessing the normality of the efficiency distribution are skewness and kurtosis.

4 Data Analysis

The main objective of this study is to investigate the profitability of the black swan investment strategy in international equity markets. For this purpose, we test two main hypotheses as a precondition for using the black swan strategy in international stock indices. First, the international stock markets' return index distribution form is abnormal. Second, international stock markets are inefficient regarding information (the second condition and the second sub-hypothesis are considered the same). If these two Hypothesizes are confirmed, it can be concluded that there has been a sharp fluctuation in the international stock markets. As a result, its recurrence is possible in the future.

The occurrence of black swan events in the capital market causes a change in the distribution of the conditional return distribution; in other words, the chart of the distribution of returns takes the form of a "broad, abnormal sequence." The black swan strategy emphasizes that if the distribution of returns is considered normal in the wrong way, investors will be less likely to take measures of the risks of the investment appropriately. Thus they will be exposed to unexpected losses (Taleb, 2008).

Determining whether the collected sample belongs to an average statistical population is done by various tests. Most of these methods are known as the "Normality Tests." This research tests the normality of the indices through the "Jarque-Bera Test." "Jarque-Bera Test" measures compliance with the normal distribution based on the Skewness and Kurtosis symmetry indices.

$$\mathrm{JB} = n\left\{\frac{(S)^2}{6} + \frac{(K-3)^2}{24}\right\} \tag{7}$$

where S is the Skewness coefficient, K is the Kurtosis coefficient and n is the freedom degree. Table 2, shows the normality test result through international stock indices' return distributions and descriptive statistics.

According to the results in Table 2, the null hypothesis can be rejected, indicating that the return distributions are not normal for international stock market indices. Furthermore, all of the indices' return distributions are right-skewed.

The second hypothesis is related to mean reversion in different international indices; Moreover, this sub-hypothesis determines the inefficiency in the international stock markets and is examined through a unit root test based on Dicky Fuller's augmented unit root test (Table 3).

According to the results obtained from the unit root test, the existence of the unit root is rejected, and the mean reversion hypothesis is confirmed. Thus. All of the international indices returns have mean reversion characteristics and can be used to form a black swan investment strategy portfolio. The study determines the black swan events date with the associated fluctuation degree in the next step for each country's stock market index. Tables 4, 5, and 6 present the days considered for a positive and negative black swan event from 2006 to 2021.

Table 4 Shows the positive and negative black swan event occurrence dates between 2007 to 2020 for countries: Argentina, Brazil, Eurozone, France, and Germany, with corresponding positive and negative volatility degrees for each country's stock market. The volatility rate shows the times that form a portfolio to gain profit or sell shares to prevent losses during the occurrence of positive and negative shocks on the market to obtain a higher average return than the market returns according to the black swan investment strategy. As seen in Table 4. The first day of portfolio formation and the number of black swan events differ for each country's market. According to Table 4, some black swan occurrences have been repeated in a row. So several positions lead to the purchase and sale of the portfolio, based on the solid black strategy.

Table 5 shows the positive and negative black swan event occurrence dates between 2007 and 2020 for India, Japan, Russia, South Korea, and Turkey, with

Table 2 International stock indices' return distribution and descriptive statistics

N	Countries	Mean	Median	Max	Min	Std. dev.	Skewness	Kurtosis	J-B	Prob
1	Argentina	−0.0010	−0.0014	0.4769	−0.1043	0.0230	2.6195	52.0723	405923.9	0.0000
2	Australia	0.0000	−0.0005	0.1020	−0.0676	0.0110	0.6888	10.5786	10321.66	0.0000
3	Brazil	−0.0002	−0.0007	0.1599	−0.1367	0.0175	0.4304	12.2745	14571.91	0.0000
4	China	−0.0002	−0.0007	0.0925	−0.0903	0.0157	0.6466	7.8263	4125.74	0.0000
5	France	−0.0007	0.0004	0.1059	−0.1309	0.0140	−0.2689	8.1316	11518.63	0.0000
6	Germany	−0.0002	−0.0008	0.1305	−0.1079	0.0137	0.2092	11.1006	11355.18	0.0000
7	India	−0.0004	−0.0006	0.1410	−0.0859	0.0110	1.0305	18.9904	29936.73	0.0000
8	Italy	0.0001	−0.0007	0.1557	−0.1087	0.0155	0.5719	10.8329	10809.57	0.0000
9	Japan	−0.0001	−0.0005	0.1211	−0.1323	0.0148	0.4320	10.5550	9688.20	0.0000
10	Russia	−0.0002	−0.0005	0.4046	−0.2522	0.0201	2.0250	62.3942	601902.4	0.0000
11	South Korea	−0.0001	−0.0005	0.1117	−0.1128	0.0124	0.5081	12.2398	14516.59	0.0000
12	Turkey	−0.0004	−0.0010	0.1106	−0.1212	0.0163	0.4981	7.5222	3663.14	0.0000
13	UK	0.0000	−0.0002	0.1151	−0.0938	0.0116	0.3946	12.9958	17669.87	0.0000
14	US	−0.0002	−0.0005	0.1384	−0.1076	0.0120	0.4938	19.0907	44462.67	0.0000

Table 3 Dicky–Fuller augmented test results for 15 international stock indices

N	Indices	Test statistic	Critical values 1%	5%	10%	Prob
1	Argentina	−63.1185	−3.4325	−2.8620	−2.5672	0.0001
2	Australia	−69.9050	−3.4325	−2.8620	−2.5672	0.0001
3	Brazil	−67.4531	−3.4325	−2.8620	−2.5672	0.0001
4	China	−61.7217	−3.4325	−2.8620	−2.5672	0.0001
5	France	−66.6217	−3.4325	−2.8620	−2.5672	0.0001
6	Germany	−64.5688	−3.4325	−2.8620	−2.5672	0.0001
7	India	−52.1620	−3.4317	−2.8620	−2.5670	0.0001
8	Italy	−64.4491	−3.4317	−2.8620	−2.5670	0.0001
9	Japan	−65.7116	−3.4317	−2.8620	−2.5670	0.0001
10	Russia	−66.0904	−3.4317	−2.8620	−2.5670	0.0001
11	South Korea	−64.4491	−3.4317	−2.8620	−2.5670	0.0001
12	Turkey	−62.9177	−3.4317	−2.8620	−2.5670	0.0001
13	UK	−67.4448	−3.4317	−2.8620	−2.5670	0.0001
14	US	−73.5039	−3.4317	−2.8620	−2.5670	0.0001

corresponding positive and negative fluctuation degrees for each country's stock market. The volatility rate shows the times that form a portfolio to gain profit or sell shares to prevent losses during the occurrence of positive and negative shocks on the market to obtain a higher average return than the market returns according to the black swan investment strategy. As seen in Table 5. The first day of portfolio formation and the number of black swan events differ for each country's market. According to Table 5, some black swan occurrences have been repeated in a row. So several positions lead to the portfolio's purchase and sale, based on each country's strong black strategy.

Table 6 Shows the positive and negative black swan event occurrence dates between 2007 and 2020 for countries: United Kingdom, United States, Italy, China, and Australia, with corresponding positive and negative fluctuation degrees for each country's stock market. The volatility rate shows the times that form a portfolio to gain profit or sell shares to prevent losses during the occurrence of positive and negative shocks on the market to obtain a higher average return than the market returns according to the black swan investment strategy. As seen in Table 6. The first day of portfolio formation and the number of black swan events differ for each country's market. According to Table 6, some black swan occurrences have been repeated in a row. So several positions lead to the portfolio's purchase and sale, based on each country's strong black strategy.

Finally, the black swan central hypothesis has been tested for different time horizons, and the results are presented in Table 7. To evaluate the performance of the black swan strategy, index portfolios were formed after each black swan event and held until the next.

The results of the means comparison test in 10% confidence level between two investment strategies' return results in Table 8 show the significance of the mean

Table 4 The days of the occurrence of a positive and negative black swan event

	Argentina				Brazil				France				Germany			
N	Date	%	Date	%	Date	%	Date	%	Date	%	Date	%	Date	%	Date	%
1	27-Feb-07	−0.07	19-Sep-08	10.2	27-Feb-07	−6.6	24-Jan-08	5.9	21-Jan-08	−6.83	24-Jan-08	6.01	21-Jan-08	−6.83	24-Jan-08	6.01
2	29-Sep-08	−0.08	14-Oct-08	11	21-Jan-08	−6.6	30-Apr-08	6.3	29-Sep-08	−5.04	19-Sep-08	9.27	29-Sep-08	−5.04	19-Sep-08	9.27
3	15-Oct-08	−0.12	24-Nov-08	8.8	15-Sep-08	−7.5	18-Sep-08	5.4	6-Oct-08	−9.04	13-Oct-08	11.18	6-Oct-08	−9.04	13-Oct-08	11.18
4	21-Oct-08	−0.10	10-May-10	7.1	17-Sep-08	−6.7	19-Sep-08	9.5	8-Oct-08	−6.31	29-Oct-08	9.23	8-Oct-08	−6.31	29-Oct-08	9.23
5	22-Oct-08	−0.10	23-Jun-14	8.6	29-Sep-08	−9.3	30-Sep-08	7.6	10-Oct-08	−7.73	24-Nov-08	10.09	10-Oct-08	−7.73	24-Nov-08	10.09
6	24-Oct-08	−0.07	3-Jul-18	7.0	2-Oct-08	−7.3	13-Oct-08	14.6	15-Oct-08	−6.82	8-Dec-08	8.68	15-Oct-08	−6.82	8-Dec-08	8.68
7	2-Mar-09	−0.07	31-Aug-18	9.4	15-Oct-08	−11.3	20-Oct-08	8.3	16-Oct-08	−5.92	10-Mar-09	5.73	16-Oct-08	−5.92	10-Mar-09	5.73
8	8-Aug-11	−0.10	12-Oct-18	7.1	22-Oct-08	−10.1	28-Oct-08	13.4	22-Oct-08	−5.10	2-Apr-09	5.37	22-Oct-08	−5.10	2-Apr-09	5.37
9	16-Jun-14	−0.10	9-Aug-19	7.9	24-Oct-08	−6.9	30-Oct-08	7.4	6-Nov-08	−6.38	10-May-10	9.66	6-Nov-08	−6.38	10-May-10	9.66
10	31-Jul-14	−0.08	13-Aug-19	10.2	27-Oct-08	−6.5	4-Nov-08	5.2	1-Dec-08	−5.59	27-Sep-11	5.74	1-Dec-08	−5.59	27-Sep-11	5.74
11	1-Oct-14	−0.08	5-Sep-19	9.1	5-Nov-08	−6.1	24-Nov-08	9.4	5-Dec-08	−5.48	27-Oct-11	6.28	5-Dec-08	−5.48	27-Oct-11	6.28
12	2-Oct-14	−0.07	10-Mar-20	8	12-Nov-08	−7.7	8-Dec-08	8.3	10-Aug-11	−5.45	28-Nov-11	5.46	10-Aug-11	−5.45	28-Nov-11	5.46
13	9-Dec-14	−0.07	25-Mar-20	10.2	21-Nov-08	−6.4	2-Jan-09	7.1	18-Aug-11	−5.48			18-Aug-11	−5.48	20-Mar-20	5.01
14	15-Dec-14	−0.08	28-Apr-20	10.2	8-Aug-11	−8	4-Mar-09	5.3	22-Sep-11	−5.25			22-Sep-11	−5.25	24-Mar-20	8.39
15	18-Jun-18	−0.08	8-Jun-20	8.3	18-May-17	−8.8	10-Mar-09	5.5	1-Nov-11	−5.38			1-Nov-11	−5.38	18-May-20	5.16
16	27-Jun-18	−0.08	19-Jun-20	7.7	26-Feb-20	−7	23-Mar-09	5.8	24-Aug-15	−5.35			24-Aug-15	−5.35		
17	12-Aug-19	−0.37	6-Jul-20	9	9-Mar-20	−12.1	4-May-09	6.5	24-Jun-16	−8.04			24-Jun-16	−8.04		
18	20-Aug-19	−0.10			11-Mar-20	−7.6	18-May-09	5	9-Mar-20	−8.39			9-Mar-20	−8.39		
19	3-Sep-19	−0.11			12-Mar-20	−14.7	29-Oct-09	5.9					12-Mar-20	−12.28		
20	9-Mar-20	−0.13			16-Mar-20	−13.9	9-Aug-11	5.1					16-Mar-20	−5.75		
21	12-Mar-20	−0.09			18-Mar-20	−10.3	21-Nov-14	5					18-Mar-20	−5.94		
22	16-Mar-20	−0.09					3-Mar-16	5.1								
23	18-Mar-20	−0.14					17-Mar-16	6.6								
24	11-Jun-20	−0.07					10-Mar-20	7.1								
25							13-Mar-20	13.9								
26							24-Mar-20	9.6								
27							25-Mar-20	7.5								
28																

Table 5 The days of the occurrence of a positive and negative black swan event

	India				Japan				Russia				South Korea				Turkey			
N	Date	%	Date	%	Date	%	Date	%	Date	%	Date	%	Date	%	Date	%	Date	%	Date	%
1	15-May-6	−4.03	9-Jun-06	5.21	17-Aug-07	−5.42	25-Jan-08	4.10	22-May-06	−9.65	23-May-06	10.68	27-Jul-07	−4.09	20-Aug-07	5.69	22-May-06	−8.31	26-May-06	5.07
2	18-May-6	−6.77	15-Jun-06	6.31	22-Jan-08	−5.65	14-Feb-08	4.27	8-Jun-06	−7.70	14-Jun-06	6.20	10-Aug-07	−4.20	26-Nov-07	4.65	16-Aug-07	−6.79	20-Jul-06	5.24
3	22-May-6	−5.1	23-Oct-07	5.59	8-Oct-08	−9.38	2-Apr-08	4.2	13-Jun-06	−9.18	12-Sep-08	6.03	16-Aug-07	−6.93	14-Feb-08	4.02	21-Jan-08	−6.40	23-Jul-07	5.08
4	8-Jun-06	−4.76	23-Jan-08	6.21	10-Oct-08	−9.62	14-Oct-08	14.15	9-Jan-07	−7.1	19-Sep-08	28.69	22-Jan-08	−4.43	8-Sep-08	5.15	17-Mar-08	−7.46	19-Sep-07	6.70
5	13-Jun-06	−4.09	25-Jan-08	6.95	16-Oct-08	−11.41	28-Oct-08	6.41	21-Jan-08	−7.47	9-Oct-08	9.80	1-Sep-08	−4.06	19-Sep-08	4.55	6-Oct-08	−8.62	24-Jan-08	5.81
6	5-Mar-07	−4.03	14-Feb-08	5.53	22-Oct-08	−6.79	29-Oct-08	7.74	9-Sep-08	−9.08	14-Oct-08	13.33	16-Sep-08	−6.10	14-Oct-08	6.14	10-Oct-08	−7.72	12-Feb-08	5.31
7	2-Apr-07	−4.92	25-Mar-08	5.81	24-Oct-08	−9.60	30-Oct-08	9.96	16-Sep-08	−17.45	29-Oct-08	13.84	6-Oct-08	−4.29	28-Oct-08	5.57	16-Oct-08	−6.26	30-Jul-08	5.59
8	1-Aug-07	−4	2-Jul-08	5.05	27-Oct-08	−6.36	4-Nov-08	6.27	6-Oct-08	−18.66	30-Oct-08	19.46	8-Oct-08	−5.81	30-Oct-08	11.95	17-Oct-08	−6.27	19-Sep-08	12.89
9	16-Aug-07	−4.38	23-Jul-08	5.58	31-Oct-08	−5.01	5-Nov-08	4.46	8-Oct-08	−14.35	24-Nov-08	17.01	10-Oct-08	−4.13	21-Nov-08	5.80	19-Nov-08	−6.67	14-Oct-08	5.43
10	17-Dec-07	−4.48	19-Sep-08	5.13	6-Nov-08	−6.53	10-Nov-08	5.81	15-Oct-08	−8.67	8-Dec-08	9.95	16-Oct-08	−9.44	26-Nov-08	4.72	8-Jan-09	−6.03	30-Oct-08	7.38
11	21-Jan-08	−8.7	13-Oct-08	6.43	13-Nov-08	−5.25	25-Nov-08	5.22	16-Oct-08	−9.11	26-Jan-09	10.83	22-Oct-08	−5.14	8-Dec-08	7.48	8-Aug-11	−7.08	24-Nov-08	9.88
12	11-Feb-08	−5.14	28-Oct-08	6.35	20-Nov-08	−6.89	8-Dec-08	5.20	24-Oct-08	−14.24	9-Feb-09	6.49	23-Oct-08	−7.48	15-Dec-08	4.93	3-Jun-13	−10.4	29-Apr-09	5.33
13	3-Mar-08	−5.18	31-Oct-08	6.99	2-Dec-08	−6.35	15-Dec-08	5.21	6-Nov-08	−9.62	13-Feb-09	6.07	24-Oct-08	−10.57	28-Jan-09	5.91	20-Jun-13	−6.82	10-May-10	7.14
14	17-Mar-08	−5.11	3-Nov-08	5.48	12-Dec-08	−5.56	27-Jan-09	4.93	11-Nov-08	−12.64	26-Feb-09	6.25	6-Nov-08	−7.56	9-Apr-09	4.30	18-Jul-16	−7.08	20-Sep-11	5.10
15	27-Jun-08	−4.15	10-Nov-08	5.89	14-Mar-11	−6.18	11-Mar-09	4.55	13-Nov-08	−7.62	10-Mar-09	8.90	20-Nov-08	−6.70	16-Aug-11	4.83	12-Mar-20	−7.26	19-Sep-13	6.44
16	15-Jul-08	−4.42	21-Nov-08	5.50	15-Mar-11	−10.04	13-Mar-09	5.15	1-Dec-08	−7.21	23-Mar-09	7.29	12-Dec-08	−4.38	27-Sep-11	5.02	16-Mar-20	−8.07	30-Dec-13	6.42

(continued)

Table 5 (continued)

	India				Japan				Russia				South Korea				Turkey			
N	Date	%	Date	%	Date	%	Date	%	Date	%	Date	%	Date	%	Date	%	Date	%	Date	%
17	6-Oct-08	−5.66	10-Dec-08	5.18	23-May-13	−7.32	2-Apr-09	4.40	17-Feb-09	−9.38	2-Apr-09	6.44	15-Jan-09	−6.03	20-Mar-20	7.44			2-Nov-15	5.40
18	7-Jan-09	−6.18	4-May-09	5.18	30-May-13	−5.15	7-May-09	4.55	3-Jun-09	−7.46	1-Jun-09	7.37	17-Feb-09	−4.11	24-Mar-20	8.60				
19	17-Aug-09	−4.2	18-May-09	17.74	13-Jun-13	−6.35	16-Mar-11	5.07	22-Jun-09	−7.80	24-Jun-09	7.37	2-Mar-09	−4.16	25-Mar-20	5.89				
20	22-Sep-11	−4.13	20-Sep-19	5.32	9-Feb-16	−5.40	22-Mar-11	4.36	22-Sep-11	−7.82	30-Jul-09	6.05	27-Nov-09	−4.69						
21	24-Aug-15	−5.94	13-Mar-20	4.04	24-Jun-16	−7.92	10-Jun-13	4.94	3-Mar-14	−10.79	19-Mar-20	7.72	19-Aug-11	−6.22						
22	9-Mar-20	−5.17	20-Mar-20	5.75	9-Nov-16	−5.36	31-Oct-14	4.83	9-Apr-18	−8.34	24-Mar-20	7.22	5-Sep-11	−4.39						
23	12-Mar-20	−8.18	25-Mar-20	6.98	25-Dec-18	−5.01	9-Sep-15	7.71	10-Mar-20	−8.11			23-Sep-11	−5.73						
24	16-Mar-20	−7.96	26-Mar-20	4.94	9-Mar-20	−5.07	22-Jan-16	5.88	12-Mar-20	−8.28			10-Nov-11	−4.94						
25	18-Mar-20	−5.59	7-Apr-20	8.97	13-Mar-20	−6.08	15-Feb-16	7.16					11-Oct-18	−4.44						
26	23-Mar-20	−13.15					10-Nov-16	6.72					9-Mar-20	−4.19						
27	30-Mar-20	−4.61					24-Mar-20	7.13					18-Mar-20	−4.86						
28							25-Mar-20	8.04					19-Mar-20	−8.39						
29							6-Apr-20	4.24					23-Mar-20	−5.34						
30													15-Jun-20	−4.76						

Table 6 The days of the occurrence of a positive and negative black swan event

	UK				US				Italy				China				Australia			
N	Date	%	Date	%	Date	%	Date	%	Date	%	Date	%	Date	%	Date	%	Date	%	Date	%
1	16-Aug-07	−4.10	24-Jan-08	4.75	15-Sep-08	−4.42	30-Sep-08	4.68	21-Jan-08	−5.17	19-Sep-08	8.62	27-Feb-07	−8.84	20-Aug-07	5.33	22-Jan-08	−7	20-Aug-07	4.61
2	21-Jan-08	−5.48	19-Sep-08	8.84	17-Sep-08	−4.06	13-Oct-08	11	6-Oct-08	−8.24	13-Oct-08	11.4	30-May-07	−6.50	4-Feb-08	8.13	30-Sep-08	−4.3	23-Jan-08	4.35
3	29-Sep-08	−5.30	13-Oct-08	8.26	29-Sep-08	−6.98	16-Oct-08	4.68	8-Oct-08	−5.68	29-Oct-08	9.87	4-Jun-07	−8.26	24-Apr-08	9.29	8-Oct-08	−4.9	25-Jan-08	5.02
4	6-Oct-08	−7.85	17-Oct-08	5.22	7-Oct-08	−5.11	20-Oct-08	4.67	10-Oct-08	−7.14	4-Nov-08	6.78	22-Jan-08	−7.22	18-Jun-08	5.24	16-Oct-08	−6.6	19-Sep-08	4.27
5	8-Oct-08	−5.18	20-Oct-08	5.41	9-Oct-08	−7.33	28-Oct-08	10.8	15-Oct-08	−5.33	24-Nov-08	7.37	28-Jan-08	−7.19	20-Aug-08	7.63	6-Nov-08	−4.3	1-Oct-08	4.22
6	10-Oct-08	−8.85	29-Oct-08	8.05	15-Oct-08	−7.87	13-Nov-08	6.67	16-Oct-08	−6.78	8-Dec-08	7.49	10-Jun-08	−7.73	19-Sep-08	9.45	13-Nov-08	−5.8	13-Oct-08	5.55
7	15-Oct-08	−7.16	4-Nov-08	4.42	22-Oct-08	−5.69	21-Nov-08	6.54	24-Oct-08	−5.61	10-Mar-09	6.99	19-Jun-08	−6.54	22-Sep-08	7.77	15-Jan-09	−4.2	30-Oct-08	4.04
8	16-Oct-08	−5.35	24-Nov-08	9.84	5-Nov-08	−5.05	24-Nov-08	4.93	6-Nov-08	−5.06	23-Mar-09	5.77	27-Oct-08	−6.32	10-Nov-08	7.27	3-Jul-09	−4	25-Nov-08	5.79
9	22-Oct-08	−4.46	8-Dec-08	6.19	6-Nov-08	−4.85	16-Dec-08	4.20	11-Nov-08	−6.20	10-May-10	11.2	18-Nov-08	−6.31	19-Nov-08	6.05	26-Oct-10	−5.7	8-Dec-08	4.06
10	24-Oct-08	−5.00	10-Mar-09	4.88	12-Nov-08	−4.73	10-Mar-09	5.80	1-Dec-08	−6.25	27-Oct-11	5.49	31-Aug-09	−6.74	4-Mar-09	6.12	8-Aug-11	−4	10-Mar-09	6.32
11	6-Nov-08	−5.70	31-Mar-09	4.34	19-Nov-08	−5.07	23-Mar-09	6.84	20-Feb-09	−5.88	29-Jun-12	6.59	19-Jan-15	−7.70	30-Jun-15	5.53	14-Jun-13	−7.6	19-Mar-09	5.91
12	19-Nov-08	−4.82	2-Apr-09	4.28	20-Nov-08	−5.56	30-Nov-11	4.24	2-Mar-09	−6.02	26-Jul-12	5.62	28-May-15	−6.50	9-Jul-15	5.76	22-Jul-19	−4.7	26-May-09	4.03
13	1-Dec-08	−5.19	10-May-10	5.16	1-Dec-08	−7.70	26-Dec-18	4.98	5-Mar-09	−5.85	3-Aug-12	6.34	19-Jun-15	−6.42	27-Aug-15	5.34	12-Mar-20	−4.7	21-Jul-09	4.96
14	14-Jan-09	−4.97	27-Sep-11	4.02	20-Jan-09	−4.01	2-Mar-20	5.09	30-Mar-09	−6.57	25-Aug-15	5.86	26-Jun-15	−7.40	25-Feb-19	5.60	16-Mar-20	−8.7	11-Sep-09	4.89

(continued)

Table 6 (continued)

	UK				US				Italy				China				Australia			
N	Date	%	Date	%	Date	%	Date	%	Date	%	Date	%	Date	%	Date	%	Date	%	Date	%
15	2-Mar-09	−5.33	24-Mar-20	9.05	10-Feb-09	−4.62	4-Mar-20	4.53	14-May-10	−5.26	10-Feb-16	5.03	27-Jul-15	−8.48			18-Mar-20	−4.7	16-Sep-09	4.58
16	5-Aug-11	−6.01	25-Mar-20	4.45	2-Mar-09	−4.24	10-Mar-20	4.89	4-Aug-11	−5.16	13-Mar-20	7.12	18-Aug-15	−6.15			7-Apr-20	−5.9	25-Oct-10	15.30
17	18-Aug-11	−4.49			5-Mar-09	−4.09	13-Mar-20	9.36	10-Aug-11	−6.65	24-Mar-20	8.93	24-Aug-15	−8.49			4-Sep-20	−5	13-Mar-20	5.67
18	22-Sep-11	−4.67			4-Aug-11	−4.31	17-Mar-20	5.20	18-Aug-11	−6.15			25-Aug-15	−7.63					17-Mar-20	12.62
19	24-Aug-15	−4.67			8-Aug-11	−5.55	24-Mar-20	11.3	1-Nov-11	−6.80			4-Jan-16	−6.86					30-Mar-20	6.85
20	9-Mar-20	−7.69			10-Aug-11	−4.62	26-Mar-20	6.38	29-Jun-15	−5.17			7-Jan-16	−7.04					1-Apr-20	4.42
21	12-Mar-20	−10.8			5-Feb-18	−4.60			24-Aug-15	−5.96			26-Jan-16	−6.42					6-Apr-20	6.06
22	16-Mar-20	−4.01			8-Feb-18	−4.15			11-Feb-16	−5.63			25-Feb-16	−6.41					16-Jun-20	4.19
23	18-Mar-20	−4.05			27-Feb-20	−4.42			24-Jun-16	−12.4										
24	27-Mar-20	−5.25			9-Mar-20	−7.79			24-Feb-20	−5.4										
25					11-Mar-20	−5.86			9-Mar-20	−11.1										
26					12-Mar-20	−9.99			12-Mar-20	−16.9										
27					16-Mar-20	−12.9			16-Mar-20	−6.10										
28					18-Mar-20	−6.30														
29					20-Mar-20	−4.55														
30					27-Mar-20	−4.06														

Table 7 Black swan investment strategy comparative performance results

N	Country	Strategy	Mean	Std. dev	Average S. E.	Sharpe ratio
One month						
1	Argentina	Black swan strategy	5.20	2.99	0.65	5.3
		Market index strategy	2.53	4.65	1.62	3.4
2	Australia	Black swan strategy	4.86	5.48	1.22	0.77
		Market index strategy	3.42	7.73	2.26	0.54
3	Brazil	Black swan strategy	22.4	19.16	4.18	0.37
		Market index strategy	12.31	14.59	2.43	0.49
4	China	Black swan strategy	2.05	1.36	0.31	3.6
		Market index strategy	0.53	0.72	2.07	6.8
5	France	Black swan strategy	2.03	4.41	1.14	1.07
		Market index strategy	4.84	4.12	2.04	1.14
6	Germany	Black swan strategy	4.65	14.34	3.38	0.29
		Market index strategy	5.34	3.27	0.86	1.29
7	India	Black swan strategy	6.53	4.58	0.88	1.4
		Market index strategy	3.76	5.38	2.78	1.19
8	Italy	Black swan strategy	1.71	3.44	2.22	1.86
		Market index strategy	4.54	3.21	2.04	2
9	Japan	Black swan strategy	2.89	4.23	0.81	1.51
		Market index strategy	1.70	1.16	0.03	4.25
10	Russia	Black swan strategy	7.16	4.6	0.95	1.39
		Market index strategy	2.63	5.31	2.94	1.2
11	South Korea	Black swan strategy	3.30	6.09	1.21	0.77
		Market index strategy	4.23	3.41	1.04	1.38
12	Turkey	Black swan strategy	4.13	3.24	0.78	2.98
		Market index strategy	3.47	4.12	3.05	2.34
13	UK	Black swan strategy	5.37	8.55	1.86	0.56
		Market index strategy	3.74	2.86	0.01	1.69
14	US	Black swan strategy	4.26	5.19	1.03	0.81
		Market index strategy	3.86	2.71	0.09	0.52
Six month						
1	Argentina	Black swan strategy	44.27	30.21	6.93	0.53
		Market index strategy	25.53	31.46	7.64	0.51
2	Australia	Black swan strategy	10.78	15.93	3.75	0.26
		Market index strategy	6.34	5.94	0.01	0.71
3	Brazil	Black swan strategy	22.41	19.12	4.17	0.37
		Market index strategy	12.83	15.48	3.32	0.46
4	China	Black swan strategy	3.95	1.71	0.42	2.88
		Market index strategy	2.23	3.27	7.83	1.51
5	France	Black swan strategy	5.43	7.19	1.99	0.65
		Market index strategy	3.63	2.82	1.36	1.67
6	Germany	Black swan strategy	15.76	16.05	4.14	0.26
		Market index strategy	8.71	8.34	0.72	0.5
7	India	Black swan strategy	22.29	17.27	3.52	0.37
		Market index strategy	13.29	15.46	1.34	0.41

(continued)

Table 7 (continued)

N	Country	Strategy	Mean	Std. dev	Average S. E.	Sharpe ratio
8	Italy	Black swan strategy	4.98	6.06	1.43	1.05
		Market index strategy	4.26	3.17	2.04	2.02
9	Japan	Black swan strategy	14.55	16.31	3.33	0.30
		Market index strategy	5.32	3.12	1.8	1.58
10	Russia	Black swan strategy	24.59	19.85	4.43	0.32
		Market index strategy	14.63	14.21	1.31	0.45
11	South Korea	Black swan strategy	11.43	12.76	2.78	0.37
		Market index strategy	6.37	5.86	3.36	0.8
12	Turkey	Black swan strategy	14.02	9.24	2.47	1.04
		Market index strategy	6.34	8.53	1.76	1.13
13	UK	Black swan strategy	16.5	26.18	6.54	0.18
		Market index strategy	8.32	5.19	4.42	0.93
14	US	Black swan strategy	18.02	27.5	6	0.15
		Market index strategy	5.87	3.54	3.18	1.19
One year						
1	Argentina	Black swan strategy	49.26	32.86	8.21	0.49
		Market index strategy	23.08	41.64	6.42	0.38
2	Australia	Black swan strategy	9.35	6.6	1.7	0.64
		Market index strategy	8.37	7.32	3.06	0.57
3	Brazil	Black swan strategy	55.25	36.48	8.6	0.19
		Market index strategy	21.26	17.31	4.37	0.41
4	China	Black swan strategy	5.03	2.51	0.69	1.96
		Market index strategy	8	7	4.56	0.7
5	France	Black swan strategy	18.61	14.55	4.6	0.32
		Market index strategy	7.45	6.52	2.57	0.72
6	Germany	Black swan strategy	28.13	23.52	6.79	0.81
		Market index strategy	12.64	5.3	5.41	0.76
7	India	Black swan strategy	22.43	17.57	4.03	0.36
		Market index strategy	19.12	6.92	6.43	0.92
8	Italy	Black swan strategy	15.21	12.21	3.38	6.42
		Market index strategy	6.3	2.8	4.87	2.29
9	Japan	Black swan strategy	16.65	12.06	2.63	0.40
		Market index strategy	10	7.63	6.76	0.64
10	Russia	Black swan strategy	4.13	2.75	5.28	2.33
		Market index strategy	11.63	9.64	5.83	0.66
11	South Korea	Black swan strategy	24.97	15.06	4.03	0.31
		Market index strategy	7.32	5.47	3.78	0.86
12	Turkey	Black swan strategy	21.13	18.28	4.88	0.52
		Market index strategy	13.84	9.03	3.61	1.07
13	UK	Black swan strategy	22.28	25.02	7.54	0.19
		Market index strategy	12.09	5.6	6.17	0.86
14	US	Black swan strategy	27.31	23	5.93	0.18
		Market index strategy	10	6.8	4.47	0.62

Table 8 Investment strategies' comparison of the mean test result

N	Country	Mean	Std. dev	Std. err. of mean	t-test	p-value
One month						
1	Argentina	28.27487	50.41834	0.568006	−54.21687	0.0000
2	Australia	2.236597	12.24896	0.137334	−14.61820	0.1083
3	Brazil	7.282400	21.11012	0.241011	−29.06703	0.0000
4	China	7.564088	42.21505	0.485616	−15.22155	0.0000
5	France	2.129346	14.86823	0.166796	−11.27821	0.2327
6	Germany	5.829198	16.46791	0.185455	−30.42042	0.1727
7	India	9.940009	22.10737	0.252101	−40.03679	0.0000
8	Italy	0.160923	12.20769	0.135316	−0.819671	0.4124
9	Japan	−0.479487	30.19888	0.342242	1.5990	0.1098
10	Russia	1.187072	9.820637	0.109199	−3.634984	0.0003
11	South Korea	0.975617	7.568482	0.084687	−5.185940	0.0000
12	Turkey	2.188244	10.93630	0.121350	−9.765639	0.0000
13	UK	0.471092	6.266855	0.068800	−3.109673	0.1943
14	US	1.550018	6.509648	0.072240	−11.39815	0.0000
Six month						
1	Argentina	35.77376	50.75198	0.58572	−37.08843	0.0000
2	Australia	3.957504	16.17849	0.18408	−1.875819	0.0607
3	Brazil	9.440063	23.56626	0.270823	−17.49603	0.0000
4	China	10.32649	45.92388	0.531881	−8.889427	0.0000
5	France	2.934962	17.00452	0.192010	−5.793726	0.0942
6	Germany	7.591593	18.24704	0.206846	−18.26387	0.0826
7	India	13.08230	24.11390	0.276861	−23.41966	0.0000
8	Italy	0.287098	16.10003	0.179634	0.077271	0.9384
9	Japan	0.884703	31.73771	0.362439	−5.368239	0.0000
10	Russia	3.323718	15.65623	0.175140	10.08850	0.0000
11	South Korea	2.358382	11.83078	0.133225	7.155635	0.0000
12	Turkey	11.25928	28.21356	0.320195	26.80623	0.0000
13	UK	0.960870	8.784317	0.097036	2.850273	0.0000
14	US	3.313641	9.402499	0.105012	9.072070	0.0000
One year						
1	Argentina	45.86144	53.87435	0.626997	−16.87133	0.0000
2	Australia	3.020204	14.17009	0.159912	−7.830682	0.0362
3	Brazil	12.19398	26.57688	0.307953	−6.554003	0.0000
4	China	14.21046	54.74843	0.639426	−1.501154	0.0000
5	France	3.813749	19.40731	0.220966	−1.193517	0.0000
6	Germany	9.821488	20.33541	0.232454	−6.759321	0.0248
7	India	16.69031	26.28953	0.304378	−9.303441	0.0000
8	Italy	0.247495	19.34279	0.217555	−0.120269	0.0000
9	Japan	2.315877	34.11369	0.392839	−8.840643	0.0000
10	Russia	5.867112	21.61026	0.243706	18.42032	0.0000
11	South Korea	4.253279	15.88819	0.180338	16.39891	0.0000
12	Turkey	8.356322	23.41460	0.263568	19.83408	0.0000
13	UK	1.522005	11.24338	0.125182	6.847716	0.0000
14	US	5.510141	12.61778	0.142042	23.36752	0.0000

difference in all countries' stock markets over the one year, so the null test hypothesis was rejected for all countries and, return distributions not equal between strategies over the one-year. The t-test result also showed that the difference between the two strategies is insignificant for developed countries in the six-month investment. Therefore, the difference in the efficiency of these two investment strategies is not acceptable for developed countries over the monthly period. Moreover, except for Australia's and European countries' stock markets, the t-test result shows a significant difference between the two strategies in the international stock markets over the six months.

In the second stage, this research, by incorporating Game Theory and preparing for black swan events, aims to help investors make decisions under conditions of uncertainty and extreme risk. In this essay, we will delve deeper into the principles of Game Theory and slack swan events through practical applications of these theories. In this context, this study uses game theory to model the behavior of investors and predict their reactions to different market conditions. By analyzing the behavior of other investors in response to unexpected events. For this purpose, this study divides the global stock market actors into four groups of players:

First, the primary player is the market indicator and has the power to shape the market trend, and other market players try to defeat it by coalition with each other. Second Risk-free player: A risk-free actor does not intend to accept investment risk. Therefore, this investor only invests in risk-free securities with a fixed rate of return and two types of risky actors. Both risky actors are interested in moving in the black swan events. Aggressive players, when the market had a solid adverse black event (a sharp drop in the market index), invested intending to gain profit, and conservative players, when the market was in a positive black swan condition (a sharp increase in the index), in a risky portfolio down, they invested in reducing possible future losses. Through this classification, this study analysis can include the different behaviors of investor groups concerning positive and negative black swan events. Moreover, it is assumed that the primary player will have two strategies to play after black swan events occur in the market: first, use an upward strategy, so the market will have an upward trend, or use a downward strategy, in which case the market will experience downward trend.

Actors will participate in a coalition if the utility and income from the coalition are more significant than what would have been obtained individually. The utility of each actor will be calculated using the probability of forming a coalition and the expected income. Finally, each actor's overall weight and strategy will be calculated based on the model used in the research (Kocak, 2014).

The utility of each actor will be calculated using three criteria: If the efficiency of the player's strategy is more than the efficiency of the primary player (market), 1 unit of positive utility will belong to players. Otherwise, they will get 1 unit of negative utility. Second, if the actor's strategy returns ahead of the return of risk-free bonds, 1 unit of positive utility will belong to them. Otherwise, they will get 1 unit of negative utility. Finally, If the Sharpe ratio of the player's strategy is more than the Sharpe ratio of the primary player or the market, 1 unit of positive utility will belong to them. Otherwise, they will get 1 unit of negative utility. The total utility is the sum of the utility points of the above three criteria. The utility calculation relationship will be as an equation;

$$\text{utility} = \begin{cases} \forall r_i > r_m : U_1 = 1, \forall r_i < r_m : U_1 = -1 \\ \forall r_i > r_f : U_2 = 1, \forall r_i < r_f : U_2 = -1 \\ \forall \text{AR}_i > \text{AR}_m : U_3 = 1, \forall \text{AR}_i < \text{AR}_m : U_3 = -1 \\ U_i = U_1 + U_2 + U_3 + 3 \end{cases} \quad (8)$$

The utility of a hypothetical coalition, S, is the sum of the utility of actors participating in the coalition:

$$U_s = \sum_{i \in S} U_i \quad (9)$$

U_s as the utility of each coalition, the primary entry of the payoff matrix will be entered into Eq. (10) to calculate the optimal solution in the respective coalition.

$$\text{pay off} = \begin{bmatrix} a_{1,1} & a_{1,2} & a_{1,n} \\ a_{2,1} & a_{2,2} & a_{2,n} \\ a_{m,1} & a_{m,2} & a_{m,n} \end{bmatrix}$$

$$\text{Min } u; st : \sum_{j=1}^{m} q_j = 1, q_j \geq 0 \forall j \quad (10)$$

By calculating the optimal solution, using Eq. (11), the value of each of the coalitions obtained, the coalition that will create the most value will be the basis for the portfolio optimization model.

$$\text{Max } (v - u)$$

St:

$$u \leq \sum_{j=1}^{m} a_{1,j} q_{1,j} \forall i$$

$$v \leq \sum_{i=1}^{n} a_{i,1} p_{i,1} \forall j$$

$$\sum_{i=1}^{n} p_i = 1, \sum_{j=1}^{m} q_j = 1$$

$$p_i \geq 0 \forall i \; q_j \geq 0 \forall j \quad (11)$$

According to the synergistic in Eq. (12) the participation of all actors in the coalition leads to the highest game value and $v(s)$ utility.

$$v(s) = \sum_{i=1}^{n} \sum_{j=1}^{m} p_i q_j a_{ij}$$

$$v(S_1, S_2) > v(S_2) + v(S_1)\ \forall S_1 \subset N, \forall S_1 \subset N, S_1 \cap S_2 = \varnothing \tag{12}$$

In the next step, the surplus value of each defined player will be calculated using the Shapley value method (Shapley, 1953) through Eq. (13) to determine the fair distribution of a total payoff among the players in a game. As mentioned, the Shapley value of player i shows the entry of player i into each of the coalitions, how much it leads to an increase in the utility on average while taking into account the probability of its entry into coalitions,

$$\varphi(v) = \sum_{i \in s} \frac{(n - |s|)!(|s| - 1)!}{n!} [v(S) - v(S \backslash \{i\})]\ i \in S \tag{13}$$

This index somehow shows the bargaining value of each actor to enter coalitions. The final result of these calculations is the Shapley vector:

$$\varphi_{sv} = (\varphi_1, \varphi_2, \varphi_3, \varphi_4)$$

To calculate the optimal portfolio, first, the utility of each player's investment strategies was calculated, and the Shapley value was determined based on the participation value of each actor in coalitions. After forming the optimal portfolio using the participation of different market players in the coalition against the significant player, the performance of the proposed strategy should be compared with the performance of the total index. If the strategy's performance is superior, it is possible to prove the assumptions of the research that the proposed strategy can promote the black swan investment strategy using game theory.

The black swan investment model optimization in this research is based on the game theory and does not consider the balance between risk and return; instead, the best response of the actor to the market conditions examined. So, the difference in the performance of the two portfolios is calculated using the Sharpe index analysis. For this purpose, the significance of the difference in Sharpe ratio criteria is proven by Jobson and Korkie (1981). Based on this statistic, the null hypothesis is that the Sharpe ratio is equal or smaller in the traditional and classic portfolio optimization methods and the H_1 is the better performance of the introduced research strategy.

$$\begin{cases} H_0\text{:SR}_1 - \text{SR}_2 = 0 \\ H_1\text{:SR}_1 - \text{SR}_2 \neq 0 \end{cases}$$

Table 9 evaluates the performance of two investment strategies based on actual risk through the Sharpe ratio with Jobson Korkie's significance level. Except for the one-month investment period for China, Germany, Japan, Russia, and the United Kingdom, the suggested coalition strategy has presented a better performance than the research's general black swan strategy in six months and one year from the perspective of the Sharpe criterion. Moreover, the Jobson & Korkie test statistics, except for France and South Korea in the mid-term, show significance levels and H_0 rejected for the rest.

Our next crucial step involves the use of sophisticated simulation techniques after laying the groundwork for our research, including the integration of the black swan investment strategy within a game theory framework for 14 international stock markets. By doing this, we hope to offer data-driven insights into how well the black swan strategy works to reduce contagion risks, thereby assisting investors and policymakers in navigating the complexities of the global financial market.

In the final level of research, we use the different scenarios that play out over various time horizons to investigate international stock market contagion through players' proportion and their interaction in the context of the black swan investment strategy. By dividing the research's 14 global stock markets into "developing" and "developed" markets in this part, we try to conduct a comparative analysis across a wide range of markets by reducing the complexity involved in studying individual markets separately in different scenarios. Second, this division enables us to investigate how player interactions and contagion effects differ within various risk environments in each scenario. The generalizability of the research findings, which makes it applicable to a wider audience, including policymakers and financial institutions, is also improved by this approach, which aligns with accepted financial practices.

The research simulation takes place in three different time horizons, in one month after black swan events occur as short term, which causes quick changes in investor sentiment. These quick decisions frequently occur during emotional highs, making the market erratic and unpredictable. And, in six months when markets and investors gradually stabilize as we move into the mid-term after a crisis or period of volatility, this phase is a crucial time for reflection and adjustment. Finally, one year as long-term scenarios depict persistent market conditions over a considerable amount of time. This scheduling helps us consider players' development strategies that align with the current financial landscape and make informed decisions.

According to this information, we deviate the three scenarios for developed and developing stock markets:

In the context of developed markets over various time frames, First, players respond quickly in the short-term scenario, characterized by an unexpected black swan event, frequently due to fear, rapid market declines, increased volatility, and general uncertainty. While risk-averse investors seek safety in less risky assets, major players engage in panic selling. In this scenario, risk-taking investors who are aggressive actively search for assets that are vastly undervalued, while conservative risky players who take a more cautious approach limit their exposure to volatile assets to manage risk. Second, Mid-term scenario: Following the initial crisis, developed markets go through a period of consolidation and stabilization. Market conditions gradually improve during this period, and investor confidence gradually returns. Selectively reentering the market, major players do so while making wise investment choices. To seek modest returns, risk-averse investors start switching to moderately riskier assets. Aggressive, risky investors find appealing long-term opportunities and gradually build up their assets in this situation, while conservative, risky investors maintain a conservative approach and carefully control

Table 9 Performance of investment strategies based on the Sharpe ratio & Jobson & Korkie test

N	Market	Black swan strategy	Behavioral black swan strategy	Sig
One month				
1	Argentina	5.3	6.2	0.0000
2	Australia	0.54	0.96	0.0000
3	Brazil	0.49	1.23	0.0000
4	China	6.8	4.8	0.0000
5	France	1.14	2.36	0.0300
6	Germany	1.29	1.10	0.0000
7	India	1.19	2.13	0.0000
8	Italy	2	2.72	0.0200
9	Japan	4.25	2.18	0.0000
10	Russia	1.2	3.24	0.0000
11	South Korea	1.38	2.46	0.0000
12	Turkey	2.34	3.78	0.0400
13	UK	1.69	1.37	0.0000
14	US	0.52	1.64	0.0000
Six month				
1	Argentina	0.51	2.3	0.0000
2	Australia	0.71	1.5	0.0300
3	Brazil	0.46	1.8	0.0000
4	China	1.51	3.4	0.0100
5	France	1.67	1.9	0.0700
6	Germany	0.5	1.17	0.0000
7	India	0.41	2.1	0.0000
8	Italy	2.02	2.43	0.0000
9	Japan	1.58	2.21	0.0000
10	Russia	0.45	1.72	0.0000
11	South Korea	0.8	1.47	0.0600
12	Turkey	1.13	2.42	0.0000
13	UK	0.93	1.24	0.0400
14	US	1.19	1.73	0.0000
One year				
1	Argentina	0.38	1.86	0.0000
2	Australia	0.57	2.03	0.0000
3	Brazil	0.41	2.12	0.0000
4	China	0.7	3.17	0.0000
5	France	0.72	1.36	0.0000
6	Germany	0.76	1.93	0.0000
7	India	0.92	3.37	0.0000
8	Italy	2.29	4.73	0.0000
9	Japan	0.64	1.48	0.0000
10	Russia	0.66	3.27	0.0000
11	South Korea	0.86	2.73	0.0000
12	Turkey	1.07	2.34	0.0000
13	UK	0.86	1.47	0.0000
14	US	0.62	1.82	0.0000

their risk exposure. Finally, the markets transition into a long-term scenario marked by consistent economic growth and market optimism, in which risky investors, both aggressive and conservative, actively look for opportunities to take advantage of the market's ongoing optimism.

In the context of developing markets over various time frames, several dynamic scenarios play out. The market is volatile in the short term, frequently brought on by localized political unrest or outside shocks. Players proceed cautiously through this stage, with major players keeping an eye on political developments and evaluating risks. Aggressive, risky investors engage in speculative trading to profit from short-term market fluctuations, while risk-averse investors look for safety in non-volatile assets. Contrarily, conservative risky investors take a more cautious stance and limit their exposure to volatile assets. Moving to the mid-term horizon, the developing stock market enters a phase of steady growth, propelled by infrastructure investments and economic reforms. Consistent market index value growth and decreased volatility define this phase. Major players grow more upbeat and continue to make long-term investments, while risk-averse players gradually start to cautiously investigate moderately riskier assets in search of higher returns. Risk-taking investors who are aggressive pursue sustainable growth strategies while gradually raising their level of risk tolerance. Conservative risky investors keep diversified portfolios and take advantage of growth opportunities while being prudent. Long-term growth in the developing market is characterized by steady and strong increases in index value. Increased investor confidence prompts major players to make sizable long-term strategic investments.

The proportions of different player types are estimated in this study using Monte Carlo simulation in a variety of market contexts, time scales, and positive or negative black swan events scenarios. By defining key parameters, modeling various scenarios in the three mentioned time horizons, and incorporating probability distributions to account for inherent uncertainty, we establish a strong framework. Furthermore, Monte Carlo simulation was applied to estimate the interactive effects of changing proportions of investor types in diverse market contexts and time frames in each scenario, with a specific focus on their influence on contagion dynamics between international stock markets. This approach integrates complex parameters encompassing player behavior, market conditions, and interdependencies, incorporating probability distributions to address inherent uncertainties. Through multiple simulation iterations, we evaluate the potential contagion effects under varying conditions, revealing how shifts in player proportions and market scenarios impact the degree and direction of contagion. Our findings offer critical insights into the interconnectedness of international stock markets. Setting the stage for the subsequent estimation table results provides a comprehensive analysis of contagion effects across diverse scenarios.

As can be seen in Table 10, each scenario's duration is specified by the time horizon; the estimated proportions of the various player types are essential elements in these scenarios. In Table 10. Player 1 stands for Major player, Player 2 represents risk-free players, player 3 shows the Aggressive risky player, and Player 4 stands for conservative risky player. Finally, the last column of Table 10 shows the contagion effect of interaction between different proportions of the players for each scenario.

Table 10 Different players' proportion & interactions contagion estimation result

Time horizons	Scenario	Player 1	Player 2	Player 3	Player 4	Contagion effect
Developing stock markets						
Short-term (one month)	Positive black swan	0.30	0.25	0.20	0.25	0.45
	Negative black swan	0.20	0.40	0.10	0.30	0.75
Midterm (six months)	Positive black swan	0.25	0.35	0.20	0.20	0.55
	Negative black swan	0.25	0.35	0.10	0.30	0.70
Long-term (one year)	Positive black swan	0.35	0.20	0.25	0.20	0.40
	Negative black swan	0.25	0.35	0.10	0.30	0.65
Developed stock markets						
Short-term (one month)	Positive black swan	0.35	0.20	0.30	0.15	0.35
	Negative black swan	0.25	0.35	0.15	0.25	0.60
Midterm (six months)	Positive black swan	0.35	0.25	0.25	0.15	0.30
	Negative black swan	0.30	0.30	0.15	0.25	0.55
Long-term (one year)	Positive black swan	0.40	0.15	0.30	0.15	0.25
	Negative black swan	0.20	0.40	0.10	0.30	0.50

"Risk-Free Players" depict the percentage of risk-averse participants seeking security, while "Major Players" depict the share of the most influential investors in the market. "Aggressive Risky Players" are people who are willing to take big risks in exchange for potential rewards, and "Conservative Risky Players" are people who take more calculated risks. Collectively, these ratios shed light on the dynamics of investor behavior over a range of market environments and timescales.

In this research, we are tracking cross-market correlations to simulate contagion effects. Higher cross-market correlations suggest greater contagion, which means that when one market moves, others often follow suit. We'll rate the strength of cross-market correlations on a scale from 0 to 1in Table 10:

0: There is no contagion; markets operate independently.
1: Full contagion (perfect convergence of market movements).

According to Table 10, there is the highest cross-market correlation of 0.75 during a "Short-Term" in a "Developing" market, indicating strong contagion effects where most markets move together during the black swan event. This research finding is supported by studies by Liu H et al. (2020). The cross-market correlation is lowest, at 0.25, during "Long-Term positive black swan" in a "Developed" market, indicating less contagion and more independent market movements. Compared to developed markets, "developing" markets typically have considerably more cross-market correlations, which could indicate higher contagion in these markets during positive and negative black swan events.

5 Conclusion

This research seeks to apply and develop a black swan investment strategy based on insights from game theory and investigate the contagion effect based on different scenarios to capture the dynamics of different stock market players during black swan events. Accordingly, game theory is used to model the behavior of individual investors in black swan events situations, where the outcome of an investor's decision depends on the decisions made by other investors. Accordingly, this research assumes zero-sum games to develop investment strategies that are based on exploiting market inefficiencies and that can generate abnormal returns. In this term, the research results align with those of Bhattli et al. (2021).

The research results demonstrate that the proposed behavioral model outperforms the traditional black swan investment strategy regarding risk management and profitability. Moreover, the zero-sum game theory approach can capture market competition dynamics. By modeling the interaction between market participants as a zero-sum game, the proposed model can identify optimal investment strategies that consider the actions of other investors in the market, and the inclusion of game theory allows for a more realistic modeling of market dynamics and investor behavior (Kliger, 2014) in the times of black swan events occurrence.

Overall, the article provides evidence for the effectiveness of a zero-sum game theory approach to promoting the black swan investment strategy and shows that the model can generate efficient portfolio allocations under various market conditions and different risk preferences in the six-month and one-year periods. The proposed model failed to outperform the general black swan strategy in the main developed and two developing stock markets out of 14 analyzed markets. According to our analysis, contagion effects are typically more pronounced in developing stock markets than in developed stock markets, with the highest levels of contagion occurring during short-term negative events. On the other hand, developed markets typically exhibit lower levels of contagion, indicating a higher degree of independence in their market dynamics under similar circumstances. These results highlight the significance of considering market development status and event duration when evaluating contagion risks in global stock markets.

Although the black swan investment strategy has shown suitable performance in minimizing losses during crises, it may not be the best strategy for all investors and market players. So, investigating the performance of other investment strategies with relative players, such as Swing trading, Arbitrage, and Value investing, compared to the performance of the black swan strategy is a suitable field for future research. Furthermore, consideration of diverse periods, such as daily and weekly in the short term and several years in the long term, with risk tolerance consideration and contribution of the transaction costs in analysis, can be considered as a suitable field for future research. Finally, expanding the analysis to different asset classes and incorporating behavioral finance theories to comprehend investor sentiment during black swan events are the potential directions for potential future research.

References

Alhassan, A. L. (2016). Insurance market development and economic growth: Exploring causality in 8 selected African countries. *International Journal of Social Economics, 43*(3), 321–339. https://doi.org/10.1108/IJSE-09-2014-0182

Ang, A., Chen, J., & Xing, Y. (2006). Downside risk. *Review of Financial Studies, 19*(4), 1191–1239.

Arago, V., & Fernandez, M. A. (2007). Influence of structural changes in transmission of information between stock markets: A European Empirical Study. *Journal of Multinational Financial Management, Elsevier, 17*(2), 112–124.

Baker, H. K., & Haslem, J. A. (1974). The impact of investor socioeconomic characteristics on risk and return preferences. *Journal of Business Research, 2*, 469–476.

Bertrand, M., & Mullainathan, S. (2000, February). *Agents with and without principals*, Industrial Relations Section Working Paper No. 430. Available at SSRN: https://ssrn.com/abstract=223592

Bhatti, O., Awais, M., Aziz, S., & Usman, U. (2021). Role of game theory in stock's investment: having loss-aversion bias during the stressed consition. *International Journal of Management, 12*, 872–893. https://doi.org/10.34218/IJM.12.3.2021.084

Brunaker, F., & Nordqvist, A. (2013). *Evaluation of black swan investment.* Department of Economics and law of Gothenburg.

Burnie, D., & De Ridder, A. (2010). Far tail or extreme day returns, mutual fund cash flows and investment behavior. *Applied Financial Economics, Taylor & Francis Journals, 20*(16), 1241–1256.

Chen, Y., Lu, W., & Wang, S. (2019). An evolutionary game model of portfolio optimization. *Journal of Systems Science and Complexity, 32*(5), 1391–1406.

Cocco, J., Gomes, F., & Maenhout, P. (2015). Consumption and portfolio choice over the life cycle. *Review of Financial Studies, 18.*

Cole, S., & Shastry, G. K. (2009). Smart money: The effect of education, cognitive ability, and financial literacy on financial market participation.

Cornell, E. P. (2019). Mean reversion in the US and international short rates. *North American Journal of Economics and Finance, 20*(8), 286–296.

Darrat, A. F., & Benkato, O. M. (2003). Interdependence and volatility spillovers under market liberalization: The case of Istanbul stock exchange. *Journal of Business Finance & Accounting, Wiley Blackwell, 30*(7–8), 1089–1114.

Eisenbach, T. M., & Schmalz, M. C. (2016). Anxiety in the face of risk. *Journal of Financial Economics, 121*(2), 414–426, ISSN 0304-405X. https://doi.org/10.1016/j.jfineco.2015.10.002

Enisan, A. A., & Olufisayo, A. O. (2009). Stock market development and economic growth: Evidence from seven sub-Sahara African countries. *Journal of Economics and Business, Elsevier, 61*(2), 162–171.

Enke, D., & Thawornwong, S. (2005). The use of data mining and neural networks for forecasting stock market returns. *Expert Systems with Applications, 29*(4), 927–940.

Estrada, J. (2009). Black swans, market timing, and the Dow. *Applied Economics Letters, 16*, 1117–1121. https://doi.org/10.2139/SSRN1086300

Estrada, J., & Vargas, M. (2012). Black swan, beta, risk, and return. *Journal of Applied Finance.*

Fama, E. F. (1970). Efficient capital markets: A review of theory and empirical work. *The Journal of Finance, 25*(2), 383–417.

Fogli, A., & Veldkamp, L. (2021). Germs Social Networks and Growth Abstract *The Review of Economic Studies, 88*(3), 1074–1100. https://doi.org/10.1093/restud/rdab008

French, K. R. (1980). Stock returns and the weekend effect. *Journal of Financial Economics, 8*(1), 55–69.

Ghon Rhee, S., & Wu, F. H. (2020). Conditional extreme risk, black swan hedging, and asset prices. *Journal of Empirical Finance, 58*, 412–435., , ISSN 0927-5398. https://doi.org/10.1016/j.jempfin.2020.07.002

Gilboa, T., Minardi, S., & Samuelson, L. (2020). Theories and cases in decisions under uncertainty. *Games and Economic Behavior, 123*, 22–40, ISSN 0899-8256. https://doi.org/10.1016/j.geb.2020.06.001

Goodell, J. W. (2020). COVID-19 and finance: Agendas for future research, 101512, ISSN 1544-6123. *Finance Research Letters, 35*. https://doi.org/10.1016/j.frl.2020.101512

Grinblatt, M., & Titman, S. (1989). Mutual fund performance: An analysis of quarterly portfolio holdings. *Journal of Business, 62*, 394–415.

Hannafey, K. (2021). *Modeling the stock market through game theory*, Honors College Theses (p. 590). https://digitalcommons.georgiasouthern.edu/honors-theses/590

Hassan, M. R., Nath, B., & Kirley, M. (2007). A fusion model of HMM, ANN, and GA for stock market forecasting. *Expert Systems with Applications, 33*(1), 171–180.

Jalil, A., & Feridun, M. (2011). Long-run relationship between income inequality and financial development in China. *Journal of the Asia Pacific Economy, 16*(2), 202–214. https://doi.org/10.1080/13547860.2011.564745

Jobson, J. D., & Korkie, B. (1981). Performance hypothesis testing with the Sharpe and Treynor measures. *Journal of Finance*.

Nihlén Jonas & Malm Jakob (2017). Mean reversion in Stock Prices: New evidence from Panel Unit Root Tests for 07 European countries, Economic Bulletin, Vol. 8, 82, pp. 0–6.

Krygier, D. (2014) *Measuring systemic risk in the Nordic countries. An application of CoVaR*, Master's Thesis, Supervisor: Professor Hans Byström, Lund University.

Kliger, D., van den Assem, M., & Zwinkels, R. (2014). Empirical behavioral finance. *Journal of Economic Behavior & Organization., 107*, 421–427. https://doi.org/10.1016/j.jebo.2014.10.012

Kocak, H. (2014). Canonical coalition game theory for optimal Portfolio selection. *Asian Economic and Financial Review*, 1254–1259.

Kaufman, G. G., & Scott, K. E. (2003). What Is Systemic Risk, and Do Bank Regulators Retard or Contribute to It? *The Independent Review, 7*(3), 371–391.

Li, X., & Zhao, X. (2015). Portfolio optimization based on game theory: A survey. *Quantitative Finance, 15*(8), 1289–1311.

Liu, H., Manzoor, A., Wang, C., Zhang, L., & Manzoor, Z. (2020). The COVID-19 outbreak and affected countries stock markets response. *International Journal of Environmental Research and Public Health, 17*(8), 2800. https://doi.org/10.3390/ijerph17082800. PMID: 32325710; PMCID: PMC7215540.

Narayan, P. K., & Smyth, R. (2017). Mean reversion versus a random walk in G7 stock prices: evidence from multiple trend break unit root tests. *International Financial markets, Institutions, and Money, 07*(2), 052–066.

Nihlén, J., & Malm, J. (2014). *Excess returns with Black Swan investing on the Indian stock market*. Department of economics Lund university.

Nofsinger, J. R., & Sias, R. W. (1999). Herding and feedback trading by institutional and individual investors. *The Journal of Finance, 54*(6), 2263–2295. http://www.jstor.org/stable/797994

Philipp, Hornung Ulrike, Leopold-Wildburger Roland, Mestel Stefan, Palan (2015). Insider behavior under different market structures: experimental evidence on trading patterns manipulation and profitability. *Central European Journal of Operations Research, 23*(2), 357–373. https://doi.org/10.1007/s10100-014-0359-2

Serletis, A., & Rosenberg, A. A. (2009). Mean reversion in the US stock market. *Chaos, Solitons & Fractals, Elsevier, 40*(4), 2007–2015.

Shapley, L. S. (1953). A value for n-person games. In H. W. Kuhn & A. W. Tucker (Eds.), *Contributions to the theory of games* (Vol. 2, pp. 307–317). Princeton University Press. This is the original paper by Lloyd Shapley in which he introduced the concept of the Shapley vector.

Shiller, R. J. (1981). Do stock prices move too much to be justified by subsequent changes in dividends? *The American Economic Review, 71*(3), 421–436.

Szpunar, P. J., & Glogowski, A. (2012). Lending in foreign currencies as a systematic risk. Macroprudential Commentaries Issue No: 4, ESRB, 5.

Taleb, N. N. (2007). *The Black Swan: The impact of the highly improbable*. Random House.

Taleb, N. N. (2008). *The Black Swan: The impact of the highly improbable*. Random House.

Taleb, N. N. (2011). *Flood by randomness* (1st ed., pp. 806–821). Random House.

Thach, N. N. (2023). Applying Monte Carlo simulations to a small data analysis of a case of economic growth in COVID-19 times. *SAGE Open, 13*(2), 21582440231181540. https://doi.org/10.1177/21582440231181540. PMID: 37362768; PMCID: PMC10285188.

Wu, J.-L., Hou, H., & Cheng, S.-Y. (2010). The dynamic impacts of financial institutions on economic growth: Evidence from the European Union. *Journal of Macroeconomics, Elsevier, 32*(3), 879–891.

Xiong, L., Luo, J., Vise, H., & White, M. (2023). Distributed least-squares Monte Carlo for American option pricing. *Risks, 11*(8), 145. https://doi.org/10.3390/risks11080145

Zhang, W., Gao, L., & Huang, X. (2018). A portfolio optimization model based on zero-sum game theory. *PLoS One, 13*(8), e0202587.

Impact of Country-Level Factors on Green Bonds Issuance: Comparison Between BRICS and G7 Countries

Mani Pouyan, Karlygash Zhangaliyeva, and Alimshan Faizulayev

1 Introduction

Climate change has impacted human life and has brought many concerns among scholars and market participants. Economists such as Nordhaus (1990), the first to merge global warming into endogenous growth models, and Stern (2007) have attempted to incorporate climate policies into economic theories. The Socially Responsible Investing (SRI) movement, which originated in the 1970s, paved the way for the introduction of green bonds in 2008. Since adopting the Paris Climate Agreement in 2015, the green bond market has experienced significant growth (Otek Ntsama et al., 2021).

Green bonds represent a type of financial debt instrument tailor-made to finance ecologically sustainable projects. They are offered by a range of entities, including governments and corporations, with the aim of funding projects that have a positive impact on the environment. Such projects may incorporate initiatives related to energy efficiency, sustainable water management, or the preservation of other natural resources. Green bonds encourage investors to support environmentally friendly projects with low carbon impact, promoting sustainable development. For the past several years, green bonds' issuance increased rapidly (Yadav et al., 2023). Investors can integrate ethical criteria into investment choices with green bonds while generating sustainable and financial value. Green bonds, like conventional bonds, provide periodic interest payments and principal repayments upon maturity (Dan & Tiron-Tudor, 2021).

M. Pouyan · K. Zhangaliyeva · A. Faizulayev (✉)
KIMEP University, Bang College of Business, Almaty, Republic of Kazakhstan
e-mail: a.faizulayev@kimep.kz

N. Ozatac et al. (eds.), *Sustainable Development in Banking and Finance*, Springer Proceedings in Business and Economics,
https://doi.org/10.1007/978-3-031-65533-3_11

Despite the challenges posed by the COVID-19 pandemic, there continues to be a strong and varied growth trend for sustainable and socially responsible investments such as green bonds. For those committed to supporting environmentally friendly initiatives, green bonds are one option available to both private sector companies and public institutions. Globally, the cumulative amount of green bond issues hit more than $2613 billion in Q3 2023 At the end of Q3 2023. There are few emerging markets other than China that rank in the top countries. Strong policy support has contributed to the growth of robust local and international markets in all three cases (Climate Bonds Initiative, 2023).

The Green Bonds market is expanding, and private investors tend to invest in global capital markets with better control over the social, economic, and political context. Due to the difference in financial market sizes, some regions may attract less investment than others. Some developed markets are leading the way in this field by establishing regulatory frameworks and issuing several green and sustainable bonds. So, it is crucial to understand the factors that drive the development of the green bond market.

Several studies have produced varying and even conflicting findings on the relationship between country-level variables and green bond issuance. This presents an opportunity for further investigation. In light of this, utilizing a quantitative approach, our research aims to provide a more comprehensive understanding of the relationship between macroeconomic factors and the green bond market. Additionally, we will explore the factors that could impact this relationship.

The design of a green bond closely resembles a traditional bond, differing primarily in the earmarked utilization of funds for eco-friendly projects. According to the Green Bond Principles (GBP), the fundamental elements of a green bond encompass the following:

1. Allocation of Funds: The finances from a green bond must fund eco-friendly projects that offer evident environmental advantages. The issuer will evaluate and attempt to quantify these benefits.
2. Project Assessment and Selection Procedure: The issuer must articulate the evaluation process for project qualification using the funds from the green bond. This entails defining sustainability goals, determining project alignment with specified eligible categories, outlining related criteria for eligibility (including exclusions if relevant), and disclosing processes for identifying and managing potential environmental and social risks linked to the projects.
3. Fund Handling: The net proceeds from the green bond, or an equivalent amount, should be meticulously recorded in a designated sub-account, sub-portfolio, or a similar tracking mechanism, verified by an established internal procedure subject to annual auditing.
4. Disclosure: Issuers are obliged to provide and maintain current information regarding fund utilization, which will be updated annually until full allocation and as needed in case of significant developments. This should encompass a comprehensive list of allocated projects, brief project descriptions, allocated amounts, and anticipated impacts.

The green bond market has seen significant growth since its inception. The market started with less than $1 billion in 2007 and has grown substantially over the years. In 2013, more green bonds were issued than the previous six years combined, and by 2017, new issues totaled $162.1 billion. The market continued the upward trend, and new issues reached a new record of $257.7 billion in 2019. The growth of the green bond market is closely related to the rise of green finance, where the stock market plays an important role in environmental preservation. The ratification of the Paris Agreement in 2015 and subsequent political decisions to promote international investments in green bonds have also contributed to the growth of the market.

Several studies have produced varying and even conflicting findings on the relationship between country-level variables and green bond issuance. This presents an opportunity for further investigation. In light of this, our research aims to provide a more comprehensive understanding of the relationship between macroeconomic factors and the green bond market, utilizing a quantitative approach. Additionally, we will explore the factors that can potentially impact this relationship.

2 Literature Review

2.1 Theoretical Background

The relationship between country-level factors and investment in bond securities can explained by neoclassical investment theory, which argues the issuance and investment of financial securities depend on various economic and financial factors, which also influence bond market securities (Aman et al., 2023). At the same time, Capital structure theories have been a subject of theoretical discourse in the context of the issuance of bond securities. One of the most important theories is information asymmetry (Myers and Majluf, 1984). They analyzed capital structure and investment decisions to reduce inefficiencies caused by information asymmetry, including knowledge as a factor in obtaining debt financing. Based on the theory, due to asymmetric information, managers know the real value of the company, and they try to finance by bonds instead of stocks, especially in case of high information asymmetry in the market (Halim et al., 2017; Klein & Weill, 2016; Nagano, 2017). Theoretically, the issuance of financial securities, including green bonds, is mostly related to country-level variables such as economic and financial factors.

2.2 Macroeconomic Factors and the Bond Market

There is a rich literature about analyzing the market sentiments or company-specific features of bonds, but at the same time, some studies have also emphasized the significance of macroeconomic and financial factors in the development of the bond market (Aman et al., 2023). Eichengreen and Luengnaruemitchai (2004) found relationships between economic size, institutional environment, exchange rates, and fiscal balance with bond market expansion in Asian countries. Taking larger samples, Burger and Warnock (2007) and Claessens et al. (2007) found some determinants of bond markets, such as inflation and institutional environment. Later Adelegan and Radzewicz-Bak (2009) found the impacts of the legal environment and national savings on African bond markets. Similar results were repeated in different regions, including South America (Eichengreen et al., 2008), Asia (Bhattacharyay, 2013), and Africa (Mu et al., 2013).

Recently, Ahwireng-Obeng and Ahwireng-Obeng (2019) found that macroeconomic factors such as Inflation, domestic debt, external debt, GDP, fiscal balance, and international trade impact African sovereign bond market development. Cepni et al. (2021) research on emerging sovereign bond markets has the same results regarding factors such as inflation and country financial variables. Gottschalk and Ndang (2023) showed that institutional factors, including country income level, government effectiveness, rule of law, and quality of regulations, can influence firms' capital structure, and macroeconomic performance influences leverage and corporate bond spreads.

2.3 Factors Influencing Green Bonds Issuance

Determining variables for green bond valuation is crucial as they provide the basis for understanding the relationships and interactions within green bond issuance. The variables stated below allow us to measure and evaluate the green bond issuance at the country level. Tolliver et al. (2021) categorized drivers into three groups: macroeconomic factors (such as the size of the economy, stock market capitalization, and trade openness), institutional factors (including capital account openness, the rule of law, and regulatory quality), and environmental factors, as assessed by "Nationally Determined Commitments." Several variables can be considered when examining the green bonds market in low- and middle-income countries, according to (Otek Ntsama et al., 2021):

1. Market Capitalization: The size of the green bond market and the total market capitalization of a country can indicate the level of development and acceptance of green bonds.
2. Government Initiatives: The presence and effectiveness of government initiatives to support the development of the green bond market can significantly influence its growth.
3. Standardization: The existence of clear and standardized eligibility criteria for green bonds can reduce the risk of greenwashing and increase investor confidence.
4. Political Stability: Political instabilities can pose challenges to developing the green bond market.

5. Quality and Availability of Information: The accessibility and reliability of information on green investments can influence investor decisions and the overall growth of the green bond market.
6. Green Label Assets: The availability of green label assets can also impact the development of the green bond market.
7. Climate Change Risks: Exposure to climate change risks can influence the urgency and necessity of developing the green bond market.
8. Economic Development Trajectory: The ability of a country to decarbonize its economy while maintaining a sustainable economic development trajectory can also be a significant factor.

Summarizing Tolliver et al. and Otek Ntsama et al., factors that influence the performance of Green Bonds can be categorized into three major categories: macroeconomic/financial, demographic/environmental, and governmental.

Macroeconomic and Financial Category: Inflation Rate, GDP, Unemployment, Fiscal Balance, Trade Openness, Financial Development Index, Credit Rating

Tolliver et al. (2020) mentioned that the economic status of a country plays a crucial role in determining its borrowing costs.

Green bond issuance is evaluated using the GDP indicator to estimate the progression of green finance. This indicator serves as a stand-in for the costs associated with environmental pollution and is computed by dividing the GDP by the environmental pollution expenses (Lin & Hong, 2022). The Gross Domestic Product (GDP) is a key metric in comprehending economic advancement and its connection to environmental elements. It is commonly employed alongside other metrics to scrutinize diverse economic and environmental performance facets. For instance, GDP per capita is employed to evaluate the economic well-being of a nation's residents (Prajapati et al., 2021). Moreover, research conducted by Lin & Hong (2022) has indicated a correlation between GDP growth and environmental indicators like CO_2 and N_2O emissions, highlighting the influence of economic development on environmental pollution. Additionally, econometric models exploring the association between GDP and environmental factors have unveiled both positive and negative relationships with variables such as CO_2 and N_2O (Ioan et al., 2020).

The indicator of export-to-GDP trade openness is used in measuring green bond issuance because it reflects a country's economic openness and its engagement in international trade. This indicator is relevant to green bond issuance as it can influence a country's economic development, access to capital, emerging technologies, and knowledge needed for sustainable economic growth (Tolliver et al., 2020).

The inflation rate is an important indicator to consider in the context of green bond issuance Anh Tu et al. (2020). It is perceived as a measure of economic management that directly influences default risks. Higher inflation rates can lead to macroeconomic instability, which in turn can lower the government's creditworthiness and affect the cost of borrowing for government bonds. Additionally, higher inflation can negatively affect investor decisions in the green market, as it influences the cost of financing energy efficiency projects.

The Financial Development Index (FDI) is used in measuring green bond issuance because it reflects a country's financial development level, which can impact the availability of funds for green projects and the overall development of the green finance market.

Wang et al. (2019) highlight the high costs involved in the search, discovery, and processing of information, suggesting that truly efficient information markets are hard to achieve. They note the role of credit rating agencies in analyzing debtor credit, ensuring third-party reputation, and providing both objective and subjective insights into credit risks. These agencies are pivotal in lowering the information gathering and processing costs, thereby enhancing market dynamism. The function of credit ratings in the bond market is also emphasized, aiding in market equilibrium and stability. The impact of these ratings on the market value of green bonds is significant. High-rated green bonds benefit more from green evaluation certifications in terms of reduced financing costs for the issuer. Conversely, lower-rated green bonds may diminish these certifications' impact, affecting investor inclination towards green investments. The explanatory variables in the multiple linear regression equation for green bond issuance hold a high level of interpretation for each credit rating category, indicating a comprehensive understanding of the factors at play.

Countries with higher economic complexity are more likely to have the capacity to develop and implement green technologies and projects, making them attractive for green bond investments. Additionally, economic complexity can indicate a country's ability to transition towards a more sustainable and environmentally friendly economy, which is essential for the success of green bond issuance.

Governmental Category: Government Effectiveness, Sustainable Development

ESG consists of three dimensions, and one of them is governance. Let's consider the World Governance Indicator (WGI). WGI evaluates six governance aspects: responsibility, political constancy minus terrorism, governance efficacy, norms quality, adherence to the law, and anti-corruption measures. This indicator is a part of the broader New Public Governance (NPG) framework, which aims to safeguard public economy foundations while enhancing societal welfare (Osborne, 2006). When analyzing panel data, standard methods present limitations, as noted by Kociemska et al. (2023). According to their research, pooled linear regression models fail to account for country-specific variances, whereas models focusing on individual nations rely on limited data and overlook shared characteristics and progress influences among countries. Their research indicates that yearly increases in WGI values correspond with GB values. However, an increase in WGI may negatively impact the value of GB, especially in rich countries.

A highly effective government is more likely to create a conducive environment for green finance, including the development of supportive policies, regulatory frameworks, and incentives for green projects. This, in turn, can influence the issuance and success of green bonds by providing a stable and supportive environment for investors and project developers (Tolliver et al., 2020).

Demographic/Environmental Variables: Population, CO_2 Emission

CO_2 emissions are used in measuring green bond issuance because they are a critical environmental indicator that reflects a country's carbon footprint and environmental impact. Green bonds are specifically designed to finance projects that contribute to environmental sustainability and climate change mitigation. Reducing CO_2 emissions is a key goal of green finance, and measuring CO_2 emissions helps to evaluate the success and impact of green bond investments in achieving environmental objectives (Kasman, 2015). Tu et al. (2020) state that higher unemployment rates can lead to an increase in the debt level obtained with higher costs, which can impact the issuance of green bonds. The country's population size is a measure of its citizens, and it has to meet the needs and requests of a large population. Tu et al. (2020) mentioned that financing a low-carbon economy directly impacts a higher standard of living for its population. The population growth will require reliable and affordable green finance for climate change projects.

Authors		Data	Period	Method	Variables	Results	
#	Name of Article	Name(s) of authors	Date	Variables	Model	Country	Level
1	Exploring the Relationship Between ESG Performance and Green Bond Issuance	Wang Sh. And Wang D.	27.05.2022	Green loan volume, ESG Scores, Environmental dimension, Social dimension, Governance dimension, Financial performance, Leverage, Firm size, Firm IPO age, Firm ownership, Firm growth	Probit model. Non-linear method: maximum likelihood estimates. Ordinary least squares OLS regression	China	Company
3	Research on the Factors Affecting the Risk Premium of China's Green Bond Issuance	Qinghua Wang Q., Zhou Y., Luo L., and Ji J	14.11.2019	Risk premium, Shibor, Certificate GB, Leverage, ROE, Credit rating, GB issuance, Term, Debtor, Soe	Multiple linear Regression model, ordinary least squares (OLS) model had a heteroscedasticity problem	China	Company
4	Does compliance to Green Bond Principles matter? Global Evidence	Nanayakkara M., Colombage S.	2022	Bid-ask spread ratio (BAS), bond turnover ratio, GDP per capita and the 10-year Treasury bond rate as indicators	Cross-sectional regression analysis, The Wald test	World	Country
1	The determinants of green bond issuance in the European Union	Dan, Anamaria; Tiron-Tudor, Adriana	2021	Issue, ESG, Rating, Fiscal_balance, Trade, Inflation, Unemployment, Population, GDP per capita	Regression	EU	Country

3	Governance Effectiveness and Green Bonds. An Empirical evaluation	Kociemska H., Frydrych S., and others	2023	WGI index and GB emissions	Linear regression model, Fixed effects model (for country-level approach), generalised least squares (GLS), heteroscedasticity problem	World	Country
4	The New Public Governance?	Stephen P. Osborne	2014	NPM, NPG and PA	PAM theory	UK	Country
5	Green bonds issuance: insights in low- and middle-income countries	Otek Ntsama, U. Y., Yan, C., Nasiri, A., Mbouombouo Mboungam, A.H	2021	Use-of-proceeds, use-of-proceeds revenue, project, Securitisation (ABS), Covered bond types and loan	Managerial implications	China, India, Brazil, Poland, Chile, Indonesia, South Africa, the Philippines, and others	Country
6	Green Innovation and Finance in Asia	Tolliver, C., Fujii, H., Keeley, A.R., Managi, S.	2021	GDP, air pollution flows, labor, produced capital, and natural capital, time	Environmentally adjusted multifactor productivity (EAMFP)	Japan, China, Asia, OECD	Company and Country
7	Drivers of green bond market growth: The importance of Nationally Determined Contributions to the Paris Agreement and implications for sustainability	Clarence Tolliver, Alexander Ryota Keeley, Shunsuke Managi	2020	Green bond issuance, Capital controls (TF), Regulatory quality (RQ), Rule of law (RL), Stock market capitalization (ST), GDP, Trade openness (TO)	Exploratory factor analysis (EFA) and hypothesis formulation, Structural equation modelling (SEM)	World	Country
8	Investigating solutions for the development of a green bond market: Evidence from analytic hierarchy process	Tu, C.A., Rasoulinezhad, E., Sarker, T	2020	Green bond development: inflation, interest rate, exchange rate, economic stability, monetary policy, fiscal	Multi-criteria decision-making (MCDM) method called the analytic hierarchy process (AHP) method	World	Country

(continued)

(continued)

Authors		Data	Period	Method	Variables	Results	
#	Name of Article	Name(s) of authors	Date	Variables	Model	Country	Level
				policy, political stability, social support, higher education of the population, legal			
9	Research on the Factors Affecting the Risk Premium of China's Green Bond Issuance	Wang, Q., Zhou, Y., Luo, L., Ji, J.	2019	Green bond issuance risk premium, three-month Shanghai interbank offered rate, certificate, leverage, ROE, credit rating, size, term, debtor, soe	The multiple linear regression model	China	Company and Country

3 Data and Methodology

Yearly macroeconomic data for 64 countries from different regions for the period from 2014 to 2022 were downloaded from different sources such as the World Bank (World Bank, 2023), Emissions Database for Global Atmospheric Research (European Commission. Joint Research Centre, 2022), International Monetary Fund (IMF, 2023). However, a year lag is considered for two factors, so data collected from 2013 to 2021 is used. The research variables by type and their measurement are shown in Table 1. As the table shows, the research variables are categorized into different groups: one dependent and independent variable at three levels: macroeconomic/financial, demographic/environmental, and governmental.

In addition to Green bond issuance as the dependent variable in the research model, a set of country-level factors are considered independent variables based on the literature. There is a regression model to determine the elements that influence green bond issuance:

Table 1 Research variables

Variable	Source	Definition
Dependent variable		
Green Bond Issuance	IMF	The gross value of green bond issuances in the year t
Macroeconomic/financial variables		
Inflation rate	World Bank	Consumer price index
GDP	World Bank	The gross domestic product of the country divided by its population
Unemployment	World Bank	Unemployment rate
Fiscal balance	World Bank	General government net lending/borrowing % GDP
Trade openness	World Bank	Export % GDP
Financial development	IMF	FD index for year t-1
Credit rating	Fitch	Numerical codes are used to rate and measure the credit-worthiness and risk level of a country.
Governmental variables		
Government effectiveness	World Bank	Government effectiveness index
Sustainable development	UNstat	SDG Index Score
Demographic/environmental variables		
Population	World Bank	Logarithms of total population
CO_2 emission	European Commission	Logarithms of total CO_2 emission for country i and year t-1

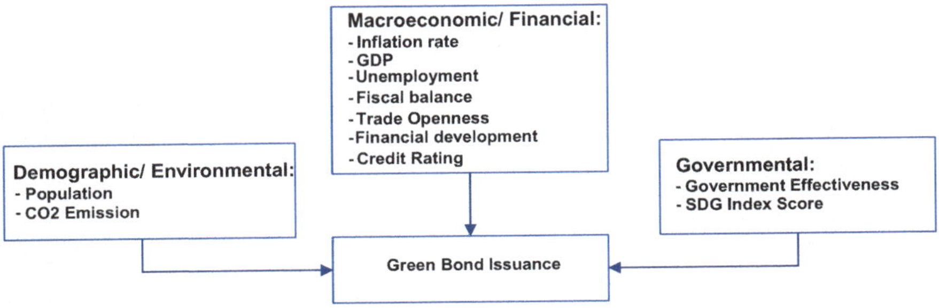

Fig. 1 Conceptual Model

$$\begin{aligned}\text{GB Issuance}\,i,t = &\beta 0 + \beta 1\ \text{CPI}\,i,t + \beta 2\ \text{GDP}\,i,t + \beta 3\ \text{UNEMPLOY}\,i,t \\ &+ \beta 4\ \text{POP}\,i,t + \beta 5\ \text{FB}\,i,t + \beta 6\ \text{TRADE}\,i,t + \beta 7\ \text{CO}_2 i,t \\ &+ \beta 8\ \text{FD}\,i,t + \beta 9\ \text{GE}\,i,t + \beta 10\ \text{SDG}\,i,t + \beta 11\ \text{RATE}\,i,t + \text{U}i,t\end{aligned}$$

In these equations, *i* represents the country and *t* represents the time. GB issuance shows Green Bonds issuance as the dependent variable. CPI, GDP, UNEMPLOY, FB, TRADE, FD, and RATE are macroeconomic and financial that evaluate inflation rate, GDP per capita, unemployment rate, fiscal balance, trade openness, financial development, and rating.

POP and CO_2 represent demographic and environmental variables including population and CO_2 emission. Finally, Governmental variables such as GE and SDG show government effectiveness and SDG index. The conceptual model of research is shown in Fig. 1, which explains the relationship between variables in the model.

As this research delves into the relationship between variables across various countries and years, it is crucial to identify the suitable model for estimation among OLS regression, Fixed, and Random Effect models. To achieve this, all three models will be tested, and the Redundant Fixed Effects Tests and Hausman Test will be utilized to determine the optimal model. If the fixed effect model is found to be the most appropriate, models will be scrutinized for heteroscedasticity.

To determine the most appropriate analysis model, three different models are executed. Subsequently, the Redundant Fixed Effects Test and Hausman Test are utilized to select the optimal model. For the validity of the model and to check regression assumptions, different tests were used to determine autocorrelation, normality of residuals, heteroscedasticity, and multicollinearity.

4 Results

This study collected data from 64 countries over nine years, spanning from 2014 to 2022. The dataset comprises 576 observations across all variables without any missing values. Outliers were addressed through winsorization, while variables with large numbers were normalized using logarithmic transformation. Table 2 presents descriptive statistics of the dataset.

The regression model in this study involves eleven independent variables, which introduces the possibility of correlations between them. To ensure their independence and avoid issues with multicollinearity, correlation coefficients were calculated for each variable. In Table 3 a detailed display of the variables' correlations is shown.

Based on the findings, there appears to be a high correlation between Rating and governmental variables. To prevent multicollinearity from negatively impacting the accuracy of results, it is advisable not to include all variables in the model. However, it is worth noting that in theory, the correlation is not absolute; therefore, the regression model should not be biased.

p-value related to the Breusch-Pagan test in the models is less than 0.05 that the null hypothesis consisting of homoscedasticity is rejected, so models suffer from heteroscedasticity, Durbin-Watson statistics must be between 1.8 and 2.2 is not fulfilled by the test results so all the models have autocorrelation problems. At the same time, P-values for the Jarque Bera test are less than 0.05, showing that residuals are not distributed normality but based on the VIF test. There is no multicollinearity among variables.in general, the model violates regression assumptions, so they are biased.

Based on the regression results, the F-Limer statistic probability is less than 0.05, leading to the rejection of the null hypothesis that assumes the model is Pooled OLS. Instead, it is shown that the appropriate model is the panel model. In addition, the Husman test supports the fixed effect model as the alternative to the random effect model. The null hypothesis is rejected in all models with a P value less than 0.05, indicating that the fixed effect model is the suitable choice for this study (Table 4).

Table 2 Descriptive statistics

	Mean	Standard deviation	Minimum	Maximum	Observation
GB-issuance	4.06	13.08	0.00	130.81	576
Inflation rate	0.04	0.05	−0.02	0.72	576
GDP per capita	4.00	1.09	0.16	7.63	576
Unemployment	0.07	0.05	0.01	0.34	576
Population	6.18	2.03	1.55	8.44	576
Fiscal balance	−0.03	0.05	−0.42	0.25	576
Trade openness	0.53	0.39	0.08	2.13	576
CO_2 emission	2.01	0.75	0.25	4.06	576
FD index	0.54	0.22	0.15	0.98	576
Government effectiveness	0.79	0.81	−0.85	2.28	576
SDG index	74.69	6.64	50.63	86.76	576
Rating	7.08	4.61	0.00	24.00	576

Table 3 Correlation

		1	2	3	4	5	6	7	8	9	10	11	12
1	*GB-issuance*	1.00											
2	*Inflation rate*	−0.03	1.00										
3	*GDP per capita*	0.05	−0.18	1.00									
4	*Unemployment*	−0.09	0.07	−0.31	1.00								
5	*Population*	−0.36	0.09	0.33	−0.15	1.00							
6	*Fiscal balance*	−0.10	−0.08	0.28	−0.27	0.11	1.00						
7	*Trade openness*	−0.07	−0.12	0.36	−0.22	0.20	0.32	1.00					
8	CO_2 *emission*	0.29	0.09	−0.42	−0.10	−0.42	−0.21	−0.40	1.00				
9	*FD index*	0.30	−0.29	0.27	−0.09	−0.41	0.10	0.10	0.33	1.00			
10	*Government effectiveness*	0.16	−0.38	0.61	−0.27	−0.17	0.33	0.43	−0.21	0.67	1.00		
11	*SDG index*	0.19	−0.18	0.59	−0.28	−0.05	0.23	0.24	−0.22	0.35	0.60	1.00	
12	*Rating*	−0.25	0.37	−0.51	0.41	0.19	−0.30	−0.33	−0.01	−0.65	−0.86	−0.53	1.00

Table 4 Fixed/random effect testing

Redundant fixed effects test	*Statistic*	*d.f.*	*Prob.*
Cross-section F	16.871436	−82323	0
Cross-section Chi-square	690.77691	82	0
Hausman test			
Test summary	*Chi-Sq. statistic*	*Chi-Sq. d.f.*	*Prob.*
Cross-section random	25.452846	9	0.0025

Table 5 Regression results

Determinants of Green Bond Issuance, 2014–2022				
Variable	Coefficient	Std. Error	Prob.[1]	Sig level
Constant	−245.39	246.30	0.31	Not significant
Inflation rate	−3.23	11.24	0.77	Not significant
GDP per capita	26.22	3.10	0.000***	99% confidence level
Unemployment	−13.69	27.63	0.62	Not significant
Population	26.90	42.73	0.52	Not significant
Fiscal balance	−36.58	11.81	0.002***	99% confidence level
Trade openness	3.87	10.38	0.70	Not significant
CO2 emission	−48.48	10.55	0.000***	99% confidence level
FD index	32.39	17.84	0.07*	90% confidence level
Government effectiveness	−7.37	3.58	0.04**	95% confidence level
SDG index	0.82	0.47	0.08*	90% confidence level
Rating	0.17	0.39	0.65	Not significant
R-squared	0.55	*Observations*	576	
Adjusted R-squared	0.48	*Number of countries*	64	
Prob(F-statistic)	0			

[1]Source: Significant at the * 10% level; ** 5% level; ***1% level

The R squared value of 0.55 in regressions is significantly higher compared to the OLS model (0.24) and the random effect model (0.14), demonstrating that the fixed effect model has a much greater explanatory power.

Because of using a fixed effect model, it was necessary to test the regression models for heteroscedasticity via Breusch-Pagan. All the test P-values are 0, which is less than 0.05. These results show that the research models are not homoscedastic and can negatively affect the validity of the results.

The findings (Table 5) indicate that there is a significant relationship between the issuance of green bonds and certain research variables, including GDP per capita, fiscal balance, and financial development, among macroeconomic and financial variables. Additionally, the issuance of green bonds is significantly influenced by CO_2 emissions and governmental variables. Greater levels of fiscal balance, CO_2 emission, and government effectiveness index hurt green bond issuance, whereas countries with greater levels of GDP per capita, financial development, and dedication to reaching sustainable development goals typically issue more green bonds. The population, trade openness, unemployment rate, inflation, and credit rating are among the research factors for which the results do not indicate a meaningful association.

5 Conclusions

The research on the green bond market suggests that country-level factors play a significant role in the issuance of green bonds. The study found that variables such as GDP per capita, fiscal balance, CO_2 emissions, SDG index, and government effectiveness correlate with green bond issuance. This indicates that economic, environmental, and governance factors are influential in shaping the green bond market. Additionally, the study highlights the limitations of pooled linear regression models in capturing country-specific variances and emphasizes the importance of using fixed effect models for more accurate analysis. These findings underscore the need for a nuanced understanding of the diverse factors that drive green bond issuance across different countries.

Furthermore, the research sheds light on the factors that do not show a meaningful association with green bond issuance, such as inflation, population, credit rating, and trade openness. This suggests that while certain economic and environmental variables are significant drivers of green bond issuance, others may have less impact. Understanding these nuances can help policymakers, investors, and market participants make more informed decisions regarding green bond investments and market development. Overall, the study provides valuable insights into the complex interplay of macroeconomic, social, and environmental factors in the green bond market, contributing to a deeper understanding of the market's dynamics and potential avenues for future research and policy development.

References

Adelegan, O. J., & Radzewicz-Bak, B. (2009). *What determines bond market development in sub-Saharan Africa?* International Monetary Fund.

Ahwireng-Obeng, A. S., & Ahwireng-Obeng, F. (2019). Macroeconomic determinants of sovereign bond market development in African emerging economies. *International Journal of Emerging Markets, 15*(4), 651–669.

Aman, A., Isa, M. Y., & Naim, A. M. (2023). The role of macroeconomic and financial factors in bond market development in selected countries. *Global Business Review, 24*(4), 626–641. https://doi.org/10.1177/0972150920907206

Bhattacharyay, B. N. (2013). Determinants of bond market development in Asia. *Journal of Asian Economics, 24*, 124–137.
Burger, J. D., & Warnock, F. E. (2007). Foreign participation in local currency bond markets. *Review of Financial Economics, 16*(3), 291–304.
Cepni, O., Guney, I. E., Kucuksarac, D., & Hasan Yilmaz, M. (2021). Do local and global factors impact the emerging markets' sovereign yield curves? Evidence from a data-rich environment. *Journal of Forecasting, 40*(7), 1214–1229.
Claessens, S., Klingebiel, D., & Schmukler, S. L. (2007). Government bonds in domestic and foreign currency: the role of institutional and macroeconomic factors. *Review of International Economics, 15*(2), 370–413.
Dan, A., & Tiron-Tudor, A. (2021). The determinants of Green Bond Issuance in the European Union. *Journal of Risk and Finance Management, 14*, 446. https://doi.org/10.3390/jrfm14090446
Eichengreen, B., & Luengnaruemitchai, P. (2004). Why doesn't Asia have bigger bond markets?, NBER Working Paper, No. 10576, *National Bureau of Economic Research Cambridge*, USA.
Eichengreen, B., Panizza, U., & Borensztein, E. (2008). *Prospects for Latin American bond markets: A cross-country view*. The MIT Press.
Gottschalk, S., & Ndang, B. (2023). Institutional and geopolitical aspects of bond spreads impacts on corporate capital structure in emerging markets. *Global Business and Economics Review, 28*(3), 266–297.
Halim, Z. A., How, J., & Verhoeven, P. (2017). Agency costs and corporate sukuk issuance. *Pacific-Basin Finance Journal, 42*, 83–95.
Kasman, A., & Duman, Y. S. (2015). CO2 emissions, economic growth, energy consumption, trade and urbanization in new EU member and candidate countries: a panel data analysis. *Economic modelling, 44*, 97–103.
Klein, P. O., & Weill, L. (2016). Why do companies issue sukuk? *Review of Financial Economics, 31*, 26–33.
Kociemska, H., Frydrych, S., Szczech-Pietkiewicz, E., Radło, M., Kasprzak, R., Rokita, P., Pietrzyk, R., Biegun, K., & Półtorak, B. (2023). Governance effectiveness and green bonds. An empirical evaluation. *Economics and Environment, 85*, 30–51. https://doi.org/10.34659/eis.2023.85.2.561
Ioan, B., Mozi, R. M., Lucian, G., Gheorghe, F., Horia, T., Ioan, B., & Mircea-Iosif, R. (2020). An empirical investigation on determinants of sustainable economic growth. *Lessons from Central and Eastern European Countries. Journal of Risk and Financial Management, 13*(7), 146.
Lin, L., & Hong, Y. (2022). Developing a green bonds market: lessons from China. *European Business Organization Law Review, 23*(1), 143–185.
Mu, Y., Stotsky, J. G., & Phelps, P. (2013). Bond markets in Africa. *Review of Development Finance, 3*(3), 121–135.
Myers, S. C., & Majluf, N. S. (1984). Corporate financing and investment decisions when firms have information that investors do not have. *Journal of Financial Economics, 13*(2), 187–221.
Nagano, M. (2017). Sukuk issuance and information asymmetry: why do firms issue sukuk? *Pacific-Basin Finance Journal, 42*, 142–157.
Nordhaus, W. D. (1990). *A general equilibrium model of policies to slow global warming. In Economic Models of Energy and Environment*. Proceedings of a Workshop, Washington, DC, October.
Osborne, S. P. (2006). The new public governance? *Public Management Review, 8*, 377–387. https://doi.org/10.1080/14719030600853022
Otek Ntsama, U. Y., Yan, C., Nasiri, A., & Mbouombouo Mboungam, A. H. (2021). Green bonds issuance: Insights in low- and middle-income countries. *International Journal of Corporate Social Responsibility, 6*, 2. https://doi.org/10.1186/s40991-020-00056-0
Prajapati, D., Paul, D., Malik, S., & Mishra, D. K. (2021). Understanding the preference of individual retail investors on green bond in India: An empirical study. *Investment Management and Financial Innovations, 18*(1), 177–189.

Stern, N. (2007). *The economics of climate change: the Stern review*, Cambridge University press.

Tolliver, C., Keeley, A. R., & Managi, S. (2020). Drivers of green bond market growth: The importance of Nationally Determined Contributions to the Paris Agreement and implications for sustainability. *Journal of Cleaner Production, 244*(118), 643. https://doi.org/10.1016/j.jclepro.2019.118643

Tolliver, C., Fujii, H., Keeley, A. R., & Managi, S. (2021). Green innovation and finance in Asia. *Asian Economic Policy Review, 16*, 67–87. https://doi.org/10.1111/aepr.12320

Tu, C. A., Rasoulinezhad, E., & Sarker, T. (2020). Investigating solutions for the development of a green bond market: Evidence from analytic hierarchy process. *Finance Research Letters, 34*(101), 457. https://doi.org/10.1016/j.frl.2020.101457

Wang, Q., Zhou, Y., Luo, L., & Ji, J. (2019). Research on the factors affecting the risk premium of China's Green Bond Issuance. *Sustainability, 11*, 6394. https://doi.org/10.3390/su11226394

Yadav, M., Mishra, N., & Ashok, S. (2023). Dynamic connectedness of green bond with financial markets of European countries under OECD economies. *Economic Change and Restructuring, 56*, 609–631. https://doi.org/10.1007/s10644-022-09430-3

The Impact of Board Characteristics on R&D Investments: The Role of Education Level and Age

Sedat Çerez, Abdullah Kürşat Merter, Yavuz Selim Balcıoğlu, and Gökhan Özer

1 Introduction

In the contemporary dynamic and highly competitive landscape, it is imperative for organizations to prioritize expenditures in R&D because it serves as the primary catalyst for fostering innovation and sustaining operational endeavors. R&D investments are recognized as a very important factor in fostering innovation and ensuring long-term growth. It is argued that investments in R&D enable firms to engage in innovative activities, providing firms with a more competitive advantage (David et al., 2008; Chen, 2014). But what influences these crucial investment decisions? Stiles and Taylor (2001) argue that it is the board's mandate to determine how firm resources are allocated within the organization. This shows that the board has a direct influence on the strategic outcomes of the firm (Kim et al., 2009). The members of the board of directors make recommendations to the firm on strategic actions. They establish a link between the firm and the external environment and support the formulation and implementation of strategies.

Examining the relationship between board characteristics and R&D investments has received significant attention in the corporate governance literature. Previous studies have shown that board size (Ginesti et al., 2023; Hernandez et al., 2010), independence (Balsmeier et al., 2017; Lu & Wang, 2015), CEO duality (Chen & Hsu, 2009; Li & Yang, 2019) and diversity (Azzam & Alhababsah, 2022; Almor

S. Çerez (✉) · A. K. Merter · Y. S. Balcıoğlu
Gebze Technical University, Faculty of Business Administration, Gebze, Turkey
e-mail: sedatcerez@gtu.edu.tr

G. Özer
Gebze Technical University, Faculty of Business Administration, Gebze, Turkey

Kyrgyz-Turkish Manas University, Faculty of Economics and Administrative Sciences, Bishkek, Kyrgyzstan

N. Ozatac et al. (eds.), *Sustainable Development in Banking and Finance*, Springer Proceedings in Business and Economics,
https://doi.org/10.1007/978-3-031-65533-3_12

et al., 2022) are related to R&D investments. The relationship between the board and R&D investments differs depending on the specific characteristics of the board. While some studies suggest that larger boards may have difficulty reaching consensus, leading to delays or reductions in R&D investments (Chen, 2012; Zhaohui & Ding, 2012), some studies have not found a significant relationship between board size and R&D investments (Azzam & Alhababsah, 2022; Ginesti et al., 2023). According to Linck et al. (2008), companies with larger growth possibilities allocate more resources toward research and development and experience major volatility in stock returns. They are more likely to have smaller boards with fewer independent members. Conversely, larger companies typically have more substantial and more independent boards.

The primary objective of this research is to investigate how board members' age and educational backgrounds affect the amount of R&D expenses that companies invest. Developing countries often strive for rapid economic growth and innovation. R&D plays a crucial role in driving technological advancements, improving productivity, and fostering innovation. However, resources, both financial and human, are often limited in developing countries. Ensuring that these resources are directed towards impactful R&D projects can maximize returns on investment. Boards with a higher education level can facilitate better knowledge transfer, forming partnerships with international organizations, or adopting best practices from developed markets. Due to their vast experiences and the nature of generational values, older board members might be more risk-averse than younger board members. This risk aversion can lead to a conservative approach toward R&D investments, which are inherently risky and uncertain. Examining the impact of education level and age on R&D expenditures is of great importance due to the essential role that research and development plays in promoting economic progress. This significance is further heightened by emerging countries' distinct problems and opportunities.

In this study, the effects of the education level and age factors of the members of the board of directors on the R&D expenditures of the firm are analyzed over 1282 observation values of the firms operating in Borsa Istanbul between 2010 and 2019. All observation values obtained were used in the study where panel data analysis was preferred, and operations were performed on unbalanced panel data. Financial institutions such as banks, real estate investment trusts, and holdings are not included in the study since they are subject to different regulations and legislations. The results show that more educated and younger board directors are substantially and positively related to R&D investments. These results suggest that boards with higher levels of education tend to have a deeper understanding of the intricacies and potential payoffs of R&D projects. Their educational backgrounds might provide them with a better grasp of the long-term benefits of R&D investments, making them more inclined to champion and prioritize such ventures within the company's strategic plans. Furthermore, younger boards seem to bring a fresh perspective and a more adaptable mindset towards innovation and technological advancements. They might be more attuned to the rapid changes in the market, the evolving needs of consumers, and the potential disruptive technologies on the horizon.

2 Literature Review and Hypothesis Development

Studies indicate the critical role of R&D in launching new products and boosting productivity, leading to sustainable growth (Bustinza et al., 2019; Grossman & Helpman, 1994, 2015; Pindado et al., 2015). Innovation is key in today's fast-paced and competitive market, and R&D plays a crucial part in driving innovation. By investing in research and development, companies can stay ahead of their competitors by creating groundbreaking products and services (Andersson, 2012). However, such investments come with significant uncertainties, substantial initial costs, and extended returns on investment (Khan et al., 2020). Therefore, the creation and execution of R&D strategies is vulnerable to conflicts of interest that may arise among shareholders and managers (Lee & O'neill, 2003; Muhammad et al., 2022).

The study by Hernández et al. (2010) examined the influence of board qualities and ownership structure on the R&D investments of 86 technological companies in Spain. Results of the study indicate that an increase in the number of executive members on a firm's board is associated with a negative impact on the firm's investments in R&D. Additionally, the ownership structure is found to moderate the relationship between board characteristics and R&D investments. He et al. (2010) investigated the correlation between the educational attainment of board members and the level of investments in research and development (R&D) within a sample of 623 firms publicly listed on the Chinese Stock between 2004 and 2007. The researchers find that the educational attainment of the board members does not significantly influence R&D spending as a whole. However, they revealed that the educational attainment of the board members has a more pronounced impact on R&D investments in sectors that heavily rely on capital and technology, as opposed to more labor-intensive sectors.

Chen (2012) found a negative association between R&D expenditure, board size, and educational attainment when examining the effects of board composition on R&D spending for electronics companies listed on the Taiwan Stock. Furthermore, there is no discernible relationship between the number of board meetings and R&D spending. Zhaohui and Ding (2012) examined the connection between the R&D spending and board composition of information technology businesses that were listed in China from 2007 to 2010. The results indicate that the number of independent directors on the board has a positive influence on R&D expenditures. However, the size and average age of the board of directors have a negative impact on the firm's R&D spending.

Chen et al. (2013) used the resource dependency theory to assess how the CEO's attributes affected the company's R&D spending. The findings indicated that while CEO tenure and R&D investments are negatively correlated, CEO education level and expenditure are positively correlated. Chen (2014), based on the resource dependence theory, examined the relationship between board structure and R&D investments of electronics firms operating in Taiwan. At the end of the study, they found that board education level, members' industry-specific experience and commitment to each other have a positive effect on the firm's R&D investments and CEO power has a positive moderating effect on this effect.

Kuo et al. (2018) examined the impact of managers' education level on R&D investments due to the moderating effects of corporate ownership, family participation in management, and type of control over 437 firms operating on the Taiwan Stock between 2006–2012. In the study's findings, they observed that managers with higher education levels attach more importance to R&D investments. They also found that executive professionalism strengthens the positive impact of managers on R&D investments, while corporate ownership and family participation in management weaken this relationship. Wang et al. (2019) examined if there is a relationship between R&D expenditures and managers' postgraduate education experience using the ordinary least squares (OLS) regression method over 1374 firms operated on the Chinese Stock Exchange. According to the findings, it is observed that the percentage of managers with PhD increases the firm's impact on R&D expenditures. Feng et al. (2021), in their study of firms listed on the Shanghai and Shenzhen Stock, obtained empirical evidence that board members with experience in academia positively affect the R&D expenditures of companies. Azzam and Alhababsah (2022) found that the tenure of the chairman of the board of directors had a negative effect on R&D investments, whereas the chairman's age did not have a significant effect on R&D investments.

Managers with advanced education (postgraduate) have more knowledge than others (Chen, 2012; Wally & Baum, 1994). This accumulation of knowledge constitutes superior information processing capability (Chen, 2014). In a constantly evolving and rapidly changing environment, real-time information processing capability and forward-looking forecasts on environmental issues are important (Bantel & Jackson, 1989). This creates significant information processing demands on company managers. Advanced education gives business leaders skills that make it easier to judge research and development projects (Dalziel et al., 2011). Hence, adding more highly educated directors to the board helps the company better manage its R&D investments by looking at the short- and long-term effects of R&D investments and coming up with the best strategies. This also helps the company find projects with a positive net present value (Chen, 2014). Also, managers with more schooling may be better able to learn how to use technology (Lin et al., 2011) and get the information they need to solve R&D problems (Wincent et al., 2010).

In summary, it can be concluded that R&D investments are very important in fostering innovation within businesses. Additionally, the allocation of resources towards R&D activities is of significant importance. The educational background of board members determines their ability to effectively oversee and regulate the financial aspects of R&D investments. It is anticipated that managers with higher levels of education will exhibit a greater inclination towards innovation, thereby positively influencing the magnitude of R&D investments.

H1 The postgraduate education of the board directors is positively related to the firm's R&D investments.

Older managers tend to be more risk-averse and conservative than their younger counterparts (Zhaohui & Ding, 2012). R&D investments are risky investments due to their uncertain future. For this reason, older managers are more hesitant about R&D investments compared to younger managers. In addition, due to the difficulty of acquiring new knowledge, older managers may have difficulty in accepting new ideas. On the contrary, younger managers may be more willing to try and accept new ideas because they are more curious and have more recent knowledge.

H2 Younger board members are positively related to a firm's R&D investments.

3 Methodology

3.1 *Sample*

The sample of the research includes firms operating in Borsa Istanbul between the years 2010–2019. Financial institutions such as real estate investment trusts, banks, and holdings are excluded from the sample as they have different regulations and legislation. Data on the board of directors are obtained from the Public Disclosure Platform (KAP) and firm-specific financial data are obtained from the Finnet database. To minimize the effect of outliers in the data set on the analysis results, the financial data variables are equalized to the observation values corresponding to the 5% to 95% quintiles. All analysis procedures were performed using the Stata 17 statistical package program.

3.2 *Research Model and Variables*

The following study model has been designed to quantify the effect of age and board education status on the firm's R&D investments.

$$\mathrm{R\&D_{it}} = \beta_{0it} + \beta_1 \mathrm{POSTGRADUATE_{it}} + \beta_2 \mathrm{CONTROL_{it}} + \mu_i + v_{it} \quad (1)$$

$$\mathrm{R\&D_{it}} = \beta_{0it} + \beta_1 \mathrm{YOUNG_{it}} + \beta_2 \mathrm{CONTROL_{it}} + \mu_i + v_{it} \quad (2)$$

The R&D variable in the model follows the previous studies and consists of firms' R&D expenditure ratio (R&D1) (Azzam & Alhababsah, 2022; Chen et al., 2013; Kuo et al., 2018; Sing & Gaur, 2013; Zhaohui & Ding, 2012; Feng et al., 2021) and R&D investment ratio (R&D2) (Greve, 2003; Kuo et al., 2018; Chen, 2012; Chen et al., 2013). Postgraduate and young variables represent the independent variables of the models. First, each board member's education level is ranked as follows in the educated variable: 1 represents high school and lower, 2 is a bachelor's degree, 3 is a master's degree, and 4 is a PhD. Each rating ranges from 1 to 4. The average education level is then calculated by dividing the total education level of all board members by the total number of members. Last but not least, the boards with postgraduate education averages higher than 2 were marked as 1, while the remaining boards were coded as 0. In the young variable, the average education level of each board is taken and the boards with an average education level below

Table 1 Definitions and explanations of variables

Variables	Explanations of variables
R&D1	R&D expenditure ratio; R&D expenses / net sales
R&D2	R&D investment ratio; R&D expenses / total assets
Postgraduate	The board's average education level is 1 if it is postgraduate; 0 otherwise.
Young	The board's average age is 1 if it is under 50; 0 otherwise.
Size	Firm size; natural logarithm of total assets.
Leverage	Firm leverage; total liabilities / total assets
MV	Market value ratio; market capitalization/book value
Boardsize	Natural logarithm of total board members
Independent	Number of independent board members divided by the total number of board members.
Gender	If there is a female member on the board of directors, 1; otherwise, the value 0 is given.
Financial	Number of financial expert board members / Total board members
Overlapped	Number of board members overlapping in committees / Total board members

50 are coded as 1 and the others as 0. Control refers to the control variables tested for their effect on R&D expenditures and used in previous studies. To prevent the outliers of the financial variables in the models from negatively affecting the results of the analysis, the outliers of the variables were equalized to 5% and 95% observation values. The entire analysis process was carried out using the Stata 17 statistical package program. Abbreviations and detailed explanations of the variables in the models are given in Table 1.

Table 2 shows the descriptive statistics of the variables in the model. As can be seen from the table, 1328 observations were obtained in all variables except the market value ratio. To prevent outliers in the data set from affecting the analysis results, the variables' outliers were equalized to the observation values corresponding to 5% to 95%. The enterprises' R&D expenditure ratio (R&D1) in the sample varies between 0% and 2.4%, with an average of 0.37%. The R&D investment ratio (R&D2) has an average value of 0.35%. The rate of postgraduate education among the board of directors is 81.2%. The young variable, which expresses the probability that the mean age of the board of directors in the sample is less than 50, has an average value of 22.8%.

Table 3 shows the correlation matrix that shows how the variables used in the study are correlated. Based on the table, the independent variables don't have a strong correlation to each other. This shows that there is no multicollinearity problem in the model. Furthermore, the Variance Inflation Factor (VIF) and tolerance values were computed for each independent variable to conduct additional tests for multicollinearity. VIF values ranging from 1.06 to 1.79 are less than 10. At the same time, tolerance values ranging from 0.55 to 0.96 are greater than 0.1. This shows that the regression models do not have potential multicollinearity problems. In addition, there is a positive correlation that is statistically significant between the Postgraduate variable added to the model and both R&D1 and R&D2 variables that

Table 2 Descriptive statistics

Variables	Number of observations	Mean	Standard deviation	Median	Min	Max
Boardsize	1,328	1.924	0.293	1.946	1.099	2.708
Independent	1,328	0.262	0.135	0.286	0	0.571
Gender	1,328	0.553	0.497	1	0	1
Financial	1,328	0.397	0.215	0.400	0	1
Overlapped	1,328	0.465	0.186	0.500	0	1
Postgraduate	1,328	0.812	0.391	1	0	1
Young	1,328	0.228	0.420	0	0	1
R&D1	1,328	0.0037	0.006	0.000	0	0.024
R&D2	1,328	0.0035	0.006	0.000	0	0.021
Size	1,328	19.91	1609	19.68	17.35	23.27
Leverage	1,328	0.515	0.214	0.539	0.156	0.864
MV	1,282	1.875	1.287	1.480	0.500	5.400

represent R&D investments. The *youth* variable, which expresses the probability that the average age of the board of directors is below 50, is found to have a statistically significant and negative relationship with both the R&D expenditure ratio and the R&D investment ratio.

4 Research Findings

In order to examine the effects of education and age factors within the board of directors on the firm's R&D investments, it is necessary to determine which estimation method is more appropriate. For this purpose, the F test, the Breusch-Pagan test, and the Hausman test were applied to the model. In the models where both R&D expenditure ratio (R&D1) and R&D investment ratio (R&D2) dependent variables are included, the F test yielded fixed effects results. The Breusch-Pagan test yielded random effects results, and the Hausman test was performed. Since the P values obtained as a result of this test were greater than 0.10, the H0 hypothesis could not be rejected (P: 0.6490). This result shows that the most optimal estimation method for the model is the random effects method.

To check whether the random effects panel data analysis method determined from the estimator tests will provide accurate and unbiased analysis results, deviations from assumptions tests were applied. Variation, autocorrelation, and cross-sectional dependence, which are expressed as hypothetical problems, are measured by Levene, Brown and Forsythe, Durbin-Watson and LBI and Pesaran, respectively.

When the test statistics (W0, W50, W10) of the Levene, Brown and Forsythe test results of the model with the dependent variable R&D1 are compared with the Snedecor F table with (142,1139) degrees of freedom, it is understood that there is variance between units (Tatoğlu, 2021: 266–267). Bahargava et al.'s Durbin-Watson

Table 3 Correlation matrix

		1	2	3	4	5	6	7	8	9	10	11
R&D1	1	1.000										
R&D2	2	0.940***	1.000									
Postgraduate	3	0.118***	0.102***	1.000								
Young	4	−0.052*	– 0.065**	– 0.128***	1.000							
Size	5	0.007	0.019	0.221***	– 0.231***	1.000						
Leverage	6	−0.006	0.019	0.045	−0.087	0.251***	1.000					
MV	7	0.024	0.075***	0.122***	0.015	0.006	0.188***	1.000				
Boardsize	8	−0.029	−0.007	0.217***	– 0.236***	0.590***	0.017	0.020	1.000			
Independent	9	0.043	0.022	0.115***	−0.0150	0.009	0.126***	0.028	– 0.133***	1.000		
Gender	10	0.056**	0.059**	0.039	– 0.099***	0.059**	0.088***	– 0.072***	0.096***	−0.044	1.000	
Overlapped	11	0.072***	0.042	0.055**	0.018	0.039	0.099***	−0.061**	– 0.091***	0.464***	−0.012	1.000
Financial	12	0.041	0.049*	0.106***	– 0.075***	0.103***	0.102***	0.059**	0.087***	0.094***	0.119***	0.012

Notes: The symbols ***. **, and * denote statistical significance at the 1%, 5%, and 10% levels of confidence, respectively

and Balgati-Wu's LBI tests, which test the presence of autocorrelation in the model, are both lower than the critical value (2). Therefore, autocorrelation problem is encountered in the model (Tatoğlu, 2021: 268). The Pesaran test result, which tests horizontal cross-sectional dependence in the model, is significant at the one percent level (P:0.000). This indicates that the model has a cross-sectional dependence problem.

When the statistics of Levene, Brown and Forsythe tests (W0, W50, W10) of the model with R&D2 dependent variable are compared with the Snedecor F table with (142,1139) degrees of freedom, it shows that there is variance between units. Moreover, Bahargava et al.'s Durbin-Watson and Balgati-Wu's LBI tests are lower than the critical value (2), indicating an autocorrelation problem in the model. The cross-sectional dependency issue in the model is shown by the Pesaran test result (P:0.000).

Both the R&D1 and R&D2 models are susceptible to altering variance, autocorrelation, and horizontal cross-sectional dependence, as demonstrated by the tests used to detect hypothetical problems. To eliminate these issues, researchers often employ the Driscoll Kraay robust standard error estimators as a suitable testing approach in samples where the number of cross-sectional units (N) exceeds the time dimension (T) (Tatoğlu, 2021: 364). The findings of the analysis conducted on the constructed model, which aimed to examine the impact of board education level and age characteristics on a firm's R&D investments, are presented in Table 4. The Driscoll Kraay robust standard error estimator was chosen as the preferred method based on the results of the assumptions tests.

The main results regarding the effect of the board of directors' education level on R&D investments show that R&D investments are given more importance when the board of directors includes members with postgraduate education. The *Postgraduate* variable, which represents the average education level of the board of directors, is statistically significant and positive on both the R&D expenditure ratio (R&D1) and the R&D investment ratio (R&D2). This finding is consistent with previous studies (Wang et al., 2019; Chen, 2012, 2014; Kuo et al., 2018) and supports hypothesis H1.

The coefficient of the *young* variable, which refers to the proportion of directors under 50 years of age in the board of directors, on R&D expenditures is statistically significant and positive. Consistent with previous studies (Zhaohui & Ding, 2012), this finding indicates that younger directors attach more importance to R&D investments and supports hypothesis H2. Older managers tend to be more conservative and take fewer risks than younger managers (Zhaohui & Ding, 2012). On the contrary, young managers tend to accept new ideas more easily due to their up-to-date knowledge and curiosity. Since R&D expenditures are risky investments with an uncertain future, older managers are less accepting of these investments.

In the study, additional tests were applied to better understand the impact of board education level and age on R&D investments. Table 5 reports the effects of the interactions of education and age variables on R&D investments. Board members who are under 50 years of age and have a postgraduate degree have a positive effect on both the R&D expenditure ratio and the R&D investment ratio. According to this finding, the fact that the directors are both young and have postgraduate education

Table 4 Driscoll Kraay analysis results

	(1)	(2)	(3)	(4)
Variables	R&D1	R&D1	R&D2	R&D2
Postgraduate	0.000** (2.42)		0.001** (2.30)	
Young		0.000** (2.62)		0.000 (1.01)
Size	0.000** (2.67)	0.000** (2.86)	−0.000 (−1.28)	−0.000 (−1.18)
Leverage	−0.000 (−0.44)	−0.000 (−0.24)	−0.000 (−0.49)	−0.000 (−0.48)
MV	−0.000* (−2.08)	−0.000 (−1.61)	0.000 (0.45)	0.000 (0.43)
Boardsize	0.001 (1.21)	0.001 (1.36)	0.001 (1.75)	0.001* (2.10)
Independent	−0.002** (−2.68)	−0.002* (−2.15)	−0.001** (−2.56)	−0.001* (−1.87)
Gender	−0.000 (−0.11)	−0.000 (−0.23)	0.000 (0.85)	0.000 (0.64)
Overlapped	0.001 (1.80)	0.001 (1.42)	0.000 (1.36)	0.000 (1.50)
Financial	0.001 (1.48)	0.001 (1.35)	0.001 (1.70)	0.001 (1.73)
Year effect	YES	YES	YES	YES
Sector effect	YES	YES	YES	YES
Intercept	0.000 (.)	0.000 (.)	0.000 (.)	0.000 (.)
Observations	1,282	1,282	1,282	1,282
R2 value	0.1187	0.1131	0.0975	0.0905
Ki-Kare	4,389.73***	1,270.57***	9,531.70***	10,135.48***

Notes: The symbols ***, **, and * denote statistical significance at the 1%, 5%, and 10% levels of confidence, respectively

has a positive effect on the firm's R&D investments. On the contrary, directors who are 50 years old or older and have a bachelor's degree or less have no significant effect on R&D investments.

Table 6 provides an in-depth look into the results of the two-step system GMM estimation, focusing on the relationship between board education, age, and R&D investments. Notably, the Hansen test's p-values are not statistically significant, which attests to the validity of our instruments across all regression analyses conducted. The accuracy of the model was additionally confirmed by assessing the insignificance of the first-order serial correlation (AR (1)). This is crucial, as it confirms that the model is appropriately structured. This is further validated by the absence of the second-order serial correlation (AR (2)), allowing us to discount both white noise processes for regression error estimations. Upon comparison, it's evident that the findings detailed in our primary table about the influence of board education and age on R&D investments are consistent, even when we employ the two-step GMM methodology.

Table 5 Panel data analysis results of interaction variables

	(5)	(6)	(7)	(8)
Variables	R&D1	R&D2	R&D1	R&D2
Postgraduate X Young	0.001** (3.25)	0.001* (2.23)		
Underpost X Old			0.000 (0.05)	−0.000 (−0.81)
Size	0.000** (3.00)	−0.000 (−1.07)	0.000** (2.78)	−0.000 (−1.25)
Leverage	−0.000 (−0.26)	−0.000 (−0.49)	−0.000 (−0.27)	−0.000 (−0.48)
MV	−0.000 (−1.62)	0.000 (0.48)	−0.000 (−1.59)	0.000 (0.41)
Boardsize	0.000 (1.09)	0.001* (1.95)	0.001 (1.63)	0.001* (2.07)
Independent	−0.002** (−2.52)	−0.001** (−2.53)	−0.002** (−2.28)	−0.001* (−2.17)
Gender	−0.000 (−0.23)	0.000 (0.63)	−0.000 (−0.18)	0.000 (0.72)
Overlapped	0.001 (1.34)	0.000 (1.39)	0.001 (1.52)	0.000 (1.54)
Financial	0.001 (1.24)	0.001 (1.62)	0.001 (1.39)	0.001 (1.75)
Year Effect	YES	YES	YES	YES
Sector Effect	YES	YES	YES	YES
Intercept	−0.009*** (−3.71)	0.000 (.)	−0.008*** (−3.73)	0.000 (.)
Observations	1,282	1,282	1,282	1,282
R2 Value	0.1135	0.0905	0.1156	0.0928
Ki-Kare	6,504.87***	8,673.15***	4,477.26***	11.485.29***

Notes: The symbols ***, **, and * denote statistical significance at the 1%, 5%, and 10% levels of confidence, respectively

5 Conclusion

This study aims to examine the effect of the education level and age of the members of the board of directors on a firm's R&D investments by using the panel data analysis method over the firms operating in Borsa Istanbul from 2010 to 2019. For this purpose, hypotheses were developed for both education and age variables, and Driscoll Kraay robust standard error estimator was used as a result of assumptive problem tests to test whether the hypotheses are supported or not.

According to the empirical findings, in line with other studies (Wang et al., 2019; Chen, 2012, 2014; Kuo et al., 2018), the educational level of board members has a positive impact on firms' R&D investments. Highly educated managers have more knowledge and information-processing skills than others. (Chen, 2012; Wally & Baum, 1994). In a constantly evolving and changing environment, the ability to

Table 6 Two-step system GMM estimation

Variables	R&D1		R&D2	
	Coeff.	t-value	Coeff.	t-value
$R\&D1_{t-1}$	1.045***	14.24		
$R\&D2_{t-1}$			1.080***	13.41
Postgraduate	0.001**	2.10	0.001**	2.51
Young	0.000*	1.71	0.000	0.78
Intercept	−0.000	−0.12	0.000	0.05
Control Variable	YES		YES	
Industry Effects	YES		YES	
Year Effects	YES		YES	
AR(1) Test	0.012		0.018	
AR(2) Test	0.124		0.128	
Hansen Test	0.192		0.158	
F Statistic	192.19***		101.11***	
Observations	1,137		1,137	

Notes: The symbols ***, **, and * denote statistical significance at the 1%, 5%, and 10% levels of confidence, respectively

process real-time data information is an important factor. In addition, since R&D projects are a type of long-term investment involving uncertainty, they require extreme caution in decision-making. For this reason, managers with advanced education can evaluate the short- and long-term effects of research and development projects and take appropriate strategic steps.

In accordance with previous research (Zhaohui & Ding, 2012), an increase in the number of youthful board members has a positive impact on a company's R&D investments. Older directors tend to be more risk-averse and conservative than their younger counterparts (Zhaohui & Ding, 2012). Due to the high risk associated with R&D investments, younger managers may place a greater emphasis on R&D investments and be more receptive to new ideas than their elder counterparts.

The study's results carry significant implications about the influence of board members' age and education level on the firm's motivation to engage in research and development (R&D). The majority of existing research on corporate governance has mostly focused on the economies of developed countries. However, there is a scarcity of empirical studies examining the applicability of corporate governance practices from established economies to those of developing countries (Chen, 2012). The use of Turkish data to investigate how board education and age affect R&D investments is anticipated to shed light on the relationship between governance and R&D in emerging economies. The institutional frameworks, regulatory environments, and cultural dynamics of these economies differ significantly from their developed counterparts. Hence, extrapolating findings from developed economies and applying them directly to emerging markets can be misleading.

References

Almor, T., Bazel-Shoham, O., & Lee, S. M. (2022). The dual effect of board gender diversity on R&D investments. *Long Range Planning, 55*(2), 101884. https://doi.org/10.1016/j.lrp.2019.05.004

Andersson, M. (Ed.). (2012). *Innovation and growth: From R&D strategies of innovating firms to economy-wide technological change*. Oxford University Press.

Azzam, A., & Alhababsah, S. (2022). Do tenure and age of board chair matter for R&D investment? *Journal of Financial Reporting & Accounting*. https://doi.org/10.1108/JFRA-01-2022-0023

Balsmeier, B., Fleming, L., & Manso, G. (2017). Independent boards and innovation. *Journal of Financial Economics, 123*(3), 536–557. https://doi.org/10.1016/j.jfineco.2016.12.005

Bantel, K., & Jackson, S. (1989). Top management and innovations in banking: Does the composition of the top management team make a difference? *Strategic Management Journal, 10*, 107–124. https://doi.org/10.1002/smj.4250100709

Bustinza, O. F., Gomes, E., Vendrell-Herrero, F., & Baines, T. (2019). Product–service innovation and performance: The role of collaborative partnerships and R&D intensity. *R&D Management, 49*(1), 33–45. https://doi.org/10.1111/radm.12269

Chen, H.-L. (2012). Board characteristics and R&D investment: Evidence from Taiwan's electronics industry. *Advances in Management & Applied Economics, 2*(4), 161–170.

Chen, H.-L. (2014). Board capital, CEO power and R&D investment in electronics firms. *Corporate Governance: An International Review, 22*(5), 422–436. https://doi.org/10.1111/corg.12076

Chen, H. L., & Hsu, W. T. (2009). Family ownership, board independence, and R&D investment. *Family Business Review, 22*(4), 347–362. https://doi.org/10.1177/0894486509341062

Chen, H.-L., Ho, M., & Hsu, W.-T. (2013). Does board social capital influence chief executive Officers' Investment decisions in research and development? *R&D Management, 43*(4), 381–393. https://doi.org/10.1111/radm.12025

Dalziel, T., Gentry, R. J., & Bowerman, M. (2011). An integrated agency-resource dependence view of the influence of directors' human and relational capital on firms' R&D spending. *Journal of Management Studies, 48*(6), 1217–1242. https://doi.org/10.1111/j.1467-6486.2010.01003.x

David, P., O'Brien, J. P., & Yoshikawa, T. (2008). The implications of debt heterogeneity for R&D investment and firm performance. *Journal of Management Studies*, 1217–1242.

Feng, C. B., Mirza, S. S., Ahsan, T., & Gull, A. A. (2021). The impact of financial flexibility and directors' academic experience on corporate R&D investments: A quantile regression approach. *Applied Economics, 54*(17), 1974–1988. https://doi.org/10.1080/00036846.2021.1983145 © 2021 Informa UK Limited, trading as Taylor & Francis Group.

Ginesti, G., Campa, D., Allini, A., & Maffei, M. (2023). The role of CSR committee characteristics on R&D investments. *International Business Review*, 102147.

Greve, H. R. (2003). A behavioral theory of R&D expenditures and innovations: Evidence from shipbuilding. *The Academy of Management Journal, 46*(6), 685–702. https://doi.org/10.2307/30040661

Grossman, G. M., & Helpman, E. (1994). Endogenous innovation in the theory of growth. *Journal of Economic Perspectives, 8*(1), 23–44.

He, Q., Chen, S., & Zhang, J. (2010). Board education level distribution and R&D investment: Empirical study based on listed manufacturing firms. *Picmet 2010 Technology Management for Global Economic Growth.*

Hernandez, A. B., Camelo, C., & Valle, R. (2010). The effects of boards of directors on R&D investments: The case of Spain. *International Journal of Human Resources Development and Management, 10*(2), 152–165. https://doi.org/10.1504/ijhrdm.2010.031441

Khan, M. A., Qin, X., Jebran, K., & Ullah, I. (2020). Uncertainty and R&D investment: Does product market competition matter? *Research in International Business and Finance, 52*, 101167. https://doi.org/10.1016/j.ribaf.2019.101167

Kim, B., Burns, M. L., & Prescott, J. E. (2009). The strategic role of the board: The impact of board structure on top management team strategic action capability. *Corporate Governance: An International Review, 17*(6), 728–743. https://doi.org/10.1111/j.1467-8683.2009.00775.x

Kuo, H.-C., Wang, L.-H., & Yeh, L.-J. (2018). The role of education of directors in influencing firm R&D investment. *Asia Pacific Management Review, 23*(2), 108–120. https://doi.org/10.1016/j.apmrv.2017.05.002

Lee, P. M., & O'neill, H. M. (2003). Ownership structures and R&D investments of US and Japanese firms: Agency and stewardship perspectives. *Academy of Management Journal, 46*(2), 212–225. https://doi.org/10.5465/30040615

Li, M., & Yang, J. (2019). Effects of CEO duality and tenure on innovation. *Journal of Strategy and Management, 12*(4), 536–552. https://doi.org/10.1108/JSMA-04-2019-0049

Lin, C., Lin, P., Song, F. M., & Li, C. (2011). Managerial incentives, CEO characteristics and corporate innovation in China's private sector. *Journal of Comparative Economics, 39*(2), 176–190. https://doi.org/10.1016/j.jce.2009.12.001

Linck, J. S., Netter, J. M., & Yang, T. (2008). The determinants of board structure. *Journal of Financial Economics, 87*(2), 308–328. https://doi.org/10.1016/j.jfineco.2007.03.004

Lu, J., & Wang, W. (2015). Board independence and corporate investments. *Review of Financial Economics, 24*, 52–64. https://doi.org/10.1016/j.rfe.2015.01.001

Muhammad, H., Migliori, S., & Consorti, A. (2022). Corporate governance and R&D investment: does firm size matter? *Technology Analysis & Strategic Management*, 1–15. https://doi.org/10.1080/09537325.2022.2042508

Pindado, J., de Queiroz, V., & De la Torre, C. (2015). How do country-level governance characteristics impact the relationship between R & D and firm value? *R&D Management, 45*(5), 515–526. https://doi.org/10.1111/radm.12115

Sing, D. A., & Gaur, A. S. (2013). Governance structure, innovation and internationalization: Evidence from India. *Journal of International Management, 19*(3), 300–309. https://doi.org/10.1016/j.intman.2013.03.006

Stiles, P., & Taylor, B. (2001). *Boards at work: How directors view their responsibilities*. Oxford University Press.

Tatoğlu, F. Y. (2021). *Panel Veri Ekonometrisi: Stata Uygulamalı*. Beta Basım Yayım Dağıtım A.Ş.

Wally, S., & Baum, J. R. (1994). Personal and structural determinants of the pace of strategic decision making. *Academy of Management Journal, 37*(4), 932–956. https://doi.org/10.5465/256605

Wang, C., Yang, J., Cheng, Z., & Ni, C. (2019). Postgraduate education of board members and R&D investment—Evidence from China. *Sustainability, 11*(22), 6524. https://doi.org/10.3390/su11226524

Wincent, J., Anokhin, S., & Örtqvist, D. (2010). Does network. Does network board capital matter? *A Study of Innovative Performance in Strategic SME Network, 63*(3), 265–275. https://doi.org/10.1016/j.jbusres.2009.03.012

Zhaohui, Z., & Ding, W. (2012). The board structure and R&D investment—A study on the Chinese listed IT companies. *International Symposium on Management of Technology (ISMOT)*, 226–229.

Green Finance Dynamics: Exploring the Factors Impacting Global Bond Markets

Dana Moldakulova, Yeran Baishan, and Alimshan Faizulayev

1 Introduction

The globe is at a critical turning point when environmental preservation is more necessary than ever amid mounting worries and discussions about climate change. In the pursuit of achieving the ambitious 1.5 °C target outlined in the Paris Agreement, a profound transformation in investment strategies is imperative (McCollum et al., 2018). This necessitates a shift towards sustainable financial mechanisms, with a particular focus on green finance (GF) initiatives. Green bonds, a key component of GF, have gained significant traction globally and across Asia, emerging as a vital instrument for funding low-carbon developments (Durrani et al., 2020).

Green bonds, often defined as fixed-income securities designed to raise capital for projects with environmental benefits, have witnessed a remarkable evolution. From a modest \$3.4 billion market in 2012 to an impressive \$156 billion in 2017, their growth underscores the increasing importance of financial instruments aligned with environmental sustainability (Bracking, 2015). This journey began with Europe's pioneering green bonds in 2007 and 2008, with China later becoming the world's largest issuer in 2015. The rise of green bond award schemes has further propelled issuance, reflecting a heightened commitment to environmentally conscious financial practices.

While green bonds have traditionally been associated with funding renewable energy or energy efficiency projects, their role has expanded to encompass broader environmental initiatives, including climate change mitigation, natural resource conservation, and biodiversity preservation (Chugan et al., 2017). This expansion

D. Moldakulova · Y. Baishan · A. Faizulayev (✉)
Bang College of Business, KIMEP University, Almaty, Republic of Kazakhstan
e-mail: a.faizulayev@kimep.kz

N. Ozatac et al. (eds.), *Sustainable Development in Banking and Finance*, Springer Proceedings in Business and Economics,
https://doi.org/10.1007/978-3-031-65533-3_13

has been accompanied by the emergence of various green finance initiatives, such as green bond standards, grant programs, and sovereign green bonds (Li et al., 2021).

The urgency of addressing climate change and the imperative to transition to a low carbon-intensive economy have prompted a reevaluation of the financial sector's role in driving green growth (Alemzero & Huaping, 2021). The critical role of the financial sector in facilitating the transformation from polluted economies to green economies has elevated the discourse around green financing, positioning it as a mandatory option for sustainable economic development (Huang et al., (2022). Utilizing a linear regression model, our study aims to explore the impact of key independent variables, including GDP, inflation rate, sustainability competitiveness, natural capital, resource intensity, social capital, intellectual capital, and governance, during 2017–2022. We analyze the factors influencing green bond issuances on a global scale, offering insights into the dynamics shaping the international green bond market. The structure of the paper is as follows: Section 2 provides a comprehensive review of the literature on global green bond market development. Section 3 explains the theoretical background. Section 4 outlines the empirical model and methodology and elucidates our main hypothesis. Section 5 summarizes the main findings of the study, and Sect. 6 discusses the policy implications and offers conclusions.

2 Literature Review

The literature on global green bond market development has gained prominence, reflecting the growing significance of sustainable finance in the international arena. Studies emphasize the advantages of green bond issuances, including resilience against environmental risks, enhanced reputation, lower debt costs, diversification benefits, and access to a broad investor base (Bachelet et al., 2019; Gilchrist et al., 2021). While the green bond market represents a relatively small segment compared to conventional bonds, scholars have identified barriers and proposed solutions to foster its growth on a global scale (Tolliver et al., 2020). Challenges include difficulties in general bond market development, accessing local markets from abroad, a scarcity of domestic green investors, and perceived higher risks associated with green investments. International collaboration, increased awareness of green bond integrity, credit enhancements, tax incentives, standardization of definitions and frameworks, and labeling qualified bonds are suggested remedies (Tolliver et al., 2020).

The literature on determinants of green bond issuances is evolving, with studies analyzing security, issuer, and market characteristics (Chiesa & Barua, 2019), constructing the Nationally Determined Contribution index (Tolliver et al., 2020), and exploring legal infrastructure, interest rates, and economic stability in developing countries (Anh et al., 2020). Advancements in financial technology (FinTech) and the emergence of green finance platforms are influencing the accessibility and efficiency of green bonds. Literature highlights how technological innovations contribute to the expansion of green finance and facilitate the integration of environmental considerations into investment decisions (Ge et al., 2022).

Macroeconomic and institutional factors, known to influence capital and financial market development, play a crucial role in the global context (Tolliver et al., 2020). Drivers of the green bond market align with those of conventional bonds, with climate awareness and policymakers' commitment playing pivotal roles (Banga, 2019).

Global variations in green finance priorities are evident, with the European market leading in volume, followed by the Asia-Pacific and North American markets (Cheong & Choi, 2020). The green bond market in China, driven by government policies, is expanding rapidly, with renewable energy projects dominating issuances (Xiao & Dong, 2022).

Overall, the literature presents a dynamic and evolving landscape, emphasizing the need for tailored analyses within specific regions or economic contexts to understand the multi-faceted factors influencing global green bond markets.

3 Theoretical Background

The theoretical foundation for this study draws from a synthesis of economic, environmental, and social theories that collectively contribute to understanding the dynamics of global green bond issuances. The selected theories offer a comprehensive framework for analyzing the interplay between various determinants and the volume of green bond issuances.

1. *Institutional Theory:* Institutional Theory posits that the quality of institutions shapes organizational behavior. In green bonds, governance practices are central to institutional quality. Effective governance influences investor perceptions of transparency and credibility, impacting the overall attractiveness of green bonds relative to conventional bonds. Institutions that prioritize sustainability and environmental responsibility are likely to foster a conducive environment for green bond issuances. Therefore, this theory provides a lens through which the governance variable in the study can be understood. A strong institutional framework is expected to positively influence green bond issuances by instilling confidence in investors regarding transparency and adherence to environmental standards.
2. *Resource-Based View (RBV):* The Resource-Based View emphasizes that competitive advantage arises from efficient resource utilization. Applied to nations, lower resource intensity is indicative of efficient resource use. In the context of green bonds, nations with lower resource intensity are expected to be more attractive to sustainable investments. Efficient use of resources aligns with environmental responsibility and sustainability principles, contributing to the overall appeal of green bonds.

3. Finally, our social and intellectual capital variables are based upon the *Social capital and Knowledge-based view (KBV)* theories that emphasize the role of intellectual wealth in fostering innovation and competitive advantage. Moreover, social networks and relationships contribute to the creation of value. Social capital is reflected in the level of trust and cooperation within a society in green bonds. Nations with higher intellectual capital are expected to lead in developing and adopting environmentally friendly technologies.

4 Methodology and Hypotheses Development

To explore the factors influencing the issuance of global green bonds, we utilize a linear regression model, taking into account potential multicollinearity issues through the examination of GVIF. The model is expressed as follows:

$$Yi,t = \alpha 1 + \beta 1X1i,t + \beta 2X2i,t + \beta 3X3i,t + \beta 4X4i,t$$
$$+\beta 5X5i,t + \beta 6X6i,t + \beta 7X7i,t + \varepsilon i,t$$

Given that the dataset involves panel data encompassing 67 countries spanning 2017 to 2022, it is essential to account for fixed effects (Table 1).

4.1 Economic Determinants

The Gross Domestic Product (GDP), a foundational economic indicator, is posited as a pivotal determinant in this study. The theoretical premise rests on the assumption that economic prosperity, reflected in higher GDP, engenders increased financial capacity and a proclivity toward environmentally responsible investments. This aligns with extant literature that underscores the positive correlation between economic development and sustainable financial practices (Smith et al., 2018).

Table 1 Variables in the model

Variable	Description	Data source	Expected effects
Y	Green bond issuance in logarithm	Climate Bonds Initiative	
X1	Gross domestic product in logarithm	DataBank | The World Bank	+
X2	Inflation rate in percentage		−
X3	Natural capital score	SolAbility Sustainable Intelligence	+
X4	Resource intensity score		+
X5	Social capital score		+
X6	Intellectual capital score		+
X7	Governance score		+

- H1: Higher GDP is positively associated with an increase in the volume of global green bond issuances.

Analogously, the inflation rate, as an economic variable, is theorized to exert an influence on green bond volumes. Economic instability, as indicated by inflation, may impact investor confidence and alter investment preferences, potentially affecting the issuance of green bonds.

- H2: An increase in the inflation rate is associated with a decrease in the volume of global green bond issuances.

4.2 Sustainability Determinants

The sustainability dimensions examined in this study encompass natural capital, resource intensity, social capital, intellectual capital, and governance. Essentially, these variables collectively contribute to assessing a nation's sustainability competitiveness, reflecting its capacity for sustainable economic growth and commitment to environmental responsibility, as proposed by Porter and Kramer (2011).

Natural capital, indicative of a nation's ecological wealth, is postulated to play a role in shaping green bond issuance patterns, aligning with literature that emphasizes the intrinsic link between natural capital and sustainable finance (Costanza et al., 2017).

- H3: A higher level of natural capital is positively associated with an increase in the volume of global green bond issuances.

Additionally, *resource intensity*, representing resource utilization efficiency in economic activities, is theorized to impact green bond issuance, reflecting a commitment to resource-efficient and sustainable practices (Korhonen et al., 2018).

- H4: Higher resource intensity is positively correlated with an increase in the volume of global green bond issuances.

Social capital, intellectual capital, and governance collectively contribute to the broader societal and institutional framework shaping green bond markets. Social capital, encompassing trust and social cohesion, is expected to influence investor confidence and preference for sustainable investments (Coleman, 1988).

- H5: Greater social capital is positively associated with an increase in the volume of global green bond issuances.

Intellectual capital, indicative of a nation's knowledge and innovation capacity, is postulated to align with green finance by fostering advancements in environmentally friendly technologies and practices (Edvinsson & Malone, 1997).

- H6: Higher intellectual capital is positively correlated with an increase in the volume of global green bond issuances.

Governance, representing the quality of institutional frameworks, is presumed to be a critical factor in shaping investor confidence and, consequently, green bond market dynamics (La Porta et al., 1997).

- H7: Improved governance is positively associated with an increase in the volume of global green bond issuances.

5 Results

In Table 2, we present the correlation matrix between our dependent variable and the independent variables. None of the selected variables exhibit a Pearson correlation coefficient exceeding 0.8. Variance Inflation Factor tests are employed to align with regression. The model underwent a comprehensive check for autocorrelation, and no indications of such were detected, affirming the reliability of the findings.

The regression results are given in Table 3. Overall, the model can significantly explain 53.88% of changes in green bond issuance.

In line with expectations, an increase in GDP positively influences the issuance of green bonds. In economic terms, it implies that countries with higher GDP levels are more likely to engage in or support the issuance of green bonds. This could be because a higher GDP might signify greater economic capacity, financial resources, and investor interest in sustainable or environmentally friendly projects.

As anticipated, a higher inflation rate is associated with a negative impact on the issuance of green bonds. In economic terms, this might imply that countries experiencing higher inflation rates are less likely to engage in or support green bond activities. Higher inflation can create economic uncertainties and reduce the attractiveness of long-term investments, such as those associated with green projects.

Based on the analysis, the influence of Natural Capital on the issuance of green bonds appears to be negligible or insignificant. In other words, the presence or level of natural capital doesn't seem to have a substantial effect on the decision or likelihood of issuing green bonds. This might imply that, within the context of the study, other factors or variables play a more significant role in explaining the issuance of green bonds, and the contribution of natural capital is not statistically relevant.

There is a positive association between resource intensity and the issuance of green bonds. Higher resource intensity, possibly indicating a greater use of resources in economic activities, is linked to a positive impact on the issuance of green bonds. Social capital is positively associated with green bond issuance. Higher levels of social capital, encompassing social networks, relationships, and community interactions, are connected to a positive impact on the issuance of green bonds.

The positive and substantial association between intellectual capital and the number of green bonds issued implies that countries with higher levels of intellectual capital—comprising knowledge, skills, innovation, and intangible assets—demonstrate a significant positive influence on the quantity or scale of green bonds issued.

Table 2 Correlation matrix

	Issuance	GDP	Inflation	Natural capital	Resource intensity	Social capital	Intellectual capital	Governance
Issuance	1.000							
GDP	0.524	1.000						
Inflation	−0.237	−0.086	1.000					
Natural capital	−0.085	−0.169	−0.062	1.000				
Resource intensity	0.306	0.052	−0.102	0.145	1.000			
Social capital	0.455	0.136	−0.208	0.008	0.432	1.000		
Intellectual capital	0.469	0.208	−0.257	−0.002	0.287	0.533	1.000	
Governance	0.267	−0.082	0.005	0.058	0.196	0.210	0.164	1.000

Table 3 Regression results

	Coefficients	Standard error	t Stat	P-value	Sig.	GVIF^ (1/(2*Df))
(Intercept)	−1.5435384	1.84727052	−0.8355779	0.4042		
GDP	0.58325332	0.05881518	9.91671439	0.0000	***	1.053744
Inflation	−0.0688077	0.01888071	−3.6443398	0.0003	***	1.246982
Natural capital	−0.007859	0.00953802	−0.8239618	0.4107		1.046724
Resource intensity	0.03157888	0.01283328	2.46070239	0.0146	*	1.167259
Social capital	0.03521839	0.01206234	2.91969818	0.0038	**	1.32748
Intellectual capital	0.04932765	0.01233756	3.99816965	0.0000	***	1.258902
Governance	0.02765593	0.01466651	1.88565194	0.0605	.	1.438583
Factor(Year) 2018	−0.5814092	0.35091262	−1.6568488	0.0988	.	1.121041
Factor(Year) 2019	0.02141844	0.34999551	0.06119634	0.9513		
Factor(Year) 2020	0.05535157	0.38668884	0.14314239	0.8863		
Factor(Year) 2021	0.64791277	0.39636562	1.63463412	0.1034		
Factor(Year) 2022	0.87464886	0.43046596	2.03186536	0.0433	*	
Adjusted R square = 0.5388				Observations = 257		
Significance F = 2.2e-16				F = 25.93		

Signif. codes: 0 '***' 0.001 '**' 0.01 '*' 0.05 '.' 0.1 ' '1

For instance, a higher level of intellectual capital may contribute to the development of innovative and impactful green projects, attracting more investor interest and financial support. Additionally, effective intellectual property management and expertise in sustainability practices may enhance the credibility and attractiveness of green bond issuances.

6 Conclusion and Policy Implications

In conclusion, utilizing the latest available data, this study represents a pioneering effort to examine the multi-faceted relationship between economic and sustainability variables and their impact on global green bond issuance. The findings underscore the pivotal role of Gross Domestic Product (GDP) in driving green bond volumes, indicative of a positive association between economic prosperity and environmentally responsible investments. Simultaneously, the study reveals that inflation rates influence green bond issuance, with higher inflation correlating with a decrease in issuance, signaling the impact of economic instability on investor confidence and preferences.

Exploring the sustainability aspects, which include natural capital, resource intensity, social capital, intellectual capital, and governance, the research provides highly noteworthy insights. While natural capital and governance exhibit negligible effects on green bond issuance, resource intensity, social capital, and intellectual capital emerge as significant determinants. Higher resource intensity, reflective of resource-efficient practices, and elevated levels of social and intellectual capital are linked to increased green bond issuances.

7 Policy Implications

Policymakers are urged to recognize the symbiotic relationship between economic development and sustainability competitiveness. Strategies that enhance resource efficiency, social cohesion, and intellectual capital can contribute to fostering a conducive environment for green finance. The dynamic interaction between economic and sustainability factors in the global green bond landscape illuminates new avenues for research and policy formulation. As the first of its kind on a global scale, this study provides a foundation for future investigations into the evolving dynamics of green finance, offering valuable perspectives for scholars, practitioners, and policymakers alike.

References

Alemzero, D., & Huaping, S. (2021, September 09). *What drives energy efficiency in Africa? Insights from 12 selected countries using incremental decomposition analysis*. PREPRINT (Version 1) available at Research Square. https://doi.org/10.21203/rs.3.rs-887117/v1

Anh, T. C., Sarker, T., & Rasoulinezhad, E. (2020). Factors influencing the green bond market expansion: Evidence from a multi-dimensional analysis. *Journal of Risk and Financial Management, 13*(6), 126. https://doi.org/10.3390/jrfm13060126

Bachelet, M. J., Becchetti, L., & Manfredonia, S. (2019). The green bonds premium puzzle: The role of issuer characteristics and third-party verification. *Sustainability, 11*, 1098. https://doi.org/10.3390/su11041098

Banga, J. (2019). The green bond market: A potential source of climate finance for developing countries. *Journal of Sustainable Finance & Investment, 9*(1), 17–32. https://doi.org/10.1080/20430795.2018.1498617

Bracking, S. (2015). Performativity in the green economy: How far does climate finance create a fictive economy? *Third World Quarterly, 36*(12), 2337–2357. https://doi.org/10.1080/01436597.2015.1086263

Cheong, C., & Choi, J. (2020). Green bonds: A survey. *Journal of Derivatives and Quantitative Studies: 선물연구, 28*(4), 175–189. https://doi.org/10.1108/JDQS-09-2020-0024

Chiesa, M., & Barua, S. (2019). The surge of impact borrowing: The magnitude and determinants of green bond supply and its heterogeneity across markets. *Journal of Sustainable Finance & Investment, 9*(2), 138–161. https://doi.org/10.1080/20430795.2018.1550993

Chugan, P. K., Mungra, Y., Mehta, K., & Mehta, K. (2017, January 5). Challenges and policy implications for marketing Green Bonds. Available at SSRN: https://ssrn.com/abstract=2937627

Coleman, J. S. (1988). Social capital in the creation of human capital. *The American Journal of Sociology, 95*, S95–S120.

Costanza, R., de Groot, R., Braat, L., Kubiszewski, I., Fioramonti, L., Sutton, P., Farber, S., & Grasso, M. (2017). Twenty years of ecosystem services: How far have we come and how far do we still need to go? *Ecosystem Services, 28*(Part A), 1–16, ISSN 2212-0416. https://doi.org/10.1016/j.ecoser.2017.09.008

Durrani, A., Rosmin, M., & Volz, U. (2020). The role of central banks in scaling up sustainable finance—What do monetary authorities in the Asia-Pacific region think? *Journal of Sustainable Finance & Investment, 10*(2), 92–112. https://doi.org/10.1080/20430795.2020.1715095

Edvinsson, L., & Malone, M. S. (1997). *Intellectual capital: Realizing your company's true value by finding its hidden roots*. HarperCollins Publishers, Inc.

Ge, L., Zhao, H., Yang, J., et al. (2022). Green finance, technological progress, and ecological performance—evidence from 30 provinces in China. *Environmental Science and Pollution Research, 29*, 66295–66314. https://doi.org/10.1007/s11356-022-20501-w

Gilchrist, D., Yu, J., & Zhong, R. (2021). The limits of green finance: A survey of literature in the context of green bonds and green loans. *Sustainability, 13*(2), 478. https://doi.org/10.3390/su13020478

Huang, H., Chau, K. Y., Iqbal, W., et al. (2022). Retracted article: Assessing the role of financing in sustainable business environment. *Environmental Science and Pollution Research, 29*, 7889–7906. https://doi.org/10.1007/s11356-021-16118-0

Korhonen, J., Nuur, C., Feldmann, A., & Birkie, S. E. (2018). Circular economy as an essentially contested concept. *Journal of Cleaner Production, 175*, 544–552, ISSN 0959-6526. https://doi.org/10.1016/j.jclepro.2017.12.111

La Porta, R., Lopez-De-Silanes, F., Shleifer, A., & Vishny, R. W. (1997). Legal determinants of external finance. *The Journal of Finance, 52*, 1131–1150. https://doi.org/10.1111/j.1540-6261.1997.tb02727.x

Li, M., Hamawandy, N. M., Wahid, F., Rjoub, H., & Bao, Z. (2021). Renewable energy resources investment and green finance: Evidence from China. *Resources Policy, 74*, 102402, ISSN 0301-4207. https://doi.org/10.1016/j.resourpol.2021.102402

McCollum, D. L., Zhou, W., Bertram, C., et al. (2018). Energy investment needs for fulfilling the Paris Agreement and achieving the Sustainable Development Goals. *Nature Energy, 3*, 589–599. https://doi.org/10.1038/s41560-018-0179-z

Porter, M. E., & Kramer, M. R. (2011). Creating shared value. *Harvard Business Review, 89*(1–2), 62–77.

Smith, M. S., Cook, C., Sokona, Y., et al. (2018). Advancing sustainability science for the SDGs. *Sustainability Science, 13*, 1483–1487. https://doi.org/10.1007/s11625-018-0645-3

Tolliver, C., Keeley, A. R., & Managi, S. (2020). Policy targets behind green bonds for renewable energy: Do climate commitments matter? *Technological Forecasting and Social Change, 157*, 120051, ISSN 0040-1625. https://doi.org/10.1016/j.techfore.2020.120051

Xiao, Y., & Dong, X. (2022). Study on the 2-mode network characteristics of the types and issuing places of Chinese Provincial Green Bonds. In A. E. Hassanien, Y. Xu, Z. Zhao, S. Mohammed, & Z. Fan (Eds.), *Business Intelligence and Information Technology. BIIT 2021* (Lecture Notes on Data Engineering and Communications Technologies) (Vol. 107). Springer. https://doi.org/10.1007/978-3-030-92632-8_53

Dynamic Connectedness Between Uncertainty and Energy Cryptocurrencies: Evidence from TVP-VAR Connectedness Approach

Tania Klayme and Korhan K. Gokmenoglu

1 Introduction

Since the launch of Bitcoin in 2009, the cryptocurrency has attracted global attention from investors due to its performance and diversification properties. The expansion of this market brings potential benefits, including decentralization, low transaction costs, high accessibility, anonymity, and increased investment opportunities (Gallersdörfer et al., 2020). However, alongside these advantages, there are also several risks and challenges. It is imperative for policymakers and industry stakeholders to collaboratively address these challenges to ensure the sustained growth and stability of the cryptocurrency market.

One of the most significant criticisms of cryptocurrencies is their environmental impact. Environmental degradation and climate change are among humanity's foremost threats, primarily due to the substantial increase in CO_2 emissions accelerating global warming. Conventional cryptocurrencies, such as Bitcoin, contribute to this issue by consuming large amounts of energy, much of which comes from fossil fuels. The extensive energy consumption and adverse environmental effects of cryptocurrency mining are becoming a growing concern. Without clear legislative direction toward sustainable energy, bitcoin mining will likely persist in relying on fossil fuels. To mitigate these concerns, there is a pressing need for collaborative efforts among industry players, regulators, and environmental advocates to promote greener practices in cryptocurrency.

T. Klayme
Eastern Mediterranean University, Department of Banking and Finance, Famagusta, Cyprus

K. K. Gokmenoglu (✉)
Ankara HBV University, Faculty of Financial Sciences, Department of Capital Markets, Ankara, Turkey
e-mail: korhan.gokmenoglu@hbv.edu.tr

N. Ozatac et al. (eds.), *Sustainable Development in Banking and Finance*, Springer Proceedings in Business and Economics,
https://doi.org/10.1007/978-3-031-65533-3_14

The negative environmental impact of conventional cryptocurrencies has caused unrest among investors. This issue negatively affects investor confidence and leads to a loss of favor among environmentally sensitive customers and investors. This situation is expected to have an increasingly detrimental impact on the demand and price of cryptocurrencies. Simultaneously, it has prompted investors worldwide to focus more on green alternatives to diversify/reduce the environmental risk of cryptocurrencies (Pham et al., 2022; Ren & Lucey, 2022). The cryptocurrency market has gradually shifted toward more environmentally friendly mining processes in response to these issues. The shift toward sustainability not only aligns with growing environmental consciousness but also positions these cryptocurrencies as potentially more resilient investments in the long term.

Energy cryptocurrencies are energy trading platforms built on blockchain technology. These platforms employ smart contracts to facilitate direct transactions between users, enabling the purchase and sale of excess renewable energy. Powerledger (POWR), GridPlus (GRID+), and SunContract (SNC) are three popular energy cryptocurrencies included in our study. Power Ledger (POWR) is a blockchain platform revolutionizing the energy market by enabling peer-to-peer electricity trading through smart contracts. GridPlus (GRID+) focuses on blockchain solutions for the energy sector, developing blockchain-based tools for more efficient energy markets. SunContract (SNC) is a decentralized platform connecting energy producers and consumers, utilizing smart contracts to facilitate transparent and direct electricity trading. These projects collectively strive to decentralize and democratize energy systems, promoting renewable energy use, transparency, and user control in the evolving landscape of blockchain and energy technology.

The study aims to provide a nuanced examination of the dynamic connectedness between energy cryptocurrencies (Powerledger, GridPlus, and SunContract) and major uncertainty indicators (Economic Policy Uncertainty (EPU) and Climate Policy Uncertainty (CPU)). The EPU index, proposed by Baker et al. (2016), is determined by averaging three factors. The initial factor is drawn from aspects of policy uncertainty found in newspaper articles. The second component mirrors uncertainties linked to forthcoming challenges in the tax code. The ultimate element is acquired from economic forecasts. We utilize the CPU index Gavriilidis (2021) developed, derived from the scaled frequency of journals regarding climate policy and regulations published in eight major US newspapers. An understanding of the relationship between energy cryptocurrencies and uncertainty indicators can provide valuable insights for both investors and policymakers.

The structure of this study is outlined as follows: Section 2 delves into the literature review, Section 3 explicates the data and methodology, Section 4 details the results, and Sect. 5 encapsulates the conclusion.

2 Literature Review

Many studies have examined the connectedness between economic/financial risk measures and conventional cryptocurrencies. For instance, Jiang et al. (2021) employed a quantile coherency analytic technique to assess the interconnectivity of EPU, the COVID-19-induced stock market volatility index, and the returns of conventional cryptocurrencies. Most conventional cryptocurrencies proved to be efficient safeguards against elevated EPU and the equity market volatility induced by COVID-19 throughout the pandemic. Additionally, utilizing a wavelet coherence approach, Rubbaniy et al. (2021) investigated the co-movement of financial and non-financial risk proxies with the returns of Bitcoin, Ethereum, and Ripple. Their findings suggested that cryptocurrencies function as safe-haven assets for non-financial market-based proxies. Wu et al. (2021), employing a wavelet coherence technique, explored the co-movement of EPU and four cryptocurrencies (Bitcoin, Ethereum, Ripple, and Litecoin) and discovered no causal association between EPU and cryptocurrency returns amid the COVID-19 outbreak. These studies collectively underscore conventional cryptocurrencies' resilience and risk-mitigating qualities during periods of economic uncertainty.

The interrelation between energy, sustainable cryptocurrencies, and stock markets has also been scrutinized. Haq et al. (2023) probed the co-movements of green bonds, sustainable and traditional cryptocurrencies, and prominent sustainability indices across both temporal and frequency domains. They deduced that green bonds and sustainable cryptocurrencies provide opportunities for sustainable investment and risk management to cryptocurrency traders and investors. Moreover, Gallersdörfer et al. (2020) recommended categorizing cryptocurrencies as either energy-intensive or energy-efficient, aligning with Ren and Lucey's (2022) classification into 'black/dirty' or 'green/clean' based on energy usage. The latter study revealed that dirty cryptocurrencies tend to find safe havens during periods of increasing uncertainty in clean energy. Furthermore, Pham et al. (2022) utilized quantile connectedness to explore the tail dependency between carbon prices and green and non-green cryptocurrencies. During low volatility periods, the link between carbon pricing and cryptocurrency returns diminishes, and the connectivity between green cryptocurrencies and Bitcoin is minimal. These diverse investigations shed light on the multifaceted relationships between economic risks, energy considerations, and the dynamics of various cryptocurrencies, emphasizing their roles as both risk mitigators and sustainable investment options.

The impacts of uncertainty on financial assets constitute an important part of the finance literature. The relationship between uncertainty indices and cryptocurrencies has also garnered attention in the literature. One of the most frequently used proxies to represent uncertainty is the EPU index. Wang et al. (2019) estimated the risk spillover effects from uncertainty to Bitcoin using the US EPU index, stock market uncertainty index, and VIX as proxies for the uncertainty levels. They conclude that, in most market situations, the spillover is insignificant. Cheema et al. (2020) claimed that the considerable predictability of EPU for cryptocurrency returns over diverse periods challenges the perception of cryptocurrencies as effective hedges or safe havens during uncertain periods. The assertion posits that cryptocurrencies may not consistently exhibit the expected protective characteristics in the face of market uncertainty. Fasanya et al. (2021) demonstrated that the connectedness between Bitcoin and precious metals, with the US EPU, is more pronounced around the median and higher quantiles. This observation implies that the perceived investment shelter provided by connectedness may not be as robust during periods of heightened uncertainty. Moreover, Sarker et al. (2023) showed that an increase in the CPU index positively impacts the Bitcoin market in the short term, with a more pronounced effect in the long term.

Although the literature on cryptocurrencies is quite extensive, there is a notable scarcity of studies investigating shock transmission between energy cryptocurrencies and risk factors. The research of Yousaf et al. (2023) is somehow conceptually similar to ours. They investigated the connectedness between energy cryptocurrencies and other asset classes, considering the COVID-19 and the Russian-Ukraine war. Their findings indicated that the energy cryptocurrencies were the net receivers of the shock. In addition, the connectedness increased rapidly during the COVID-19 pandemic period. Although our studies share some characteristics, such as the utilization of energy cryptocurrencies and the consideration of the impact of COVID-19, they differ in that we specifically focus on risk factors.

3 Data and Methodology

3.1 Data

This study explores the connectedness between energy cryptocurrency and major uncertainty indices. In this regard, we use monthly prices of the three well-known energy cryptocurrencies: Powerledger (POWR), GridPlus (GRID+), and SunContract (SNC). The cryptocurrency data was collected from the Coinmarketcap database, while the EPU and CPU indices were extracted from the Policy Uncertainty database. The data used in this study spans January 2018 to April 2023. We used the first log-differenced series: $y_t = \log(x_{it}) - \log(x_{it-1})$.

3.2 Methodology

The time-varying parameter vector autoregression (TVP-VAR) model proposed by Antonakakis and Gabauer (2017), an extension of the Diebold and Yilmaz (2012) connectedness approach, is employed to explore the connectedness between uncertainty and energy cryptocurrency. The TVP-VAR technique enables the variance to fluctuate using a Kalman filter estimate incorporating forgetting components.

In addition, the rolling window is not randomly selected, preventing the loss of important observations and making this approach suitable for small samples. The TVP-VAR model is presented as follows:

$$Y_t = \beta_t Y_{t-1} + \varepsilon_t; \varepsilon_t \& \mathrm{N}(0, \Sigma_t) \tag{1}$$

$$\mathrm{vec}(\beta_t) = \mathrm{vec}(\beta_{t-1}) + \vartheta_t, \vartheta_t\ N(0, R_t) \tag{2}$$

Where $\mathrm{Y_t}$, ε_t, and ϑ_t are $(N \times 1)$ vectors, whereas Σ_t, R_t, and β_t are $(N \times N)$ dimensional time-varying coefficient matrix.

The Word representation of the TVP-VAR model is presented as follows:

$$Y_t = {}_{j=0}^{\infty}\Sigma\ \Theta_{jt}\varepsilon_{t-j} \tag{3}$$

Where $\Theta_{jt}$is an $N \times N$ dimensional matrix.

Based on the generalized impulse response function and the generalized forecast error variance decompositions proposed by Koop et al. (1996), the vector moving average model's dynamic coefficient forms the basis of the connectedness index developed by Diebold and Yilmaz (2012) and is defined as follows:

$$d_{ij,t}^{g} = \frac{\sigma_{jj,t}^{-1}\ \Sigma_{h=0}^{H-1}\left(e_i'\Theta_{h,t}\Sigma_t e_j\right)^2}{\Sigma_{h=0}^{H-1}\left(e_i'\Theta_{h,t}\Sigma_t\Theta_{h,t}'e_j\right)} \tag{4}$$

where $\sigma_{jj,\ t}$is the jth diagonal element of Σ_t.

The total connectedness index (TCI) represents the degree of interconnectedness between the time series and is computed as follows:

$$H_t^g = \frac{\Sigma_{i,j=1,i\neq j}^{N} d_{ij,t}^{g}}{\Sigma_{j=1}^{N} d_{ij,t}^{g}} \times 100 \tag{5}$$

The spillover received by variable j from all other variables i is known as total directional connectedness to others, and it is calculated as follows:

$$H_{i\to j}^{g} = \frac{\Sigma_{j=1,i\neq j}^{N} d_{ij,t}^{g}}{\Sigma_{j=1}^{N} d_{ij,t}^{g}} \times 100 \tag{6}$$

The spillover received by variable i from all other variables j is known as total directional connectedness from others, and it is calculated as follows:

$$H_{i\leftarrow j}^{g} = \frac{\Sigma_{j=1,i\neq j}^{N} d_{ij,t}^{g}}{\Sigma_{i=1}^{N} d_{ij,t}^{g}} \times 100 \tag{7}$$

Finally, the net pairwise directional connectedness signifies the difference between the overall directional connectedness to others and the overall directional connectedness from others.

$$H^g_{ij,t} = H^g_{i \to j} - H^g_{i \leftarrow j} \tag{8}$$

4 Empirical Results

4.1 Descriptive Statistics and Correlation Matrix

Descriptive statistics for the variables utilized in this study are presented in Table 1. We observe that the energy cryptocurrency variables depict a negative mean rate of return, while the uncertainty indices exhibit the highest mean returns. The table also indicates that GridPlus is the riskiest variable (std.dev = 0.477), whereas Powerledger presents the lowest level of risk. All variables, except for CPU, demonstrate right-skewed distributions.

The correlation matrix among the variables is displayed in Table 2. A positive correlation is observed between the uncertainty indices and energy cryptocurrencies. This observation suggests that higher uncertainty levels correspond to increased returns for energy cryptocurrencies.

Table 1 Descriptive statistics

	CPU	EPU	PWR	GRID	SNC
Mean	5.2532	5.2557	−0.0273	−0.0253	−0.0319
Maximum	6.0193	6.2225	1.0618	1.5132	0.8876
Minimum	4.3754	4.6976	−0.6987	−0.8864	−0.6714
Std.Dev	0.3365	0.3328	0.1101	0.4774	0.3474
Skewness	−0.3844	0.9186	0.6854	0.6974	0.3628
Kurtosis	3.0288	3.5988	3.8049	3.9953	3.4219
Jarque-Berra	1.5783	9.9571***	6.7384**	7.8301**	1.8791

*** and ** signify 1% and 5% significance level, respectively

Table 2 Correlation matrix among the variables

	CPU	EPU	PWR	GRID	SNC
CPU	1				
EPU	0.334	1			
PWR	0.158	0.056	1		
GRID	0.068	0.163	0.450	1	
SNC	0.115	0.153	0.464	0.412	1

4.2 Static Spillover Results

In this section, we employed the TVP-VAR model to explore dynamic connectedness across the energy cryptocurrency market and various uncertainty indices. Initially, we conducted static analysis to examine connections between energy cryptocurrency variables and uncertainty indices, and the results presented in Table 3. 'TO' represents the volatility spillover to other markets, and 'FROM' represents the spillover received by each variable from all others. The net pairwise directional connectedness was then computed by calculating the difference between 'FROM' and 'TO'.

EPU shows the highest connectedness level to other variables (38.06%), followed by CPU (31.66%). SNC (38.78%) and PWR (37.53%) are the top receivers of the system. In net terms, EPU and CPU transmit shocks to energy cryptocurrencies, while SNC, PWR, and GRID are net shock receivers. Additionally, Table 3 presents the TCI, representing the average impact of a shock in one series on all others. The TCI for all markets is 31.33%, indicating that the transmission of market uncertainty, as represented by EPU and CPU market spillover, has a moderate impact on the energy cryptocurrency market.

4.3 Dynamic Spillover Results

Table 4 presents the dynamic connectedness matrix among energy cryptocurrencies and uncertainty indices. It is evident that EPU, followed by CPU, exerts the most influence on other markets. Specifically, EPU and CPU individually contribute 42.21% and 35.14% to the energy cryptocurrency market. Likewise, SNC (40.43%), PWR (38.14%), and GRID (36.14%) are the primary net shock receivers.

The outcomes from both tables collectively indicate a moderate level of connectedness between uncertainty indices and energy cryptocurrencies. The bottom rows of Tables 3 and 4 provide the total net spillovers for each market. The findings emphasize that EPU is the main net transmitter of shocks, whereas SunContract (SNC) emerges as the primary net receiver of shocks.

Table 3 Static connectedness matrix

	CPU	EPU	PWR	GRID	SNC	FROM
CPU	70.06	21.70	1.63	2.45	4.16	29.94
EPU	8.82	84.51	1.87	3.79	1.01	15.49
PWR	6.28	4.73	62.47	12.78	13.74	37.53
GRID	7.06	5.21	13.10	65.11	9.55	34.89
SNC	9.53	6.41	13.01	9.83	61.22	38.78
TO	31.66	38.06	29.61	28.84	28.46	156.63
						TCI
Net	1.720	22.56	−7.92	−6.05	−10.32	31.33

Table 4 Dynamic connectedness matrix

	CPU	EPU	PWR	GRID	SNC	FROM
CPU	67.22	22.03	1.67	2.75	5.13	32.78
EPU	9.22	84.07	1.89	3.86	0.96	15.93
PWR	7.14	5.72	61.86	11.82	13.46	38.14
GRID	8.25	5.77	12.09	63.86	10.03	36.14
SNC	10.53	7.49	12.39	10.03	59.57	40.43
TO	35.14	42.21	28.47	28.47	29.56	163.43
						TCI
Net	2.35	26.28	−10.11	−7.67	−10.85	32.69

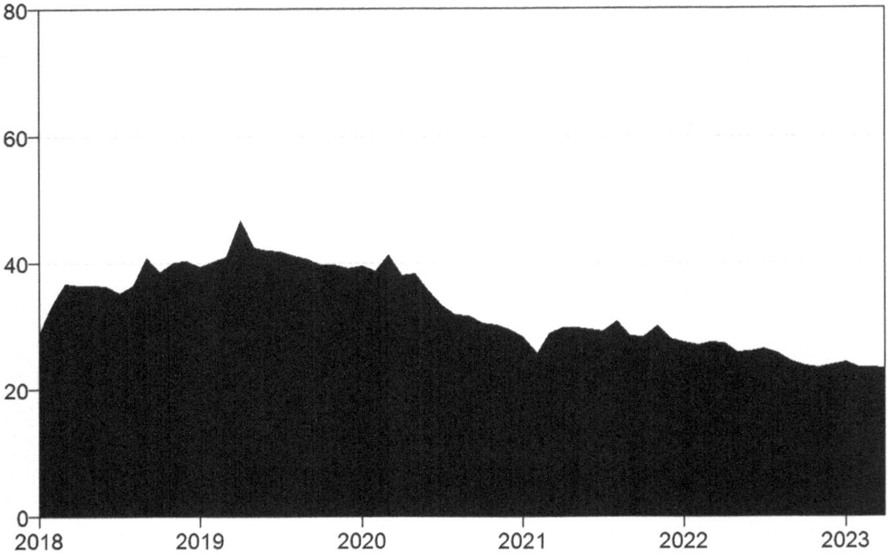

Fig. 1 Total connectedness index based on the TVP-VAR model

The average connectedness between energy cryptocurrencies and market uncertainty indices is illustrated in Fig. 1. The total connectedness remains moderate throughout our sample period. A significant surge is noticeable during the 2019–2020 period, coinciding with the onset of the COVID-19 pandemic in the first quarter of 2020. Energy cryptocurrencies appear to be more susceptible to volatility spillover during the COVID-19 pandemic period, as highlighted by Haq et al. (2023).

Figures 2a, b visually illustrate the directional connectedness from one variable to the other market and vice versa. These graphs illustrate the findings presented in Table 4. Energy cryptocurrencies have consistently been the net recipients of shocks. The results affirm that the EPU index plays a central role as the primary transmitter of uncertainty, followed by the CPU index. These outcomes align with the studies of Youssef et al. (2023) and Haq et al. (2023).

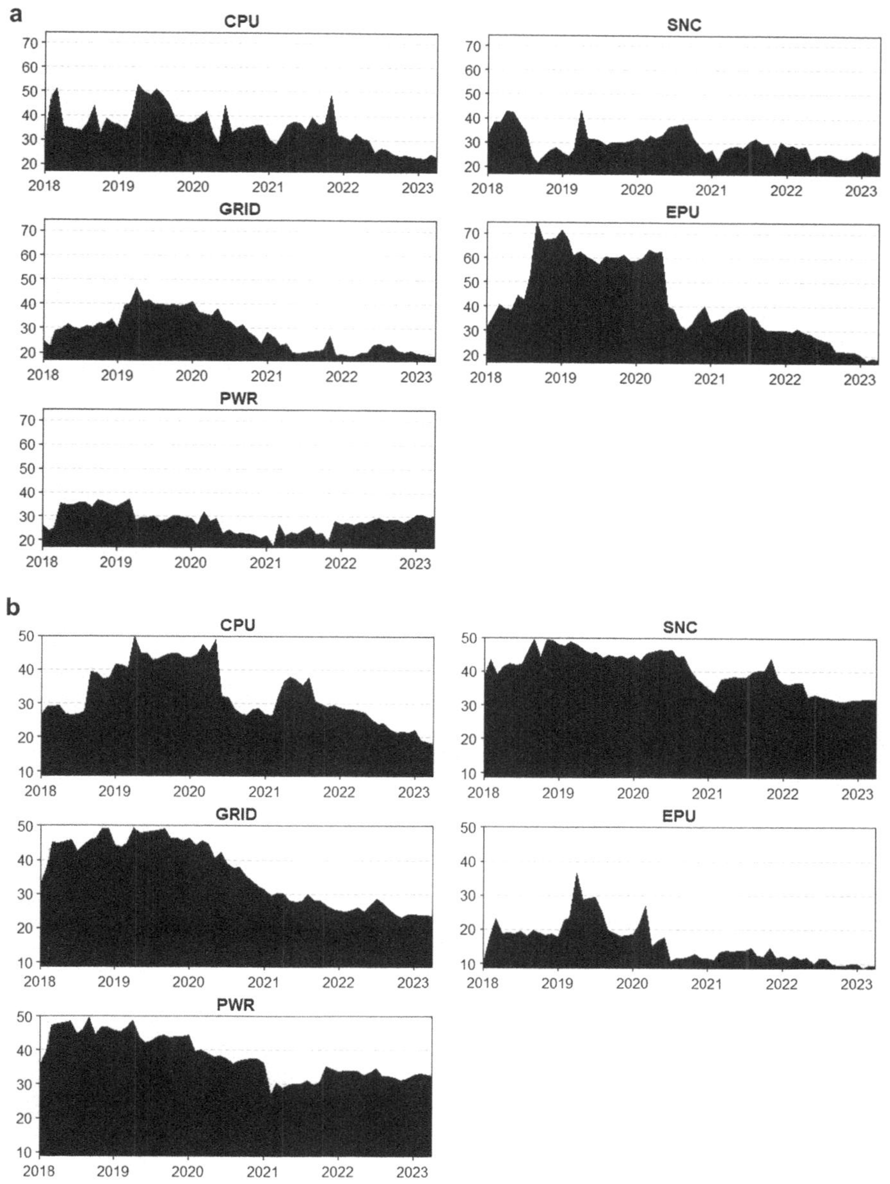

Fig. 2 (**a**) TO dynamic connectedness index. (**b**) FROM dynamic connectedness index

5 Conclusion

This study investigated the dynamic connectedness among three energy cryptocurrencies and two major uncertainty indices. We utilized monthly closing prices from January 2018 to April 2023. Static and dynamic connectedness were assessed using the TVP-VAR approach. The total connectedness indices were 31.33% and 32.69%, indicating a moderate interdependence between energy cryptocurrencies and uncertainty indices. The results reveal that the EPU tends to be the highest transmitter of shocks, while energy cryptocurrencies act as net receivers. Shocks transmitted and received were more pronounced during the COVID-19 period.

These empirical findings carry several implications for both policymakers and investors. Cryptocurrency investors are advised to exercise caution when diversifying their portfolios. Institutional investors may find value in selecting energy coins to enhance diversification and mitigate risk during economic instability. Portfolio managers are encouraged to explore various investment possibilities, emphasizing multiscale discoveries and the potential benefits of diversifying portfolios to mitigate substantial losses. Additionally, they may consider high-return, low-connectedness energy cryptocurrencies during uncertain periods. Policymakers should encourage sustainable investment portfolio diversification, contributing to reduced carbon emissions.

Appendix 1. Net Dynamic Connectedness Index

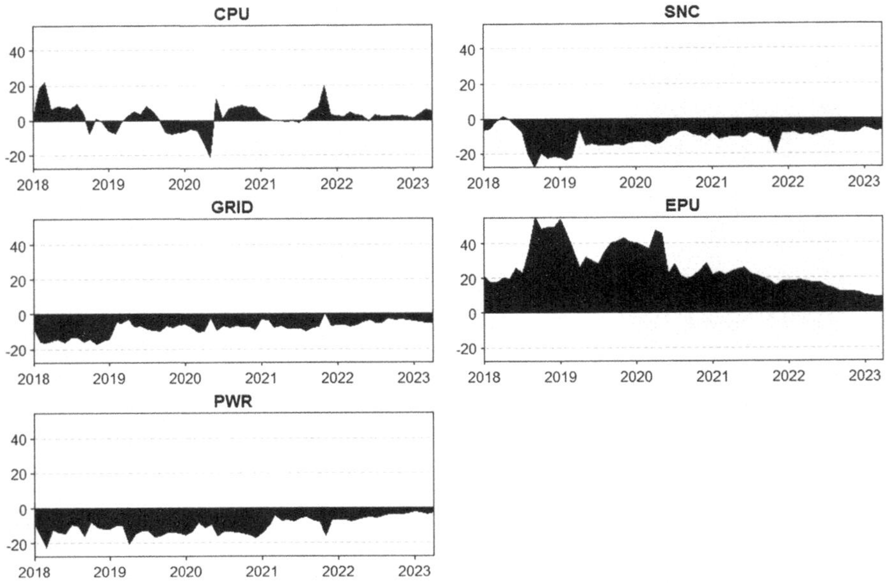

References

Antonakakis, N., & Gabauer, D. (2017). Refined measures of dynamic connectedness based on TVP-VAR. MPRA Paper. Available at: https://mpra.ub.uni-muenchen.de/78282/

Baker, S. R., Bloom, N., & Davis, S. J. (2016). Measuring economic policy uncertainty. *The Quarterly Journal of Economics, 131*(4), 1593–1636.

Cheema, M. A., Szulczyk, K., & Bouri, E. (2020). Cryptocurrency returns and economic policy uncertainty: A multicountry analysis using linear and quantile-based models. Available at SSRN 3567635.

Diebold, F. X., & Yilmaz, K. (2012). Better to give than to receive: Predictive directional measurement of volatility spillovers. *International Journal of forecasting, 28*(1), 57–66.

Fasanya, I. O., Oliyide, J. A., Adekoya, O. B., & Agbatogun, T. (2021). How does economic policy uncertainty connect with the dynamic spillovers between precious metals and bitcoin markets? *Resources Policy, 72*, 102077.

Gallersdörfer, U., Klaaßen, L., & Stoll, C. (2020). Energy consumption of cryptocurrencies beyond Bitcoin. *Joule, 4*(9), 1843–1846.

Gavriilidis, K. (2021). Measuring climate policy uncertainty. Available at SSRN 3847388.

Haq, I. U., Ferreira, P., Quintino, D. D., Huynh, N., & Samantreeporn, S. (2023). Economic policy uncertainty, energy and sustainable cryptocurrencies: Investigating dynamic connectedness during the COVID-19 pandemic. *Economies, 11*(3), 1–23.

Jiang, Y., Wu, L., Tian, G., & Nie, H. (2021). Do cryptocurrencies hedge against EPU and the equity market volatility during COVID-19? New evidence from quantile coherency analysis. *Journal of International Financial Markets, Institutions and Money, 72*, 101324.

Koop, G., Pesaran, M. H., & Potter, S. M. (1996). Impulse response analysis in nonlinear multivariate models. *Journal of Econometrics, 74*(1), 119–147.

Pham, L., Karim, S., Naeem, M. A., & Long, C. (2022). A tale of two tails among carbon prices, green and non-green cryptocurrencies. *International Review of Financial Analysis, 82*, 102139.

Ren, B., & Lucey, B. (2022). A clean, green haven? Examining the relationship between clean energy, clean and dirty cryptocurrencies. *Energy Economics, 109*, 105951.

Rubbaniy, G., Khalid, A. A., & Samitas, A. (2021). Are cryptos safe-haven assets during Covid-19? Evidence from wavelet coherence analysis. *Emerging Markets Finance and Trade, 57*(6), 1741–1756.

Sarker, P. K., Lau, C. K. M., & Pradhan, A. K. (2023). Asymmetric effects of climate policy uncertainty and energy prices on bitcoin prices. *Innovation and Green Development, 2*(2), 100048.

Wang, G., Tang, Y., Xie, C., & Chen, S. (2019). Is bitcoin a safe haven or a hedging asset? Evidence from China. *Journal of Management Science and Engineering, 4*(3), 173–188.

Wu, W., Tiwari, A. K., Gozgor, G., & Leping, H. (2021). Does economic policy uncertainty affect cryptocurrency markets? Evidence from Twitter-based uncertainty measures. *Research in International Business and Finance, 58*, 101478.

Yousaf, I., Riaz, Y., & Goodell, J. W. (2023). Energy cryptocurrencies: Assessing connectedness with other asset classes. *Finance Research Letters, 52*, 103389.

SPRINGER NATURE

GPSR Compliance

The European Union's (EU) General Product Safety Regulation (GPSR) is a set of rules that requires consumer products to be safe and our obligations to ensure this.

If you have any concerns about our products, you can contact us on ProductSafety@springernature.com

In case Publisher is established outside the EU, the EU authorized representative is:

Springer Nature Customer Service Center GmbH
Europaplatz 3
69115 Heidelberg, Germany

The manufacturer's authorised representative in the EU is Springer Nature Customer Service Centre GmbH, Europaplatz 3, 69115 Heidelberg, Germany. If you have any concerns regarding our products, please contact ProductSafety@springernature.com

Printed and bound by CPI Group (UK) Ltd, Croydon, CR0 4YY
01/10/2026
02225961-0006